TRADE, FDI AND REMITTANCES
SELECTED WRITINGS

TRADE, FDI AND REMITTANCES
SELECTED WRITINGS

Bhubanesh Pant

ADROIT

Adroit Publishers

NEW DELHI • KATHMANDU

ISBN : 978-81-87393-91-7

2021

Published by
ADROIT PUBLISHERS 4675/21, Ganpati Bhawan, Ansari Road, Daryaganj, New Delhi-110 002 Phone : 011-23266030
adroitpublishers@gmail.com

Typeset in Garamond Premier Pro by Arun, Akriti Graphic Solution, Delhi-110081 E-mail: arun263923@gmail.com, Ph: 9999414390

Preface

This book contains several articles and papers I initially wrote over a period of three decades and encompasses three important subjects of the external sector, namely trade, foreign direct investment (FDI), and remittances. While trade is a general topic, both FDI and remittances are more specific in nature.

The main reason I took to reprint my earlier writings, primarily based on the experiences of Nepal, is that many of the challenges concerning trade, FDI and remittances which I previously examined continue to persist both in Nepal as well as in other developing countries. While the selections in this book retain my original premises and analyses, they are equally relevant to the present-day issues of the developing world. Although I am aware that these pages do not synthesize and present the entire range of current issues, I am nevertheless optimistic that the key suggestions expressed in this book will still be beneficial to policymakers in the course of formulating appropriate policies and strategies for economic development in general, and external sector development in particular.

This book is divided into three sections, with the writings on each topic presented chronologically. Section 1 covers issues on trade, Section 2 deals with topics on FDI, and Section 3 includes different aspects of remittances. I have made some minor changes to the main text and headings from the original publications. Additionally, I have removed the technical and quantitative analyses so that the core issues are understood by a wider audience.

Finally, I am very thankful to the editors of the respective journals and newspapers for their kind permission to reproduce the materials for this collection.

Bhubanesh Pant

Contents

Section III: Remittances

Abbreviations and Acronyms

ADB	Asian Development Bank
AFTA	ASEAN Free Trade Area
ASEAN	Association of South-east Asian Nations
ATC	Agreement on Textiles and Clothing
BFTA	Bilateral Free Trade Agreement
BIMSTEC	Bay of Bengal Initiative for Multi-Sectoral Technical and Economic Cooperation
BIPPA	Bilateral Investment and Protection Agreement
BMET	Bureau of Manpower Employment and Training
BOI	Board of Investment
BoP	Balance of Payments
CDIS	Coordinated Direct Investment Survey
CTH	Changes in Tariff Heading
DER	Dual Exchange Rate
DOI	Department of Industries
EBA	Everything But Arms
EC	European Community
EPZ	Export Processing Zone
ESCAP	Economic and Social Commission for Asia and the Pacific
EU	European Union
FDI	Foreign Direct Investment
FITTA	Foreign Investment and Technology Transfer Act
FTA	Free Trade Area
FY	Fiscal Year
GATS	General Agreement on Trade in Services
GATT	General Agreement on Tariffs and Trade
GCC	Gulf Cooperation Council
GDP	Gross Domestic Product
GEP	Group of Eminent Persons
GOE	Group of Experts

GPZ	Garment Processing Zone
GSP	Generalized System of Preferences
HTA	Hometown Association
ICT	Information and Communication Technology
IDP	Investment Development Path
IMF	International Monetary Fund
IPA	Investment Promotion Agency
IPO	Initial Public Offering
LDC	Least-developed Country
LMIC	Low- and Middle-income Countries
MDGs	Millennium Development Goals
MFA	Multifibre Arrangement
MFI	Microfinance Institution
MFN	Most Favored Nation
MIGA	Multilateral Investment Guarantee Agency
MNC	Multinational Corporation
MWF	Migrant Welfare Fund
NAFTA	North American Free Trade Area
NEFT	National Electric Fund Transfer
NELM	New Economics of Labor Migration
NGO	Non-governmental Organization
NIC	Newly Industrializing Country
NPC	National Planning Commission
NRB	Nepal Rastra Bank
NRI	Non-resident Indian
NTB	Non-tariff Barrier
NTIS	Nepal Trade Integration Strategy
ODA	Official Development Assistance
OGL	Open General License
OLI	Ownership, Location and Internationalization
OWS	One Window Service
POL	Petroleum, Oils, and Lubricants
PRI	Pakistan Remittance Initiative

PTA	Preferential Trading Arrangement
QR	Quantitative Restriction
R&D	Research and Development
RoO	Rules of Origin
RTA	Regional Trading Arrangement
SAARC	South Asian Association for Regional Cooperation
SAFTA	South Asian Free Trade Area
SAPTA	South Asian Preferential Trading Agreement
SDGs	Sustainable Development Goals
SDT	Special and Differential Treatment
SER	Single Exchange Rate
SITC	Standard International Trade Classification
SME	Small and Medium Enterprise
TNC	Trade Negotiation Committee
TPC	Trade Promotion Center
TRIMs	Trade-related Investment Measures
TRIPs	Trade-related Aspects of Intellectual Property Rights
UNCTAD	United Nations Conference on Trade and Development
WTO	World Trade Organization

1

Introduction

Many developing countries have been undertaking programs of external economic liberalization in the past decades. In 1960, only 22 percent of all countries had such openness, but by 2016, 56 percent of countries were open to international trade (World Bank, 2018). In recent decades, countries have been not only open to trade, but also to other international flows such as foreign direct investment (FDI) and remittances, among others.

Indeed, the expansion of trade has been unique by historical standards. Likewise, the globalization of capital flows has emanated due to the of policy initiatives undertaken in different countries. Among the capital flows, FDI has been a growing avenue of capital in developing countries and there have been evidences showing that FDI can have a positive impact on economic growth.

Remittances, on the other hand, are a principal avenue of external development finance and have played an instrumental role in lowering poverty in developing countries. They have grown steadily and have proved to be more stable than other external flows.

As this book focuses on trade, FDI and remittances, the rest of this chapter underlines the significance of each of these topics and provides a synopsis of the major issues included.

Trade

Trade is an important stimulator of economic growth. It enlarges a country's consumption capacities, increases world output, and provides access to scarce resources and worldwide markets for products without which poor countries would not have been able to develop. It also assists countries to achieve development targets by promoting and rewarding those sectors of the economy where individual countries possess a comparative advantage either with respect to labor efficiency or factor endowments.

It is generally agreed that the trade sector plays an instrumental role in attaining high and sustainable economic growth. However, in Nepal's case, the country's policy regime has not been successful in improving trade competitiveness. Though policy measures were formulated both to identify new exportable products and promote diversification of export markets, these were hardly executed. Weak infrastructure, poor human resources, lack of quality standardization of exports, absence of a strong legal framework, and frequent policy reversals, among others, have limited the country in improving its international competitiveness. Market and product concentrations of exports have resulted in volatile export proceedings. Structural difficulties of trade-related services and infrastructures have hampered in materializing potential comparative advantages.

Against the above perspective, I have devoted a number of articles in the first section of this book on trade. I begin with an article on "Import Substitution Strategy" where I have suggested that the private sector should be encouraged to engage in import substitution activities by providing them more incentives. The next article on "Export Promotion Measures" makes some suggestions for promoting exports including an aggressive infrastructure policy, providing guidance to exporters on export costing and pricing as well as on export quality control, and formulation of national trade promotion strategy, among others.

Devaluation is another topic which I have critically examined focusing on the impact of the devaluation undertaken both in 1985 and in 1991. Though the government did implement some measures to mitigate the adverse impact of devaluation, the results were not promising. It should have taken some more strict measures which are also discussed.

Nepal's trade strategy covering the period from the Sixth Plan (1980/81-1984/85) to the Seventh Plan (1985/86-89/90) period is also examined. The different trade policies enunciated during this period such as the Single Exchange Rate System, the Basket System, and the New Trade Policy, among others, are reviewed. The trade dispute of March 1989 with India is also explained. As the country is susceptible to external changes, I conclude that the country's trade strategy for the maintenance of balance of payments (BoP) stability and growth must emphasize the need for a flexible economy which is able to respond swiftly to exogenous changes.

Other topics deliberated in Section I include the Uruguay Round, the World Trade Organization (WTO) and regional trade, among others. I have noted that regional trade agreements (RTAs) generally can support the WTO's multilateral trading system. Moreover, the WTO agreements acknowledge that regional arrangements and closer economic integration can be beneficial to countries. I suggest that countries should abide by the two-track approach, according priority to promoting multilateral trade negotiations under the WTO as well as pursuing meaningful RTAs.

A detailed review of Nepal's trade sector up to FY 2003/04 is also presented separately. This paper includes a discussion on the Trade Policy of 1992, the Nepal-India Trade and Transit Treaty, as well as the major constraints to Nepal's trade sector. A number of recommendations are made for resolving the trade hurdles such as technological upgrading, investment in infrastructure, designing an appropriate legal framework compatible with regional and multilateral agreements, and formulation of new trade policy, among others.

FDI

Though capital flows comprise of FDI, portfolio investment and other kind of investments, FDI is better than other flows as it is both long-term and stable.

FDI in developing countries has a long history. It has fluctuated over time, as investors have reacted to changes in the environment for investment, including government policies toward FDI and the broader economic policy framework.

The policy environment, macro-economic stability, a sound domestic financial system, good law and order conditions, and the availability of cheap energy and skilled manpower are some of the important prerequisites for FDI.

The increasing reliance of developing economies on FDI is often seen as a positive trend due to a number of good features. These include, among others, the bringing-in of improved management techniques and of more advanced technologies as well as the easier access to international financial markets. All of this together generate meaningful benefits for the recipient countries in terms of economic growth and reduced external vulnerability.

However, FDI is not an automatic process and policies are also important for procuring the maximum benefits from it. Investors are guided by a number of factors including the return on their investments relative to their risks, the easiness with which their ventures in a given country can be integrated in the investor's global strategies and the quality of the host country's enabling environment.

In the above context, the articles and papers I have reproduced on FDI in this volume are diverse with some of them being quite general in nature and, hence, applicable to developing countries. I begin with an article relating to the benefits, costs and determinants of FDI where I mention that political and economic stability are indispensable for boosting this financial flow. I also indicate that FDI policy cannot be formulated or viewed in isolation, but should be regarded as an integral part of the country's overall economic development policy. In my article pertaining to increasing FDI flows during the post-conflict transition period, I point out that this financial flow can be a powerful mechanism for revitalizing industries and rebuilding infrastructure. I also stress that conflict prevention, peace and stability in the country would help in creating a favorable business environment, which would allow the execution of sound investment-friendly policies to attract FDI.

A number of short articles on different aspects of FDI have also been included where I discuss, among others, the challenges in attracting these flows, the significance of stable political climate and guarantee of security, and formulation of effective policies for improving the overall business climate. I underscore that policies and strategies should clearly indicate areas in which FDI is sought. I reiterate that while continuity and predictability of policy are essential for encouraging FDI, it is primarily the government's responsibility to make certain that these are in place so that FDI can contribute to development goals. At the same time, investor aftercare services, the aim of which is to make certain that foreign affiliates stay and continue to expand their business operations, should be an important function of FDI promotion.

Remittances

Remittances have proved to be more stable than other external flows and have helped to counterbalance the volatility of other capital flows to developing countries.

Migrants send remittances to their family members for supporting a rise in effective demand for consumption as well as for increasing investments in housing, health, education, and small business enterprises. In many instances, remittances constitute a significant percentage of total household income, performing as a substitute for earned income lost to unemployment, illness, retirement, emigration, falling wages and crop failure, among others, and ultimately protect poor families. These financial flows also furnish increased liquidity and foreign exchange to receiving countries, facilitating an upsurge in imports of goods and services (United Nations, 2017).

Remittances can also play an instrumental role in reducing poverty as they flow mainly to poor and marginalized families. Yet, the different uses of the remitted funds vary in their potential to reduce poverty and generate economic security for the household and community. Still, it must be understood that while the inflow of remittances can make a vital contribution to poverty reduction and local development in the country, it should not be considered as a substitute for national development and poverty reduction strategy.

In Nepal's case, remittances have been providing an important lifeline for many of the most vulnerable and poor households, both by contributing to basic needs such as food, health care, education, and housing, and by helping to deal with external shocks and fluctuations in income. These inflows have operated as a kind of household insurance against loss of income and other financial adversities and also have helped in lowering the overall incidence of poverty as well as maintaining a favorable balance of payments (BoP) position.

Against the foregoing perspective, I have included a number of articles and papers on remittances focusing on the impacts, uses and policy options. My first paper on this subject pertaining to the economic impact and policy choices notes that though remittances have been playing a vital role in Nepal's economic development and a number of measures have been undertaken for encouraging remittances through the official channel, there is much more to be done. A host of policy options have been spelled out.

I have also included a paper relating to the productive use of remittances where I stress that policies and programs need to be formulated by the policymakers for encouraging the utilization of remittances for productive purposes. In this regard, the government has to probe into what motivate its citizens to send money especially beyond individual family remittances, and design its policies to take benefit of it.

My other articles on remittances, among others, pertain to the impact of the global recession on remittances, the positive role played by remittances in the aftermath of the earthquake in Nepal, the involvement of microfinance institutions (MFIs) in the remittance transfer process, and the challenges brought about these transfers where I stress that while the inflow of remittances can make a major contribution to poverty reduction and domestic development in the country, I caution that too much dependence on remittances opens up the country to exposure to external shocks linked to remittance-sending countries. Hence, a crucial challenge is to search for alternatives and devise strategies to reduce this dependency.

References

United Nations (2017). "International Financial Flows and External Debt". *Development Issues* No. 10. Department of Economic and Social Affairs. 24 March. Available at https://www.un.org/development/desa/dpad/publication/development-issues-no-10-international-financial-flows-and-external-debt/

World Bank (2018). *World Development Indicators*. Washington, D.C.: World Bank. Available at: http://databank.worldbank.org/data/reports.aspx?source=world-development-indicators

Section I: Trade

2

Import Substitution Strategy*

Import substitution refers to economic development through the structural change in domestic production so that commodities formerly imported are superseded by home-made substitutes.

Various arguments have been set forward in favor of such a strategy. First, it is argued that import substitution saves foreign exchange by keeping the rate of growth of imports less than the rate of growth of exports. Moreover, where export promotion falls short of providing the foreign exchange needed for increased imports of capital goods, import substitution is the logical alternative.

However, it should be borne in mind that import substituting outputs do not immediately result in import and foreign exchange saving. This is because with the development of an import substituting industry, import saving would take place to the extent imports of finished goods are eliminated. But the very process of domestic production would create its own imports by way of imports of raw materials.

Initially, at least, the net import saving is unlikely to be significant as the process of production often does not expand beyond the 'assembly' stage. Substantial import saving would come about only when the process of production percolates downwards to various input-supplying industries. These linkages have not been witnessed in many developing countries.

Second, this strategy reduces the balance of payments (BoP) problem by curtailing imports. This is done through the technique of improved import management which includes, among others, better transit facilities and proper supply planning and procurement practices.

---

* *The Rising Nepal*, 12 April 1985.

It is important to note that import substitution cannot just be considered as one of the facets of import saving. An import substitution strategy has to be growth-oriented also. Since planners in many developing economies reiterate foreign exchange earnings and relegate the growth aspect, the formulation of a viable import substitution strategy has been misconstrued.

With respect to Nepal, imports accelerated from Rs. 1814.6 million in 1974/75 to Rs. 6514.3 million in 1983/84. The rate of growth of exports, on the other hand, has not been satisfactory. It soared from Rs. 889.6 million to Rs. 1703.9 million between 1974/75 to 1983/84. Hence, the continuous expansion of imports and lower growth of exports have led to growing trade deficits. Implementation of import substitution activities in certain areas could mollify this problem.

At present, industries that can be classified as import substitution industries are sugar, cigarette and cement, among others. As this is not adequate, a lot needs to be done. Import substitution prospects are favorable in construction materials, agricultural implements and textiles, *inter alia*.

Because the prices of third country inputs are exorbitantly high, most import substitution industries are dependent on Indian inputs especially when these inputs are in shortages. With regard to the utilization of domestic and third country inputs, the scope for import substitution exists for many commodities used by restaurants, hotels, and other services serving the tourist industry. However, to serve this purpose it is crucial to simplify the import, administrative and clearance procedures.

The formulation of an effective import substitution strategy requires some other considerations. The private sector should be given more incentives so that they get engaged in import substitution activities. There is also a need to determine the benefits flowing from import-substituting industries and other alternative activities or else resources may be drawn from sectors that are of comparative advantage.

3

Measures for Export Promotion*

An augmentation in export trade is one of the pivotal forces in economic development. The developing countries export a variety of commodities such as fertilizers and foodstuffs for valuable foreign exchange employed to import capital goods for industrialization.

A number of newly industrializing countries (NICs) such as the Republic of Korea have performed superbly on the export front as an outcome of skilful management of their economic policies. Hence, there is a significant positive correlation between export drive and economic growth.

Export promotion serves as an engine of growth through industrialization. Investment opportunities are offered in industries supplying inputs to the export sector, in industries using the export as an input and in industries producing consumer goods for factors of production employed in exports.

Developing countries vary considerably in the degree of their dependence on exports. This is related, first, to the internal division of labor in the economy and second, to the absolute size of the economy which sets a limit to the division of labor. Much more importantly, export dependence is characterized by the share of national income which is derived from the export sector. Dependence on foreign markets implies that prices of a large proportion of national output are fixed outside the economy. In addition, the proportion of domestic output produced specifically for external markets can be absorbed in domestic use to a very limited extent. The combination of these two circumstances results in the fluctuations of external receipts.

---

* *The Rising Nepal*, 4 August 1985.

Bulk of primary products exports of developing countries consists of agricultural commodities and industrial raw materials, which are both characterized by low income elasticity of demand. Thus, prospects for faster export expansion, or even for maintaining the past rate of growth are not propitious.

Exports to developed market economies have suffered from various constraints. One is the increase in domestic production of many of these commodities within the affluent countries. Another fact is that for internal economy and social reasons, many developed countries are subsidizing and protecting to a considerable degree their agricultural and mining sectors.

Developing countries have difficulty in expanding their exports because they lack the basic institutional and policy framework necessary to promote their trade successfully. While the industrialized countries generally have a long-established institutional infrastructure for trade promotion, within both the government and business sector, developing countries often do not. Further, services for exporters may also be lacking in such areas as trade information, export packaging and export financing. Unless such a framework exists at the national level, developing countries will not attain sustained export growth.

Developing countries can mitigate the obstacles to export growth through the assistance of developed countries. Three choices exist for the opulent nations: a) elimination of quantitative restrictions for greater market access for products originating in developing countries; b) general tariff reduction for trade expansion; and c) the proposal for granting temporary tariff preferences to exports of manufactures by developing countries.

In Nepal, the major export items consist of rice, jute, ghee, readymade garments, woolen carpets, and hides and skins. Exports increased from Rs. 685.6 million in 1973/74 to Rs. 1709.9 million in 1983/84. Imports, on the other hand, soared from Rs. 1163.2 million to Rs. 6533.5 million during the same period. It is palpable even to a novice that huge imports and lack of satisfactory growth in exports led to expansion in trade deficits.

To solve the trade deficit problems, certain instruments can be adopted. In the first place, an aggressive infrastructure policy for boosting foreign trade should be developed. Secondly, greater freedom for exporters, greater security of incentives, and higher levels of profitability are required for the expansion of exports. Thirdly, the Trade Promotion Centre can fulfil its objective of increasing exports only if it is guided by a national trade promotion strategy. Targets should be set at the national level in terms of potential exports and markets.

Moreover, Nepalese exporters should be advised on export costing and pricing and export quality control to compete successfully in the global market. Finally, measures for export promotion should include regular commodity surveys, maintenance of internal price stability through increasing productivity and lowering cost of production, exploitation of natural resources for creating export-oriented industries, and simplification in the administrative procedures followed in issuing licenses.

The Seventh Plan (1985-1990) accords top priority to the export sector. A five-year integrated program has been formulated for the selection of 10 to 15 items which are already being exported or are likely to be exported. Their production, quality and export value are to be properly enhanced. Analogously, for the competition of Nepalese exports in the international markets, domestic cost of production of export goods, their current export prices in the world markets, and the exchange rate of foreign currencies prevailing within the country will be constantly analyzed, and apposite techniques are to be employed to tackle the associated problems.

If the measures delineated above are implemented, a viable export sector could certainly emerge in Nepal and act as a catalyst in the overall economic progress.

4

Countertrade Practices of LDCs*

Countertrade is primarily a quasi-barter arrangement that explicitly links import and export transactions. It involves trading arrangements between private firms or government entities by which the seller is required to accept, as a partial or total settlement for his exports of goods (or, in some instances, services such as technology or industrial licences), specified goods or services, from the buyer.

There are basically four forms of countertrade: barter, compensation, buy-back and counter-purchase. Under a barter arrangement, the exporter sells specified goods to the importer in exchange for specified goods. This type of transaction, that comprises a limited number of products and excludes the involvement of a third party, is a one-time operation, and the transaction is concluded in a relatively short period. Pure barter is quite infrequent due the difficulties of locating a buyer for the product, which may not be easily marketable, and of negotiating a mutually acceptable price.

Under a compensation arrangement, the exporter agrees to take full or a partial payment in kind for the goods sold, but the exporter transfers the purchasing commitment to a third party who may be an end-user of products or a trading house. Compensation arrangements are also not very prevalent because time is required to find a suitable third party to whom the exporter can transfer the purchasing commitment.

The buy-back arrangement, covering a large volume of trade, is quite commonly used. The exporter supplies plant, equipment or technology to an importer and agrees to accept, as a partial or

* *The Rising Nepal*, 21 January 1991.

full payment, goods to be produced by the importer utilizing the exporter's equipment or technology. A variant of this arrangement is trade-related performance requirements through which foreign investors are required to export a fixed proportion of goods produced or to use a specified value of domestically produced inputs in production. The value of buy-back commitment may transcend the original export transaction.

The counter-purchase arrangement is also popular, but complex. Under this arrangement, the exporter sells goods, technology, or services and agrees to purchase from the latter, within a specified period, a specific total value of goods chosen from a list that exclude those produced by the technology being exported. Unlike barter and compensation arrangement, exporters entering into buy-back and counter-purchase arrangements must employ a trading firm to market the goods they purchase.

Least developed countries (LDCs), especially those maintaining overvalued exchange rates, have provided some explanations for their exercise of countertrade practices. In the first place, stress on the growth of manufacturing sectors, originally targeted at promoting import-substitution, has led to excess capacity and has produced pressures to find markets for surplus goods. Next, countertrade in the form of buy-back arrangements is viewed as a technique of acquiring reliable sources of essential raw materials while exporting equipment and technology that have become obsolete at home. There is also widespread agreement that in recent years the interaction of external financial stringency and depressed export demand has greatly increased pressures to engage in countertrade.

The costs of countertrade differ in accordance with such factors as the type of transaction and financing utilized in association with it. Some data are available about two components of these costs, that is, the discounts on goods' prices and the commissions paid to intermediaries. Discounts vary according to the category of goods. For easily marketed bulk commodities, they range between 1 and 3 percent, whereas for manufactured goods which are more difficult to sell, discounts of 20 percent or more are common. Commission paid to intermediaries appear to range from 0.5 percent to more than 5 percent of the value of the transactions, depending on the nature of the services provided.

While countertrade practices may, in the short run, be viewed as having some advantages, in the longer run they may have some serious repercussions. Manufacturing firms have to establish subsidiaries to tackle countertrade arrangement or utilize the services of trading companies specializing in such activities. Countertrade arrangements tend to increase the cost of trade due to the inclusion of additional risks not usually present in normal bank-financed foreign trade. Risks increase as countertrade arrangements extend over several years.

When counter-purchase or buy-back arrangements are concluded, exporters may have to obtain bridging finance for themselves or provide it for foreign buyers. This aggravates the financial costs of countertrade transactions. From the standpoint of the LDCs, the dumping of their exports in third markets by importers in the developed countries may be deleterious, as it may undercut the normal trade relations that LDCs have with these markets.

The extent of countertrade is a moot subject, reflecting uncertainty over a number of points. For example, there is still no unanimity as to just what should be included in the concept of countertrade. At the moment, there exist no international laws or agreements that deal directly with countertrade practices, though some do cover certain aspects. GATT has no provision dealing specifically with countertrade practices. Some of its important provisions, such as those on antidumping and countervailing duties, quantitative restrictions, subsidies, state trading enterprises, and emergency action on imports of particular products, may be interpreted to cover certain aspects of these practices.

If a broad definition of countertrade is used, its extent is unlikely to be much less than 15 percent of world trade and may be substantially greater. However, there is no way of making a separate estimate of the quantitative importance of financial reasons as compared to other reasons for countertrade. Nevertheless, available evidence suggests that there has been a rapid growth of such trade during a period characterized by widespread difficulties over debt service among LDCs and depressed levels of demand for much of their exports.

Very little, if anything, has been done in Nepal to promote countertrade. The concerned authorities could explore the possibilities of this type of trade more scrupulously since it is a novel tool of economizing on scarce foreign exchange resources. They should not regard countertrade to mean simply trade without cash since most countertrade transactions involve the conversion of the value of traded goods into cash equivalent.

This type of trade could be conducted with LDCs in general and the SAARC countries in particular. However, the limitations delineated above should be carefully scrutinized. Export sales related to countertrade arrangements require careful planning to ensure that the imported products will be of good quality, easily marketable, delivered on time, and efficiently priced to take account of the additional marketing costs that may be required.

5

The Uruguay Round: Issues and Options*

Developing countries, which had been marginal participants in the Kennedy Round (1964-67) were more active in the Tokyo Round (1973-79). The Tokyo Round brought tariff reductions, codes on nontariff barriers, and the "framework agreement." The framework agreement, on which the developing countries were especially active, provided through its "enabling clause" a legal basis for generalized system of preferences (GSP) to breach the most favored nation (MFN) principle.

The agreement also made it easier for developing countries to adopt trade measures to foster particular industries. In return, these countries agreed to a "graduation" principle which related the capacity to make concessions to level of development.

The eventual compromise reached at Punta del Este in the Uruguay Round Declaration (GATT, 1986) distinguished trade in services from the other subjects formally encompassed in the negotiation, including trade-related aspects of intellectual property rights (TRIPs) and trade-related investment measures (TRIMs). Some negotiation groups were to tackle problems related with tariffs and nontariff measures, textiles and clothing, agriculture, tropical products, multilateral trade agreements, TRIPs and TRIMs, among others.

The results of two years of negotiations were presented to the Montreal Mid-term Ministerial Meeting in December 1988. The Meeting ended deadlocked on four issues; agriculture, intellectual property rights, textiles and clothing, and reform of the safeguards system.

---

* *The Rising Nepal*, 5 March 1991.

Four years after Punte del Este, Brussels was to provide an indication of the final balance sheet of the Uruguay Round. However, the talks ended in a stalemate. The principal cause for the failure was the impasse between the US and the European Community (EC) regarding agricultural subsidies. It was also suspected that in the final analysis the industrial countries were not all that determined to reduce non-tariff measures to trade and to do away with the bilateral deals that were becoming increasingly more frequent.

This highlights, to a degree, the growing irrelevance of any developing country in international trade and thereby in multilateral negotiations. There are two kinds of reactions to this abhorrent recognition. The "nationalist school" underlines the validity of certain stances taken internationally, which oppose the unequitable imposition of concessions on the poorer countries. The "bandwagon school", on the other hand, claims that since the world has undergone a series of reforms, developing countries must change with it if they are to achieve rapid economic growth and proceed successfully into the 21st century. This argument concludes that more opening up of the economy must be ultimately advantageous despite initial traumas, and that liberalization of current and capital accounts should be accompanied by the abandonment of rigid and untenable stances such as those on TRIPs and TRIMs.

TRIPs, or patents as they are known, are governed by an international convention—the Paris Convention, subsequently revised on several occasions—which was agreed by a number of countries at the instance of developed countries. The aim of this Convention was to procreate monopoly rights in favor of the patent holder for a number of years, in respect of any product patented by him, on the condition that he had to be compensated, both for the intellectual exercise conducted by him in discovering the product and also for the money spent by him in doing so.

The current problem posed by TRIPs is more serious since it goes even beyond the Paris Convention. First, the proposals now before GATT tend to expand the scope of patentability by including micro-biological processes and plant varieties. Plant protection, in particular, would be a severe setback to developing countries' agricultural sector, and especially to availability of seeds.

Secondly, the obligation of the patent holders seems to be greatly weakened. It is now being affirmed that a patent is considered to have served its purpose if the patented product is available for import to the countries concerned. This would imply that a country cannot introduce measures such as compulsory licensing or revocation of a patent so long as the patented product is marketed in that country at whatever price the patent holder decides.

The other set of proposals, contained in TRIMs, is equally detrimental to developing countries. They amount to an infringement of the economic sovereignty of the country, for the crux of these proposals is that all investments including those for services, like banking and insurance, should be completely free.

All pretense of planned development should be given up, and foreign investments should be permitted, irrespective of what they produce and how much they export. Actions against multinational corporations (MNCs) cannot be taken, although many of them are known to indulge in restrictive and unfair practices in respect of purchases, sales, market allocations and price manipulations.

The Uruguay Round of Trade Negotiations did not break down in December 1990 because of the inability to resolve the 'new' GATT issues, that is, TRIPs and TRIMs. The GATT conference came to a standstill over the issue of cuts in farm subsidies by the EC. The EC had agreed to cut its farm subsidies by only 30 percent, a proposal rejected as insufficient by the US and other principal food exporting nations, who demanded a 75 percent cut in subsidies to farmers and 90 percent slashing of food export subsidies.

However, the 12-nation EC, under pressure from spiraling costs, has started reviewing its agricultural support program. Although the review process may take some time, there are hopes that the trading block may be willing to consider subsidy cuts.

6

Trade Strategy of Nepal during 1980s*

Introduction

Trade contributes to growth and development in a less-developed country in various ways. If a trade strategy is properly implemented, it expands output and provides additions to incomes through demand for local natural resources. It encourages competition, with its constant stimulus toward reducing costs and refining quality. There are also other benefits. Essential capital goods, such as machinery, raw materials, and semi-finished materials, are imported. Technical know-how, skills, and management progress into the less-developed countries through trade relationship.

Nepal has already completed seven development plans. However, the trade programs developed and executed have been unsatisfactory and the benefits mentioned above have not been achieved to the degree desired.

Between the First Plan (1956/57-1960/61) and the Fifth Plan (1975-76/1979-80), there was no significant change in trade diversification, both country-wise and commodity-wise. In 1979/80 Nepal's exports to India still accounted for 45 percent of total exports while its imports comprised 51 percent. Further, primary goods constituted the major portion of exportable goods. Imports were more heterogeneous, encompassing a wide range of manufactured goods and raw materials. Thus, it was exigent to devise sound and concrete programs both to achieve improvements in commodity-wise and country-wise trade diversification as well as to curtail the alarming trade deficit.

---

* *Nepalese Economic Review*, 5(1): 1-18, January-June 1991.

The Sixth Plan (1980/81-1984/85) and the Seventh Plan (1985/86-89/90) are examined in the light of the preceding analysis. The policies announced by the Government from time to time are also delineated. Finally, some policy implications are made.

The Sixth and the Seventh Plan

The overriding objective of the Sixth Plan with regard to trade was that the principle of diversification would be pursued on the basis of economic benefits and losses. All possibilities would be explored to procure the country's imports from the cheapest sources and exports would be directed to those countries where the prices are very favorable.[1]

During the first year of the Plan, exports equivalent to the value of Rs. 1608.7 million were recorded. This is disclosed in Table 1. Improvement in agricultural production and an upsurge in handicraft and carpet exports were responsible for this state of affairs. However, during 1981/82 and 1982/83 the value of exports took a downward trend. This was attributed to the recession in world markets, widespread drought, and the elimination of exchange incentives for exporting to overseas countries. All in all, total exports from 1980/81 to 1984/85 amounted to Rs. 8676.6 million.

Table 1: Exports, Imports and Trade Deficit

(Rs. in million)

Year	Exports	Imports	Trade Deficit
1980/81	1608.6	4428.2	2819.6
1981/82	1491.5	4930.3	3438.8
1982/83	1132.0	6314.0	5182.0
1983/84	1703.9	6514.3	4810.4
1984/85	2740.6	7742.1	5001.5
1985/86	3078.0	9341.2	6263.2
1986/87	2991.4	10905.2	7913.8
1987/88	4114.6	13869.6	9755.0
1988/89	4195.3	16263.7	12068.4
1988/89*	3407.9	12336.0	8928.1
1989/90*	3641.0	13174.7	9533.7

*indicates the figures for the first nine months only.

Sources: Nepal Rastra Bank and Trade Promotion Centre.

Imports displayed a rising trend during the Plan period. Total imports soared by 27 percent in 1980/81 as compared to 1979/80 and stood at Rs. 4428.2 million whereas the spending on imports in 1984/85 was Rs. 7742.1 million, an increase of more than 15 percent when compared to that of 1983/84. During the Plan period, imports from India and overseas accounted for 45 percent and 55 percent, respectively, of total imports.

Trade deficit was to the tune of Rs. 2329.6 million and Rs. 2819.6 million, respectively, in the last year of the Fifth Plan and the first year of the Sixth Plan, but this deficit almost doubled to Rs. 5001.5 million in 1984/85 (Table 1).

Although improved performance was registered during 1983/84 and 1984/85 because of the rise in export of carpets and readymade garments, the current account deficit was still 7.2 percent of GDP, a steep increment from the 1 percent of 1975/76. On the one hand, the exchange rate of the Nepalese rupee *vis-à-vis* the India rupee had remained virtually unchanged, while on the other, the exchange rate of the Nepalese rupee against all other currencies had been fairly unstable. Further, while imports from India did not require any licensing formalities, imports from overseas were governed by licensing and rationing arrangements. Both the unpredictability of the exchange rates of the major currencies and the licensing system paved way for substantial increases in the commercial imports from India.

During the Sixth Plan period, there were some changes in the composition of the exportable items. Till the end of the Fifth Plan, jute was accorded the top place among commodities exported to overseas countries. However, during the Sixth Plan this position was captured by woolen carpets.[2] Unprocessed and semi-processed goods which formed 91 percent of the total exports to India plummeted to 39 percent by 1983/84.

Some causes for the dismal performance of the trade sector include a) paucity of important infrastructural facilities, b) recession in the international market, c) the dearth of markets for primary products, d) limited finished exportable commodities, and e) rise in prices of construction materials, petroleum products, chemical fertilizers and other such commodities which exerted upward pressures on imports.

The main goals of the Seventh Plan were a) to create a favorable balance of payments (BoP) situation, b) to develop basic infrastructures for the smooth and well-managed imports of goods and commodities necessary for economic growth,; and c) to optimize the benefits of foreign trade by making the transit system more efficient and less expensive.[3]

Some detailed programs were to be developed to fulfill the above objectives: a) an effective plan would be executed to enhance the export sector through an expansion in domestic production coupled with the standardization of the produced goods; b) the private sector's participation in the export sector would be encouraged; c) focus would be accorded to goods essential for national development, whereas imports of other goods would be curbed; d) the structure of import trade would be revised both on a commodity-wise and country-wise basis in conformity with the trends associated with the BoP situation; and e) new transit facilities would be proposed in addition to the existing ones for reducing the exorbitant transit costs.

Trade data disclose that during the first four years of the Seventh Plan, exports soared from Rs. 3078.0 million in 1985/86 to Rs. 4195.3 million in 1988/89, an average annual rise of 12 percent (Table 1). Although total exports revealed an upward trend, exports to India fell by almost 19 percent because of heavy losses in the export of pulses, rice, herbs, raw jute and jute goods between the period 1984/85 and 1986/87.

However, in the third year of the Plan (1987/88), exports to India showed an increment of 20 percent over the previous year emanating from increased export of primary goods such as mustard, linseeds, and jute goods, *inter alia*. Nevertheless, it failed to reach the level of 1984/85. The figure for 1988/89 plummeted to Rs. 1034.9 million primarily due to the expiry of Nepal-India Trade and Transit Treaties in March, 1989. The condition even worsened during the first nine months of 1989/90 when exports to India were to the tune of Rs. 221.8 million (Table 2). The major export to India during this period was raw jute (Table 3).

Table 2: Direction of Trade

(Rs. in million)

Year	Exports		Imports	
	India	Overseas	India	Overseas
1980/81	992.4	616.3	2179.0	2249.2
1981/82	994.4	497.1	2280.9	2649.4
1982/83	843.2	288.8	2499.6	3814.4
1983/84	1160.7	543.2	3058.0	3456.3
1984/85	1601.7	1138.9	3895.8	3846.3
1985/86	1241.1	1836.9	3970.9	5370.3
1986/87	1302.6	1688.8	4262.0	6643.2
1987/88	1567.8	2546.8	4595.8	9273.8
1988/89	1034.9	3160.4	4238.7	12025.0
1988/89*	984.5	2423.4	3328.3	9007.7
1989/90*	221.8	3419.2	3476.7	9698.0

* indicates the figures for the first nine months only.
Sources: Nepal Rastra Bank and Trade Promotion Centre.

Table 3: Exports of Major Commodities to India

(Rs. in million)

Commodities	1980/81	1981/82	1982/83	1983/84	1984/85	1985/86	1986/87	1987/88	1988/89	1988/89*	1989/90*
Timber	226.2	87.2	28.8	7.9	25.7	-	-	-	-	-	-
Rice (Husked)	117.6	136.5	11.3	75.7	250.0	93.2	14.4	-	-	-	-
Maize	24.5	26.1	0.3	0.4	10.9	-	-	-	1.3	-	-
Mustard & Linseeds	-	-	-	75.5	25.6	58.1	103.1	141.3	50.8	49.8	-
Herbs	16.5	6.4	5.9	8.0	27.9	16.6	8.1	16.4	13.7	13.5	-
Ghee	54.0	26.2	36.8	45.8	39.4	47.0	46.6	46.7	49.9	49.1	0.1
Dried Ginger	10.8	15.3	19.3	37.1	38.7	30.3	35.2	37.3	30.3	29.0	1.0
Raw Jute	46.4	43.4	85.5	36.5	43.9	2.3	14.5	44.1	36.5	34.6	25.5
Jute Cuttings	17.7	18.2	5.2	1.2	-	-	0.5	8.6	10.5	10.5	-
Jute Goods	10.3	81.0	179.7	212.1	260.0	167.4	164.0	188.7	134.0	134.0	0.4

* denotes the figure for the first nine months only.
Sources: Nepal Rastra Bank and Trade Promotion Centre.

Exports to overseas countries increased from Rs. 1836.9 million in 1985/86 to Rs. 3160.4 million in 1988/89, which was equivalent to an average annual growth rate of 22 percent (Table 2). The major factor was an augmentation in cottage industry products such as carpets. But, exports to overseas countries fell to Rs. 1688.8 million in 1986/87 arising from a reduction in the export of raw jute, pulses, hides and skins, and readymade garments. During the first nine months of 1988/89 and 1989/90, the export figures stood at Rs. 2423.4 million and Rs. 3419.2 million, respectively, due to the expiry of the Indo-Nepal treaty. The principal exports constituted of carpets, garments, and hides and skins. This is illustrated in Table 4.

Table 4: Exports of Major Commodities to Overseas Countries

(Rs. in million)

Commodities	1980/81	1981/82	1982/83	1983/84	1984/85	1985/86	1986/87	1987/88	1988/89	1988/89*	1989/90*
Raw Jute	94.7	62.6	13.7	-	-	28.9	21.6	30.3	4.2	0.6	0
Jute Goods	28.6	1.5	-	-	-	-	-	0.4	4.5	3.6	4.1
Pulses	40.1	58.2	3.0	6.0	108.6	240.6	100.6	4.0	46.0	42.9	173.9
Cardamom (large)	18.0	7.4	5.8	6.5	14.6	25.7	43.3	20.0	14.9	14.1	6.7
Medicinal Herbs	0.9	0.5	0.5	0.6	0.8	0.3	0.1	0.2	0.5	0.3	1.6
Woolen Goods	10.2	5.1	4.8	3.9	4.6	3.8	5.3	9.0	16.8	14.2	19.8
Hides and Skins	137.4	93.3	95.1	155.6	242.9	233.2	161.0	165.4	161.2	101.3	200.0
Carpets	65.0	84.0	137.8	265.4	249.4	376.4	627.5	1223.7	1634.0	1176.2	1724.3
Readymade Garments	13.0	13.8	10.0	20.5	470.9	803.7	611.2	916.6	1117.8	950.3	1054.5
Handicrafts	100.2	12.2	9.4	12.6	12.1	17.7	32.4	53.8	91.6	60.4	46.11

* denotes the figure for the first nine months only.

Sources: Nepal Rastra Bank and Trade Promotion Centre.

Imports catapulted by an average annual rate of more than 20 percent between 1985/86 and 1988/89, the values amounting to Rs. 9341.2 million and Rs. 16263.7 million, respectively (Table 1). Imports from India augmented annually by 2.3 per cent, and overseas imports accelerated by almost 31 percent. This situation was ascribed to the tremendous rise in the import of construction materials, POL products, and fertilizers. Although imports from other countries increased by 29.7 percent in 1988/89 compared to 1987/1988, imports from India fell by 7.8 percent in 1988/89. The imports from India was substituted by imports from other countries through the Open General License (OGL) system. Imports remained low in 1988/89 compared to the preceding years due to the transportation hurdles created by the trade and transit deadlock with India. During the first nine months of 1989/90, total imports were to the tune of Rs. 13174.7 million (Table 1). Of this, imports from overseas formed 75 percent.

Consequently, the trade deficit figures were quite alarming between 1985/86 and 1988/89 as the figures stood at Rs. 6263.2 million and Rs. 12068.4 million, respectively. Trade deficit with India and overseas countries grew at an annual rate of 5.8 percent and 35.9 percent, respectively.

To recapitulate, the following features are notable in Nepal's trade pattern:

a) Commodity-wise and country-wise diversification of trade have undergone some changes. Trade activities seem to be characterized by a significant amount of instability with regard to the commodity and market composition. Items which were vital in one year have sometimes been abruptly dropped from the trade data of the subsequent year. The variations in the commodity composition of the exports and imports do not necessarily exhibit the pattern of the real comparative advantage of the country.

b) Among the growing imports necessary for economic growth, capital goods seem important. These imports have been financed partly by international financial resources. But besides being adequate, these resources bring about a further complication. The burden of servicing them become heavier and heavier, and in some instances the condition is very critical because the exports which supply the necessary funds for servicing are expanding slowly and losing their purchasing power, while demand for imports continue to accelerate. The payment for the sharply rising current account deficit by foreign loans is only a short-term solution, but in the long run, in addition to being an unreliable method, it will result in a rapidly rising foreign debt.

c) Exports soared almost in proportion to the increase in GDP. The proportion of import contents was seen increasing in GDP. This is revealed in Table 5.

Table 5: Selected Indicators of Trade

(in percent)

Year	Primary good Exports/Total Exports	Manufactured Good Exports/ Total Exports	Exports/ GDP	Imports/ GDP	Export/ Import
1980/81	74	26	5.9	16.2	36.3
1981/82	79	21	4.6	15.9	30.2
1982/83	62	38	3.4	18.7	17.9
1983/84	60	40	4.5	17.1	26.2
1984/85	56	44	6.6	18.5	35.4
1985/86	43	57	6.2	18.9	32.9
1986/87	44	56	5.2	18.9	27.4
1987/88	36	64	6.1	20.4	29.7
1988/89	22	78	5.4	21.0	25.8
1988/89*	26	74	N.A.	N.A.	27.6
1989/90*	11	79	N.A.	N.A.	27.6

* indicates the value for the first nine months only. N.A. means not available.
Sources: Nepal Rastra Bank and Trade Promotion Centre.

Major Trade Policies

Single Exchange Rate (SER)

Since the Dual Exchange Rate (DER) scheme, established on 30 March 1978, could not fulfill its objectives, it was substituted by a Single Exchange Rate (SER) scheme on 19 September 1981. Under this scheme, all the transactions were conducted at a uniform rate of Rs. 13.20 per US$. There prevailed no attractive incentives to exporters who wished to export to overseas countries.

Nepalese exporters encountered enormous transportation cost while conducting trade with overseas countries because of the geographical problem of land-lockedness. The exporters were of the view that it was not profitable to export to overseas countries under the prevailing subsidy rate. Moreover, the objective of trade diversification was not realized as illustrated from the fact that India's share in total exports of Nepal rose from 68 percent to 74 percent between 1981/82 and 1982/83, while the share of overseas countries went down from 32 percent to 26 percent.

The Basket System

Because of the necessity to adjust the exchange rate system towards a more flexible arrangement, an exchange rate system based on a trade weighted basket, with the US dollar as the intervention currency, was introduced on 1 June 1983. Indian currency was incorporated in the basket with effect from May, 1986.

The switch towards a basket of currencies was impelled by the extravagant volatility and misalignment of exchange rates during the early 1980s. The exchange rate of the Nepalese rupee, thus, became more pragmatic and Nepal's exports more competitive. The basket system also protected the economy from the potential shocks of greater doses of devaluation.

In managing the value of the Nepalese currency, priority was accorded in ensuring a fair degree of stability in the day-to-day rates. This is more perspicuous in the case of Nepalese rupee against the Indian currency where the demand for a fair degree of stability as well as eschewal of undue exchange risks emanating from too frequent changes are affirmed. Because of its insertion in the basket the officials may have possessed some flexibility in adjusting the Nepalese rupee-Indian rupee rate misalignments. The unrestricted movement of goods, labor and capital through the long open border, and the free and unlimited convertibility of the Indian currency in Nepal made Nepalese rupee sensitively averse to frequent adjustments.

New Trade Policy and Nine-point Program

By mid-1982 the Government realized that unless new strategies are developed and implemented efficiently, the country's BoP situation would deteriorate. Hence, in June, 1982 the "New Trade Policy" was announced. Separate, but related, policies for exports and imports were incorporated.

The objectives of the export policy included the following: (a) generation of employment opportunities by enhancing the production, productivity and qualitative standard of exportable goods; (b) creation of a wide international market for domestic products; (c) expansion of the scope of international trade and increment in the level of foreign exchange earnings to meet the growing import requirements; and (d) establishing wide links with the foreign market for promoting modern technology, skill and management capabilities.[4]

A gamut of programs were spelled out in order to fulfill the foregoing goals. They included, *inter alia,* (a) the formulation of a "product development program", (b) setting up of a National Export Trade Development Council, (c) production of processed and semi-processed agricultural exportable goods for promoting export capacity, (d) pursuance of policy of both country-wise and commodity-wise diversification of exports, (c) enlargement of the private sector's participation in the trade sector, and (f) simplification and streamlining of the procedures associated with customs assessment.

The objectives of the import policy were the following: (a) to guarantee the availability of essential commodities such as capital goods, construction materials, and industrial raw materials for speeding up the pace of economic development; (b) to provide the people with easy access to those products that cannot be locally produced or those that are produced in limited quality or those that entail high production cost; and (c) to expedite the import substitution process both in the agricultural and industrial sectors.

To meet the above goals, the relevant programs that were propounded included, among others, (a) formulation of a liberal policy towards the import of capital goods, construction materials, industrial raw materials, production inputs, and goods of daily use, (b) protection to agricultural and industrial commodities that could be manufactured internally on economically feasible terms, (c) simplification of all administrative rules and regulations relating to import trade, and (d) establishment of a Trade and Supplies Management Committee.

A new government was formed in 1983, which announced a nine-point export promotion program. The notable features of the program were the following: a) formation of a 14-member Export Product and Export Promotion Council; b) furnishing of 10 percent cash subsidy on f.o.b. value of exports; c) provision to utilize 15 percent of total earnings for the import of raw materials and capital goods for industries procuring foreign exchange through exports to overseas countries; d) lowering of custom duties to just 1 percent on goods exported to third countries; e) exemption from customs and sales tax to industries exporting their own products; f) permission to exporters to borrow a pre-export loan up to Rs. 2.5 million against letters of credit opened by importers; g) supply of necessary refinance by the Nepal Rastra Bank (NRB) to commercial banks and compensation to the banks for the losses arising from rebate on interest rate; h) investment by Nepal Industrial Development Corporation of at least 10 percent of its total investment for export-oriented industries; and i) establishment of separate units by the commercial banks for export activities at their branches situated in different parts of the kingdom.

However both the "New Trade Policy" and the nine-point program did not produce satisfactory results as trade data reveal especially due to inefficiency in the administration system and lack of implementation of the various programs. The programs were generally not supervised during implementation, bringing about constant and often *ad hoc* changes in the *modus operandi*, attenuating the effectiveness and efficiency of the on-going policies.

The Auction System and the Open General License (OGL) System

The auction system came into effect in July 1986 in order to simplify imports from overseas countries. Import licenses for items to be imported under this system were grouped into three categories: (i) category A: industrial raw materials and construction materials; (ii) category B: semi-luxury items; and (iii) category C: luxury items.

The adverse effect of the auction system was that the import of various items did not seem to be directed towards satisfying the country's internal demand. Premium rates agreed to by such firms were often guided by the prices obtained by smuggling of these commodities. Paucity of appropriate monitoring regarding the payments from banks as to ascertain whether items have actually been imported and over-invoicing of items largely escalated the probability of foreign exchange leakages. Two new categories of items (D) and (E) were added by the interim government which reduced the license values on items identified as likely smuggling goods by 50 to 75 percent. Further, certain modifications were made on the Personal Effects Rule which not only curtailed smuggling but also increased revenue in the form of premium rates that were agreed during the auctions for import licenses. Nevertheless, in spite of these modifications, cases relating to smuggling and misutilization of foreign exchange were quite common.

The OGL system was introduced in March 1989 to facilitate the import of industrial raw materials and essential commodities. Some consumer goods were also incorporated in this arrangement. An examination of goods imported under the OGL system discloses that it comprised of essential goods such as petroleum products, coal, medicines and baby foods, and raw materials required for export promoting industries such as raw wool, cotton yarn, cotton fabric, as well as tractors, trucks, and buses for a smooth and convenient transportation system.

Although the objective of the OGL system was to streamline the import procedures and reduce dependence on any one particular country, many distortions emerged due to inapposite implementation of the policy. Initially, the inclusion of luxury and semi-luxury household items in the list brought about suspicion among the local masses regarding the goals of the system. Subsequently, the interim government deleted all goods from the OGL list except raw wool, cotton yarn, petroleum products, coal and newsprint. A close monitoring on the selection of goods, its price and quality was required to check deflections and provide a smooth delivery of the basic commodities.

Export Processing Zone (EPZ)

In December 1990, the Government constituted a high level working committee under the chairperson of the Industry Minister for setting up an Export Processing Zone (EPZ) in Kathmandu to promote export-oriented industries in the country. The Committee's task was to formulate a time bound program for the project, suggest the organizational structure, prepare legal framework, and explore the possibilities for financial and capital requirement of the project as well as identify the donors.

As EPZ is an industrial area specially designed for export-oriented industries where the facility of tax exemption is provided for imports of raw materials required by the manufactures inside the region. However, the manufactured goods are not allowed to be sold inside the country, as they are strictly for export.

Increased foreign exchange earnings from exports and more job opportunities are expected when the EPZ comes up at Gothatar in Kathmandu in five years' time. The proposed EPZ is believed to generate direct employment to 15300 persons and is expected to export the industrial goods worth about 84 million dollars every year.

Three types of industries may be permitted inside the EPZ. They may either be wholly owned by a foreigner, or a joint venture with Nepalese individuals or firms, or fully owned by a Nepalese. Foreigners operating industries inside it either alone or on a joint-venture basis are to make their entire payments due to the government in foreign currency. The laborers inside the EPZ would be all Nepalese. A feasibility study was undertaken by the Government with the assistance of UNDP relating to this.

Five categories of products have been identified which could be produced by industries inside the EPZ. These are carpets, garments, leather-based products, electric and electronic goods, and products based on herbs and jewellery. Some of these products, particularly garments and carpets, are already Nepal's major exportable items. Currently, the duties, taxes and their charges paid by export-oriented industries are refunded by the government. But the process of refunding these charges to industries is time-consuming and the EPZ will try to mitigate all of these hindrances. Further, imports of all raw materials would be free of all local taxes, and all the products would likewise be exported without any local taxes.

Nepal-India Trade Prior to 23 March 1989

Nepal's land-locked position, its association with the Indian market, and its reliance on India for transit routes were responsible for creation of a special relationship in trade between these two countries. Prior to 23 March 1989, the special relationship was based on two treaties signed in March 1978. A transit treaty permitted Nepalese imports entering Calcutta by sea and pass through to Nepal at any one of fifteen points along the Nepalese-Indian border free from Indian taxes or import duties; a trade treaty, on the other hand, allowed bilateral trade to take place at twenty-one points along the common border. There were other issues that were incorporated in the special relationship: the free movement of labor between the two countries, full convertibility of the Indian rupee in Nepal, no quantitative or other restrictions on either current account or capital market transactions, preferential tariffs between the two countries, and special commodity agreements between state corporations under which Indian corporations sold petroleum products, coal, sugar, and salt to Nepal state corporations at mutually advantageous prices.

Coupled with India's transport cost advantage, the above determinants have made India Nepal's principal trade partner. Since Nepal and India, while possessing low tariffs themselves, did not have a common tariff with respect to the rest of the world, it created incentives for smuggling. Given India's high tariffs structure and Nepal's wish to keep a lower tariff structure, there was an incentive to smuggle third country goods from Nepal to India. The existence of these illegal activities brought about serious repercussions. The government budget was adversely affected because Nepal depended, to some extent, on taxes on international trade and transactions. The biased statistics that were a consequence of illegal trade also misled policymakers. In addition, the illegal activities themselves and their surveillance by the authorities necessitated resource costs. To curtail smuggling, the country devised a comprehensive structure of quantitative restrictions (QRs), import licenses, and administrative controls on third country imports and maintained its tariffs on many such products at a higher level than desirable.

Breakdown of Nepal-India Trade and Transit Treaties

Due the divergences in views, the trade and transit treaties which expired on 23 March 1989 could not be renewed. Consequently, all trade over surface routes with India was limited to just two border points. This was applicable to trade with India, third country trade crossing India, and intra-Nepal trade between Central and Western Nepal. Since trade between the far western development region of Nepal and the rest of the country took place through India and this was no longer conceivable, this gave rise to acute scarcities of some basic goods in the west and an unmarketable surplus of some agricultural products. Moreover, the special commodity arrangements on fuel and coal expired. Because of the difference in procedures and time period in arranging for fuel from overseas countries, Nepal was incapable to import the same volume of fuel for quite some time.

Both Nepal and India applied MFN tariffs to bilateral trade. Hence, Nepalese exports, which had been exempted from Indian tariffs, were subject to Indian MFN custom duties that ranged between 100 and 150 percent, successfully blocking the entry of

Nepal's exports into India. Nepal's imposition of MFN tariffs on Indian imports gave rise to a 25 to 45 percent increment in tariffs. Initially, to mollify the price rise brought about by the new tariff structure, the government reduced all import duties. However, it later altered this measure for fiscal reasons, and alternatively lowered tariffs on some essential imports. The Government also introduced some items to its OGL list, modified some special tariff rates, and promulgated selective export cash subsidies. In the meantime, BoP transactions between Nepal and India continued to be carried out in Indian currency and the exchange rate between the two currencies remained to be fixed. Moreover, the Indian currency was still convertible to the Nepalese rupee. In order to check capital flight, limitations were laid down by the Nepalese officials on the purchase of Indian currency.

Impact of Impasse and Some Measures

From 23 March 1989 to 10 June 1990 Nepal was undergoing a phase of no-treaty regime. A situation of virtual stoppage of the movement of goods, particularly essential goods, across the 1778 km. long open border emerged. Both the country and its people were highly affected.

With the eradication of the duty-free status of Nepalese exports to India and the introduction of Indian MFN tariff that ranged between 100 and 150 percent, Nepal's exports to India almost vanished as displayed in Table 3. With regard to the two major exports to third countries, exports of carpets continued to expand despite the impasse, but exports of garments initially fell due to problems in acquiring imported cloth from India. However, they have since made up and attained significant levels.

The effects of the impasse has differed significantly across regions and sectors. The critical consequences were encountered by the people of the far western and the mid-western regions, while those of the eastern and the central regions were the least affected because of their propinquity to the two border points. Agricultural output was not affected to a large degree since most crops had already been harvested prior to the impasse. Moreover, the weather conditions were favorable both in 1988/89 and 1989/90. Industrial output, especially manufacturing and construction, which constituted about 15 percent of GDP, was seriously hindered due to fuel, coal and power shortages, higher costs of imports, and the evanescence of the Indian market.

Because of the difficulties faced by the trade sector, the Government announced a number of measures to expand trade with overseas countries. These included the following:

a) Custom duties on exports were lowered to 0.5 percent.

b) Cash payments were provided to exporters on the basis of f.o.b. price on a number of items, namely, (i) leather goods (25 percent), (ii) finished leather (20 percent), (iii) crossed leather (15 percent), (iv) blue leather (10 percent), (v) pulses (15 percent), (vi) large cardamom (10 percent), (vii) clarified butter (10 percent), (viii) essential oil (15 percent), (ix) dry ginger (10 percent), (x) jute hessian (35 percent), (xi) rosin (18 percent), and (xii) turpentine (18 percent).

c) Import of raw wool under the OGL arrangement without premium was introduced to lower the production cost of carpets.

d) Additional tariffs on imports were reduced.

e) Imports of basic industrial raw materials were subsumed under OGL.

f) Arrangements were made for Royal Nepal Airlines Corporation (RNAC) to provide a 50 percent discount on air freight for cargo movement to and from Karachi and Dhaka.

Agreement of 10 June 1990

The foregoing measures were either nullified or made dormant with the signing of the joint communique by the two Prime Ministers on 10 June 1990. A salient feature of the agreement was that India would import primary products from Nepal with no quantitative restrictions or basic custom duties. It would restore twenty-two border points for entry of goods into Nepal. The standby credit facility to Nepal would also rise to Rs. 350 million from Rs. 250 million. Further, India would resume supplies of coal, coke, petroleum products and preferential goods such as sugar and cement to Nepal.

Similarly, Nepal was to resume tariff preferences to Indian goods by exempting additional custom duty, among others. It would also undertake measures for the removal of Indian nationals from the ambit of the work permit system. With reference to the terms and conditions of employment in the education sector, Indian nationals would be placed on the same status as Nepalese nationals. Further, Nepal would remove the restrictions on the flow of Indian currency between Nepal and India on the basis of reciprocity.

Conclusion

Nepal's foreign trade scenario during the last decade explicitly revealed some structural issues. Although India's share in Nepal's trade fell due to the diversification programs, other countries cannot be totally depended upon for exports of basic commodities. It has been demonstrated that the Indian market is necessary for export of these commodities. Despite the structural change in the composition of goods for exports and imports, exports to third country is principally dependent on two commodities (readymade garments and carpets).

The country should assign new productive capacity to manufacturing industries that are capable of competing in the international market. It should identify potential comparative advantage industries and their production should be undertaken at a more rapid pace than is now being exercised.

Nepal is vulnerable to external changes and cannot influence world market forces. In foreign trade, the country is a price-taker implying that it does not have any control on the determination of terms and conditions of its external transactions. Hence, changes in external factors which would be favorable to the country must be exploited optimally through timely and appropriate policy measures.

Notes

1. Details are provided in NPC (1981).
2. For instance, export of woolen carpets accounted for 48 percent of total exports to overseas countries in 1983/84.
3. This is explained in NPC (1985).
4. For a detailed discussion, see Ministry of Commerce and Supplies (1982).

References

Dixit, A. (1987). "Issues of Strategic Trade Policy for Small Countries." *Scandinavian Journal of Economics*. 89(3): 349-368

Evans, H. (1989). *Comparative Advantage and Growth*. London: Harvester Wheatsheaf.

Findlay, R. (1984). "Trade and Development: Theory and Asian Experiences." *Asian Development Review*. 2(2): 23-42.

Himarios, D. (1987). "Devaluation, Devaluation Expectations and Price Dynamics." *Economica*. 54: 299-313.

Lal, D. and S. Rajapatirana (1987). "Foreign Trade Regimes and Economic Growth in Developing Countries." *Research Observer*. 2 (2): 189-217.

Markuson, J. (1986). "Explaining the Volume of Trade: An Eclectic Approach." *American Economic Review*. 76 (5): 1002-1011.

Ministry of Commerce and Supplies (1982). *Trade Policy*. Kathmandu: Government of Nepal.

Ministry of Finance: *Economic Survey*. Various Issues.

National Planning Commission (1973). *Basic Principles of the Fifth Plan*. Kathmandu: Government of Nepal.

National Planning Commission (1981). *The Sixth Plan*. Kathmandu: Government of Nepal.

National Planning Commission (1985). *The Seventh Plan (1985-90)*. Kathmandu: Government of Nepal.

Nepal Rastra Bank. *Quarterly Economic Bulletin*. Various Issues.

7

Devaluation: Impact and Measures*

Introduction

When a devaluation occurs, relative price changes are induced domestically whereby prices of traded goods rise relative to non-traded goods, increasing the relative profitability of exports and import substitutes. Under these circumstances, resources move into the traded goods sectors. Exports increases while imports are cut down. However, in the short run, the current account balance may worsen following a devaluation as the import volume will increase immediately, while export will rise only after a substantial lag.

Devaluation has also been often associated with reduced economic growth and increased unemployment. The rise in the cost of living and the redistribution of income that it leads to have been frequently criticized for transferring the burden of adjustment to the lower income groups who are least able to afford it. This strategy has been ineffective since it can increase inflation without sufficiently improving the balance of payments (BoP) position, ultimately inducing another devaluation and plunging the country into an inflation-cum-devaluation spiral.

Against this background, the Nepalese devaluation of November 1985 and July 1991 will be scrutinized. Some recommendations are also made.

Devaluation of 1985

On 30 November 1985, the Nepalese currency was devalued by 14.7 percent against both the US dollar and the Indian rupee.

---

* *The Economic Journal of Nepal*, 14(4): 45-50, October-December 1991.

Consequently, the exchange rate of Rs. 1 IC soared from Rs. 1.45 NC to Rs. 1.70.

The related authorities were reluctant to devalue earlier because of the feared inflationary consequences. They should have conceived that where a future devaluation seems inevitable, however, postponing it for fear of inflation while maintaining the same monetary and fiscal regime simply intensifies inflationary pressures by raising both the probability and the magnitude of devaluation.

The prime objective of devaluation was to prevent the Indian reserves from falling to a level critical to the country's financial stability as well as to stimulate exports and curb down imports with an attempt to reduce the increasing trade gap. The possibilities of higher export earnings after devaluation were governed by the following propositions: (a) some of the exports forming relatively small proportion of the total export earnings face elastic demand and as a consequence of permanent stimulus provided by devaluation, their sales would expand in the international market; and (b) the government would take necessary steps to check the inflationary pressures in the economy that otherwise may nullify the advantages offered to the exports by the new exchange rate.

The government did devise some measures in order to curb the difficulties arising from devaluation. These included, among others, (a) development of a practical system for pre-shipment financing, (b) simplification of the procedures and documentation for export licensing, (c) development of an evaluation and monitoring system for receipts of foreign currencies on the basis of set export price, and (d) provision of bonded warehousing facilities to supply essential inputs for export industries at a lower price. Despite these measures, hardly any notable results were attained. The trade scenario was not satisfactory as the trade deficit soared from Rs. 5001.5 million in 1984/85 (the year prior to devaluation) to Rs. 6263.2 million in 1985/86 (the year of devaluation), to Rs. 7931.8 million in 1986/87 (the year after devaluation), and to Rs. 13166.0 million in 1989/90 (four years after devaluation).

Moreover, the remedial measures to cope with the problems of inflation were also not so effective. The inflation rates were 4.1 percent and 15.9 percent for 1984/95 and 1985/86, respectively. The double digit figures prevailed till 1987/88. Although the inflation rate dropped to 8.1 percent in 1988/89, it catapulted to 11.5 percent in 1989/90.

Devaluation of 1991

Since the devaluation of July 1991 was an upshot of the Indian devaluation it is noteworthy to make some remarks in this respect. In India, devaluation was inevitable since the rupee was over-valued. India did not have the external reserves or the borrowing capacity to anticipate a cyclical upturn nor the financial resources to bring about sufficient export augmentation within a reasonable period of time. The foreign exchange reserves were depleted, the total reserves able to meet less than a month's imports. The Indian authorities were of the view that a devaluation would restore profitability without reducing foreign exchange reserves or public savings.

The above state of affairs did not apply to the Nepalese economy. In July 1991, the country had sufficient foreign exchange reserves to satisfy about eight months' imports. Hence, the primary cause for undertaking this measure was that the Nepalese official exchange rate was basically determined by India and the country's economy was very sensitive and dependent on the changes in the Indian economy. The Nepalese devaluation can, thus, be ascribed to the devaluation of the Indian rupee by 23.1 percent that was effected twice by the Indian Government since 1 July. As a result, the Nepalese currency was devalued against the US dollar by 20.9 percent, but was kept unchanged against the Indian rupee after the second bout of the latter's steep devaluation on 3 July. The Nepal Rastra Bank (NRB) stuck to the 1.79 percent revaluation on 1 July of the Indian rupee keeping the value at Rs. 1.65 while the US dollar was devalued at Rs. 42.70. The revaluation of the Nepalese currency by 1.79 percent against the Indian currency hardly made any difference to the Nepalese consumer.

After the announcement of devaluation, a package of measures to tackle the adverse repercussions should have followed suit. The Minister of State for Finance, while presenting the budget for the fiscal year 1991/92, was well aware that he was responsible for not merely drafting an annual financial program for the government, but initiating a process of fundamental economic reforms. To minimize the serious consequences of devaluation, there was a need to reduce the size of the government budget, slash wasteful spending, put an end to the fiscal drain through the public sector and re-orient the tax system. Fundamentally, however, the State Minister should have targeted on expenditure cuts rather than revenue-raising, because the problem is not that too little money is flowing into the government treasury, but that too much of the money goes unproductive. However, no concrete measures were explicitly spelled out in the budget except that unnecessary and waste expenditures would be eliminated. The State Minister himself acknowledged that any change in the Indian economy will have its impact on the Nepalese economy indicating that the government would take steps from time to time depending on the reform measures exercised by India.

The impact of devaluation on the trade deficit may be disappointing. According to an estimate, the total deficit in 1991/92, based on past economic behavior, would be Rs. 22197.3 million without any change in the exchange rate. With changes in the exchange rate, the figure is estimated to be about Rs. 24570.6 million. Thus, the added burden on the trade deficit due to exchange rate changes is about Rs. 2373.3 million. Apart from the normal rate of inflation, there would be a further 12.2 percent increase in the inflation rate with changes in the exchange rate.

Suppose the rate of growth of imports falls slightly in 1991/92 because of devaluation of the Nepalese currency *vis-à-vis* the foreign currency. In this case the contribution of devaluation to trade deficit would be Rs. 1394.5 million and there would be a further addition of 9 percent to the normal rate of inflation.

If the Nepalese *vis-à-vis* the Indian currency had been appreciated to Rs. 1.50 and the US dollar depreciated to Rs. 38.90, the burden on the trade deficit would have amounted to Rs. 179.9 million. There would have been a further increment of the rate of inflation by only 2.2 percent in this case.

Hence, a significant decline in the rate of inflation is very unlikely in the next couple of years, unless there is some extraordinary development, like a super bumper crop. Crucial costs like higher transport cost will have widespread repercussions. Since fertilizer subsidy is reduced, this is bound to affect food-grain prices.

The heavy dose of devaluation of the Nepalese rupee *vis-à-vis* the foreign currencies has put the proposed growth target for the Eighth Plan in jeopardy. Issues such as its proposed size and sectoral allocations will have to be reformulated. The planners will have to reexamine the BoP situation under the totally different foreign trade scenario.

Some economists argue that there are crucial conditions for the devaluation theory to function in a Nepali-type economy. For instance, the price elasticities of export supplies and import demand must exceed zero. According to the famous Marshall-Lerner conditions, a devaluation would bring a positive impact on the current account only when the sum of both elasticities exceeds unity. Moreover, in Nepal, the supply of primary and agricultural commodities is quite rigid in the short run while the elasticity of import demand is likely to be low especially when they comprise of raw materials, semi-processed commodities and capital goods. Hence, a devaluation may lead to a further deterioration rather than improvement of the trade balance, measured in domestic currency. Further, this strategy also brings about grave redistributive consequences since it demands a downward movement either in the share of wages in the industrial sector or in the terms of trade which agriculture gets *vis-à-vis* industry. And the latter again is likely to demonstrate itself in terms of a decline in the share of agricultural wages.

Further, the price-cost relationship in the primary sector is not important from the point of view of the country's exports, and hence would not justify a general devaluation. This is firstly due to the domestic elasticity of supply of such products which is small and unresponsive to changes in export price; and, secondly, the export price in terms of foreign currency will be the same, irrespective of the exchange rate, so that devaluation will not stimulate world demand for the product. However, these propositions are likely to hold only within certain limits.

Suggestions

The success of a devaluation will be governed by its ability to stimulate the growth of exports. More exports may be forthcoming if there is a higher inflow of imported raw materials as well as capital equipment and spare parts to rehabilitate previously neglected plant and equipment.

If the government controls the fiscal deficit, and hence the monetary expansion immediately after devaluation, there will be a counteracting force which will help to contain inflation. When monetary expansion is kept in check, the ability of producers and traders to pass the cost increases through higher prices is greatly reduced. The crucial point, thus, is to maintain a firm check on demand and on monetary expansion. At the same time, measures to reduce fiscal deficit should, as far as possible, avoid heavy indirect taxation of commodities of mass consumption.

To counter the cost-increasing impact of devaluation, production and new investments should be stimulated, freedom of entry and exit in industry should prevail, and the resource base of the financial institutions should be strengthened, so that they can finance new investments.

The favorable outcome of devaluation also depends to a large extent on the supporting steps taken by the government. These can be classified into three types: price policies, demand management measures and policies that transform an initial increase in supply into an actual increase in exports. Price policies must ensure that the change in the exchange rate is fully reflected in the price structure of the economy. Price adjustments should take place. Restrictions on imported inputs for tradables should be relaxed, and cost and incentive distortions hindering the production of tradables will have to be removed.

In Nepal, it can be said that devaluation taxes the poor in at least three ways: by reducing the real wage, increasing unemployment, and reducing government services. A curtailment in the real incomes of the poor may not be acceptable and government expenditures on health and education, among others, may have to be sustained in real terms. Moreover, due to devaluation other government expenditures will take an upward trend, as the cost of their import content and that of debt service rise, demanding larger increases in revenues to reduce the budgetary deficit. While devaluation will also raise government revenues—through higher tax revenues on trade and incomes and higher profits from public enterprises—the impact on expenditures is more immediate and will tend to be larger. If higher profits in tradables do not generate higher private investment due to lack of confidence or uncertainty, the government will need to encourage it. This, in itself, may limit the government's options in reducing private sector consumption. The alternative to reducing consumption is to cut back investment that would reduce future growth. Whichever option is resorted to, these would be unpopular decisions for the government.

Because of these narrow options, the government has to tread a thin line between a credible adjustment effort required for devaluation to be effective and the priority it places on the social fabric. This priority can be facilitated, for instance, by curtailing government expenditures where they least affect the basic needs of the poor, or by tightening credit for consumer durables. In order to contain expenditure, massive cuts will have to be effected in subsidies and well-conceived schemes will have to be devised to ensure that the weaker sections of the population are not adversely affected.

The government will also need to frame a collaborative policy in various fields so that foreign exchange earnings and savings increase. Development expenditures could be redirected to mitigate the existing obstacles. The capital stock and export-servicing facilities may also have to be rehabilitated for facilitating the channelization for more exports to foreign markets.

Because devaluation entails sudden price changes and a fall in purchasing power, it does capture more public visibility and understandably generate more political opposition. Thus, the government should develop an overall macro-economic stabilization program which it should discuss with major opposition parties so as to enable the evolution of national consensus of economic policy reform.

References

Cooper, R. (1971). "An Assessment of Currency Devaluation in Developing Countries." In Gustav Ranis, ed., *Government and Economic Development*. New Haven and London: Yale University Press.

De Vries, M. (1966). "Trade and Exchange Policy and Economic Development Two Decades of Evolving Views." *Oxford Economic Papers*. 18:1.

Diaz-Alejandro, C. (1965). *Exchange Devaluation in a Semi-Industrialized Country: The Experiences of Argentina 1955-1961*. Cambridge, Mass., and London: MIT Press.

Dornbusch, R. (1976). "The Theory of Flexible Exchange Rate Regimes and Macroeconomic Policy." *Scandinavian Journal of Economics*. 78:2.

Himarios, D. (1987). "Devaluation Expectations and Price Dynamics." *Economica*. 54:299-313.

Ministry of Finance. *Economic Survey*. Various Issues. Kathmandu: Ministry of Finance.

Nepal Rastra Bank (NRB). *Quarterly Economic Bulletin*. Various Issues. Kathmandu: NRB. Kathmandu.

Riley, C. (1980). "The Wage-Price Mechanism and the Long-Run Effects of Fiscal and Monetary Policies under Alternative Exchange Rate Regimes." *Scandinavian Journal of Economics*. 82:3.

8

WTO: Opportunities and Challenges*

The World Trade Organization (WTO) is the only international institution that deals with the rules of trade between nations. The objectives of WTO agreements, the legal ground-rules for international commerce and for trade policy, are three-fold: to help trade flow as freely as possible, to attain further liberalization slowly via negotiation, and to establish an impartial means of settling disputes. The agreements encompass goods, services and intellectual properly.

At the time of setting up the WTO in Marrakesh, some decisions were made in favor of least-developed countries (LDCs). It was decided that LDCs will only have to undertake commitments and concessions to the extent consistent with their individual development, financial and trade needs, or their administrative and institutional capabilities.

The provisions for differential and more favorable treatment of developing country members are applicable to the LDCs. According to the Enabling Clause, developed country members shall exercise the maximum restraint in seeking concessions and contributions from LDCs. LDC members are exempted from reduction commitments on domestic support and export subsidies, together with market access according to the Agreement on Agriculture. Moreover, the Agreement on Subsidies and Countervailing Measures exempt LDCs from the prohibition on export subsidies. If a transitional period has been allowed to developing country members, LDCs have been given a longer time-frame in many cases. There are other provisions for the benefit of LDCs.

---

* *The Kathmandu Post*, 6 September 1999.

It was at the first WTO Ministerial Conference held in Singapore at the end of 1996 that the WTO action plan for LDCs was adopted. This attempted to ameliorate the trading opportunities of the LDCs and their integration into the multilateral trading system. This action plan stressed the development of LDCs through macroeconomic policies, supply-side measures and improved market access. Attention was focused particularly on human and institutional capacity building and on market access for products of export interest to LDCs.

Nepal which has been pursuing an open market economy since the early 1990s is making preparations to join the WTO. It was after India had imposed an economic blockade on Nepal following its reluctance to renew Nepal-India Trade and Transit Treaty in 1999 that the country applied for WTO membership.

The impact of Nepal's entry into the WTO is not easy to predict particularly on its enterprises. Since a couple of years, Nepalese enterprises have been functioning under restrictive regimes, restrictive in terms of foreign transactions, import of technology and goods. Under the liberalized WTO regime, Nepal needs to further liberalize its external transactions, that is, remove import restrictions, import quotas, lower import tariffs, proffer national treatment to all multinational enterprises, grant most-favored nation status to all WTO member countries and render intellectual property protection in terms of longer product and process patents.

As most countries, both developing and developed, are associated with WTO and account for 80 percent of the total world trade, Nepal cannot remain aloof, but should gradually enter the competitive international market by joining the WTO. However, it is reasonably argued by some that Nepal is not fully equipped to join the WTO, as once it gets the WTO membership it cannot discriminate against foreign investment and such a provision may have an adverse impact on domestic investors; moreover, it has to rely on competitiveness of its exportable goods while keeping its domestic market open to goods originating from other countries.

It is equally true that since many countries of this region have attained a much higher level of industrial advancement, Nepal could initially face some problems of competition after getting membership. As WTO will make the whole world a global market, its member countries will have to downscale import tariffs. This means that domestic industries need to be more competitive. An important challenge for Nepal, thus, will be to compensate for the revenue loss incurred due to the fall in revenue from import tariffs.

Nevertheless, it goes without saying that the benefits of joining WTO outweigh the costs. By not joining WTO, and going by past history and policy failures of different governments, the country will never be able to compete globally. At least, when Nepal joins the WTO it will be forced to make its products more competitive and it will get access to the international market freely. The country cannot afford to say that it will insulate its market from international competition and will make it competitive after a certain period. The prime challenge for Nepal is to raise the efficiency and international competitiveness of its economy and integrate with the global economy.

Nepal can also get some benefits as WTO guarantees unrestricted transit facilities for landlocked economies of the world. When Nepal falls in a dispute with a bigger country, its resources and expertise will not be adequate to put forward its point. In such a situation, WTO's infrastructure and expertise will assist the country to fight its case according to the dispute settlement procedure of the organization.

One crucial point to note is that while the WTO regime has liberalized trade in goods, it has not liberalized trade in technology. Developed countries, while advocating free trade in goods and services, have been introducing restrictions with regard to trade in technology. These countries are reluctant to sell machinery and components embodying new technology to unrelated third parties. Hence, Nepal together with other LDCs and developing countries should bargain and try to alter these restrictive practices which are against the spirit of WTO.

9

WTO's Seattle Conference*

On the eve of the 21st century, representatives of most of the world's governments are meeting in Seattle from 30 November to 3 December 1999 for new negotiations to further liberalize trade, and set the WTO's program and priorities for the future. The result will be viewed as a proof of confidence in WTO, and a gesture of international commitment to trade liberalization. It will have immense impact on the direction and credibility of the world trading system as we move into a new and uncertainty century.

The Seattle Ministerial Conference will only be the starting point of negotiations, just as the seven-year Uruguay Round was launched at a ministerial meeting in Punta del Este in 1986 and the six-year Tokyo Round in Tokyo in 1973.

The Uruguay Round addressed the trade challenges of the early 1980s. The WTO has to address the challenges of 2000 and beyond if it is to become relevant and effective. WTO members are already committed to negotiations in agriculture, services, and intellectual property as part of their Uruguay Round negotiations. Especially, the agreements on services and on agriculture affirm that new negotiations will resume by the beginning of 2000. These two subjects are definitely going to be in the new agenda, as these sectors comprise more than two thirds of the global output, and new agreements to liberalize trade in these areas hold the prospects of ample benefit for all member states.

Currently, many proposals to broaden and deepen the agenda have been forthcoming. As of mid-September this year, more than 150 proposals had been tabled. In addition to agriculture and services, the proposals cover tariffs, anti-dumping, subsidies,

---

* *The Kathmandu Post*, 29 November 1999.

safeguards, investment measures, trade facilitation, e-commerce, competition policies, transparency in government procurements, technical assistance, capacity-building, and intellectual property protection, among others. Moreover, for many developing countries, a very crucial issue is the implementation of the already existing agreements.

Another pivotal issue is that of integrating developing countries into the global trading system. Developing countries are not threatened by the process of globalization, but are threatened by being left out of it. Trade is their link to the 21st century, and with it comes access to markets, investment, technology, and know-how. Overall, a new round is an occasion to encourage developing countries themselves to continue utilizing openness and trade as instruments for their economic growth. This implies further liberalizing their economies, rectifying structural weaknesses and market distortions, and carrying out reforms under WTO rules.

The entry of China, Russia and other countries into WTO is also due to feature at Seattle in order to make the global trading system truly global. China is the world's third largest economy, and needs an open trading system to realize its huge potential. At the same time, China and the other accession countries are also important to WTO if it is to devise a comprehensive system of global rules. Recently, some positive headways have been made relating to China's accession.

From the perspective of the least developed countries (LDCs) such as Nepal, the Seattle conference is of considerable significance. Twenty-nine LDCs out of 48 have become WTO members. As for Nepal, it has been attending WTO meetings and conferences as an observer since 1995. It was after India imposed an economic blockade on Nepal following its reluctance to renew Nepal-India Trade and Transit Treaty in 1988 that Nepal applied for WTO membership.

Developments in LDCs over the past few years have been a source of worry. Even the sustainability of an improved economic performance is questionable given the continued vulnerability of

LDCs to external shocks, particularly adverse weather conditions and sharp movements in the prices of their exports. These countries still do not get the access they need for their products; they account for one-half of one percent of world trade. Their share has been declining and they have been marginalized in multilateral trade discussions. Most of them are highly dependent on a few selected exportable goods.

The developed and other developing markets still impose high trade barriers. Hence, the elimination of all barriers to imports from LDCs should be amongst the top priorities at Seattle. It should be noted that the notion of removing barriers to imports from LDCs was previously introduced by former WTO Director-General Renato Ruggiero in July 1996 at the Group of Eight Summit in Lyon, France.

For LDCs, strengthening their capacity to actively and effectively participate in the multilateral trading system calls for a set of concrete measures and commitments by the WTO in the following areas: a) supply-side constraints, that hamper the ability of LDCs to diversify their production and exports, and obstruct them from benefiting from existing trade preference schemes should be resolved through debt cancellation, technical assistance and capacity building, and technology transfer; and b) the accession process imposes heavy burden on the limited human and institutional capacity of acceding LDCs, and their human and institutional infrastructure must be strengthened to enable them to face these challenges.

Hence, from the LDCs' point of view, the Seattle Conference will be a success if the Ministers a) agree to eliminate barriers to LDC products, b) speed up the accession for WTO membership and ensure that they have comparable rights and procedures for LDC candidates and obligations similar to those of the current LDC members, c) concur on reducing the LDCs' debt burden, and d) work with other international organizations to enhance the supply-side capacity of LDCs.

10

Preferential Trading Arrangement: Viability and Progress in South Asia*

Over the past two decades, the upcoming of preferential trading arrangements (PTAs) in various parts of the world has witnessed a noticeable development. Countries all over the world are regrouping in trade and political blocks such as the North American Free Trade Area (NAFTA), the European Union (EU), the Association of South-east Asian Nations (ASEAN) and the Shanghai Five. Moreover, there has been a recent initiative to form a Bay of Bengal Initiative for Multi-sectoral Economic and Technical Cooperation (BIMSTEC) Free Trade Area, which is expected to come about in five years' time. Under the planned BIMSTEC Free Trade Area, member countries would reduce import tariffs to 0-5 percent, the same level of those in the ASEAN Free Trade Area (AFTA). The South Asian region is no exception as seven South Asian nations set up the South Asian Association of Regional Cooperation (SAARC) in 1985 as a first move towards regional cooperation.

It was only after the 1990s that economic integration was accorded top priority within the SAARC, and the first step towards this path was the commissioning of a Study on Trade, Manufactures and Services by the SAARC Secretariat. The South Asian Preferential Trading Agreement (SAPTA) was launched by the SAARC in 1995 as the second move.

Studies of PTAs have revealed that most of the conditions for a successful PTA do not exist in the case of South Asia. These conditions include, *inter alia*, geographical proximity, the

* *The Rising Nepal*, 17 February 2002.

presence of trade complementarity, high pre-PTA tariffs, high degree of intra-regional trade, variations in economic structure based on competitiveness, and little political tensions, if any, among member nations,

According to the natural trading blocks argument of Paul Krugman, geographical proximity does promote trade. Regional trading arrangements should be undertaken on the basis that it is natural for neighbors to indulge in trade with each other. However, the South Asian case moves away from this argument in the sense that though India and Pakistan are neighbors, trade between the two countries has been low historically. Again, in terms of trade complementarity, the trade indices developed by Peter Drysdale has revealed that there is an absence of strong trade complementarity in the bilateral trade structures of South Asia.

It has been empirically shown that the average nominal tariff rate has taken a downward trend in South Asia with the undertaking of trade liberalization reform measures over the last two decades. Still, the average for South Asia is higher compared with other regions in the world which means that high pre-PTA tariff as a precondition for creating a PTA holds true for South Asia.

The share of intra-regional trade in South Asia's total trade went up from 2.4 percent in 1990 to 4.6 percent in 1999. Yet, this figure is much less than that of other PTAs. Another concern is India's growing trade surplus with other SAARC countries. Although an increasing trend has been noticed in the exports of India to other SAARC countries (excluding Pakistan) from 3.9 percent in 1970 to 5.5 percent in 1999, its import share from the region fell from 1.4 percent to 0.9 percent during the same period. This demonstrates that India's role in attracting imports from other South Asian countries is limited.

Another principal issue related to South Asian economic integration is that countries in the region are producing and trading similar commodities. The Revealed Comparative Advantage indices estimated by economists have shown that South Asian nations have an almost identical pattern of comparative advantage in a relatively narrow range of commodities; moreover, these countries do not have comparative advantages in a wide range of capital goods and advanced manufactured goods.

The political tension between the two major countries in South Asia, India and Pakistan, has been another primary hurdle to regional integration.

Despite these constraints, progress has been made to some extent. After the launch of SAPTA in 1995, three rounds of preferential tariff reductions have been conducted, namely SAPTA-I (concluded in 1995), SAPTA-II (concluded in 1997) and SAPTA-III (concluded in 1998).

Under SAPTA-I, member countries offered trade concessions for 226 commodities that formed just about 6 percent of traded goods. The issue of non-tariff barriers was not taken up in this round. The product coverage and proposed tariff cuts appeared more significant under SAPTA-II, where concessions were provided to all countries on 1,870 commodities. Non-tariff measures were also given prominence. However, both SAPTA-I and SAPTA-II seemed artificial in the sense that there was an almost total absence of demand for the products offered. Thus, SAPTA-III appeared more significant in the sense that concessions were offered to all countries on about 3,000 commodities with the aim of boosting intra-regional trade. Still, most of the items kept in such a list of goods are those that are rarely imported by the country that has granted the so-called concessions. The negotiations for the fourth round were initiated in 1999, but no progress has been made so far.

SAPTA is considered to be a step on the path to creating the South Asia Free Trade Area (SAFTA). As SAPTA is confined to trade in goods, unless it is expanded to encompass trade in services, there is a possibility of SAFTA not being a real FTA. For landlocked countries such as Nepal and Bhutan, the service sector could be much more viable and cost-effective as compared to the manufacturing sector.

Before operationalizing SAFTA, there is a need to resolve an array of complex issues such as rules of origin, identification and dismantling of non-tariff measures, a mechanism for the compensation for revenue loss, implementation timetable, monitoring mechanism, and protection of bilateral agreements and treaties, among others. Currently, there prevails no mechanisms in SAARC for ensuring that targets agreed to are strictly pursued.

The initial target of the South Asian nations to activate the SAFTA by 2001 did not materialize, neither did the signing of the draft treaty as later envisaged.

However, the recent statements made by the South Asian leaders in Kathmandu on 6 January 2002 have raised hopes that the SAFTA would, after all, materialize sooner or later. The first action will be by finalizing the text of the Draft Treaty Framework by the end of 2002.

11

WTO, Industrial Policy and Nepal*

Introduction

The current World Trade Organization (WTO) provisions have limited the industrial policy tools available to its members. On the one hand, there is proof to demonstrate that a number of policies that distort trade are still permitted under present rules. On the other hand, the added discipline imposed by the WTO rules has reduced the flexibility of national Governments to undertake development objectives. This paper examines the issues emanating from the possible revision of the WTO provisions as they relate to the pursuit of industrial and trade policy objectives by least developed countries (LDCs) in general and Nepal in particular. It also highlights some WTO-related challenges in the area of industry and trade that should be considered by the policymakers of Nepal in the light of the country's accession to the WTO in the future.

Special and Differential Treatment

The Uruguay Round Agreements have changed both the form and content of most of the major special and differential treatment (SDT) provisions. Many post-Uruguay Round SDT provisions are denoted with respect to transitional periods, differences in threshold levels and on mandatory offers of technical assistance to fulfill specific obligations rather than in the form of substantive exemptions from specific rules, as in the pre-Uruguay Round era. Moreover, the length of transitional periods and the level at which thresholds have been fixed, seem, for the most part, to have been chosen in an *ad hoc* and haphazard way.

---

* *The Economic Journal of Nepal*, 25(2): 84-94, April-June 2002.

An important component of SDT has been special market access, through trade preferences. While its actual benefits have been short of the potential due to its many limitations, and while further negotiated tariff reductions on a most-favored nation (MFN) basis will continue to erode preferential trade margins, its continued importance should not be underestimated. Especially, it could be a significant boost to the exports of Nepal and other LDCs if current limitations relating to product coverage could be eliminated. The proposal to provide duty- and quota-free and bound access for all exports of the LDCs would lead to an elimination of these limitations; it could considerably enhance the export prospects of Nepal after it becomes a member of the WTO.

However, this proposal could proceed a little further, that is, for the developing countries to also provide special market access to the LDCs, not necessarily on the same duty-and-quota-free basis as the developed countries but perhaps at up to 50 percent of the applied tariff rates of the developing countries. Still, the "cost" to the developing countries is unlikely to be particularly burdensome. Yet, the action could be a valuable technique not only for demonstrating "South Solidarity" but also to dilute the impression that it is only the developed countries that are always asked to shoulder the "burden" of all special arrangements needed to enable the multilateral trading system accommodate the needs of its different categories of members.

It should be understood that while agriculture and trade in services are pre-determined elements of the market access negotiations in the next Round, the inclusion of trade in manufactured products does not enjoy this status. However, from the LDCs' point of view, industrial tariff negotiations should also be part of the agenda of the next Round. The proposal relating to bound duty- and quota-free market access for all exports of the LDCs in the developed-country markets needs to be formally agreed in both the agricultural and manufactured goods sectors. Moreover, the LDCs have an interest in the reduction of industrial tariff peaks and elimination of tariff escalation in the markets of advanced countries, and these can be tackled properly only if negotiations on industrial tariffs are part of the new Round.

The concessions that will be offered to Nepal after it becomes a WTO member will primarily be in the form of longer phase-in periods. The country will not gain much from tariff reduction and there could be some losses emanating from the phasing out of preferences. More important, the intensification of competition is likely to marginalize the country and increase market concentration. In order to overcome the threat of marginalization in the global economy, Nepal should undertake this task from three perspectives. One, the country should be able to pinpoint which of its existing activities need to be retained and improved, and to identify new export products in order to expand the productive base, diversify exports and build up a more secure and stable source of income. Two, Nepal should participate more effectively in regional trade groupings such as the South Asian Association of Regional Cooperation (SAARC). And three, as will be discussed later, the country could achieve market penetration through strategic alliances with developing and industrialized country firms.

Nepal should clearly understand that although LDCs are exempt from complying with several WTO obligations, but if integration with the new world trade order is a policy objective, it must regard these exemptions as of an inherently temporary nature.

Import Protection and Export Promotion

Under WTO, domestic firms could be protected from import competition through tariffs, non-tariff measures and subsidies. However, the scope for import protection continues to fall. Tariffs are declining and local content protection is on the verge of being prohibited. The scope for continued import protection under the WTO depends on the ability of LDCs and developing countries to negotiate a provision that allows for greater discretion for protection. Import protection can be attained by challenging the fairness of competition by employing anti-dumping and safeguard measures.

Nepal should employ selective, performance-related and time-bound protection of infant industries. Such protection should be employed strictly as a transitional provision to address market failures and promote learning and capacity-building for future competitiveness.

With regard to export promotion, direct intervention by Governments to boost exports is being increasingly restricted by the WTO rules. This leaves LDCs little room for maneuver in the area of export subsidies for industrial products. However, there is a wide range of alternatives that are still undertaken by Governments. These include export credit and insurance schemes below market rates, concessional tax and duty provisions as well as export processing zones (EPZs). While some of them remain WTO consistent, LDCs need to reassess the degree to which other policies, which discriminate in favor of particular producers, are in their national interest. This will determine the degree to which LDC members should negotiate further restrictions on export subsidies in the next Round. The focus should be on reducing fiscal and procedural constraints on exports, trade facilitation, and generic policies to make the country more competitive such as infrastructure development and an appropriate exchange rate policy. Human capital formation, innovation policies, joint venture agreements and infrastructure are important for determining export competitiveness, and are allowed within the framework of the WTO.

Trade-related Investment Measures

The Uruguay Round agreements also incorporate provisions with respect to Trade-related Investment Measures (TRIMs). They commit signatory LDCs to phase out over a period of seven years the following: (a) local content requirements; (b) import restrictions related to foreign exchange earnings; and (c) export obligations that they may have imposed on foreign firms.

Temporary deviations from TRIMs obligations for BoP are permitted.

The final text of the Agreement on TRIMs merely clarifies some policies against the GATT 1947 context. It is argued by many countries that the list of illustrative TRIMs should not be extended. Moreover, the transition period should be extended, as the policies included in the illustrative list are important in fulfilling their development objectives. The seven-year transition period (to expire on 1 January 2002) is not adequate for LDC members to benefit from those policies.

As the TRIMs text now stands, there is no scope for implementing a performance requirement (based on the prevailing illustrative list) in a discriminatory fashion. If developing and LDCs believe that the TRIMs on the illustrative list are needed to satisfy their other objectives and must be implemented with regard to foreign firms, this will have to be negotiated.

Extending the illustrative list will demand intense negotiations. As it currently stands, the list is very much a compromise with regard to the initial negotiating positions. Some developed countries will try to extend the list, while developing and LDCs are likely to oppose such an initiative. It will be hard to predict the result of the negotiations since the negotiations, by definition, will focus around those performance requirements that are directly related to trade.

Trade-related Aspects of Intellectual Property Rights

The impact of Trade-related aspects of Intellectual Property Rights (TRIPs) on LDCs seems to be continuously debated. It involves various changes in national legislation. Some adverse effects have been estimated. These are, among others, higher prices for protected technologies and products as well as restricted possibilities for diffusion through reverse engineering.

The TRIPs Agreement envisages restrictions on replication of violation of registered trademarks, patents, industrial and textile design and layout design of integrated circuits. The production of counterfeited products is prohibited. Intellectual property is overwhelmingly concentrated in developed countries. The present owners of patents, design and trademarks will be the major beneficiaries of the implementation of the TRIPs. Royalty payments for the acquisition of technology and information by LDC firms will increase. Patent holding firms may refuse to sell the technology preferring to serve the LDC market by exports.

The implementation of the TRIPs could make the transfer of technology of Nepal more expensive. Reverse engineering opportunities may be seriously reduced, while innovation and technological adaptation will become more difficult. The liberalization of the investment and technology transfer regime will increase the financial marginalization of Nepal. Hence, as mentioned earlier, it is very important to construct strategic alliances between firms in Nepal and firms based in developing and industrialized countries to overcome these systemic biases.

As Nepal does not possess comparative advantage in innovation, attempts to develop certain sectors within the WTO imply that the country will have to depend largely on the transfer and diffusion of technology from foreign countries.

Certain changes are required in the Agreement on TRIPs as disclosed by the fact that about 70 members have not been able to fulfill the conditions of TRIPs within the prescribed deadline. Moreover, Nepal lacks the required financial, legal, institutional and human resources to carry out the provisions of the Agreement before the deadline.

The foregoing issues should be seriously considered by the policymakers and the transition period provided by the Agreement should be exploited to the maximum. It should be noted that the time to comply with this Agreement has been extended to 2016.

Competition Policy

Competition policy is a set of policies, which enhances competition among producers in markets. As markets become globalized, competition is international.

WTO plays an instrumental role in promoting competition. One of the most significant determinants of competition in markets is the free movement of goods across borders and, particularly in the service industries, the free movement of foreign direct investment (FDI). These are subject to WTO rules and discipline. One plus point of the WTO rules in this regard is that they are neutral between foreign and domestic producers. This helps to ensure that domestic and foreign producers are able to compete on equal terms.

Nepal, especially after being a WTO member, could be concerned about the restrictive business practices, such as price fixing and market allocation, of the MNCs, which set up affiliates in its economy. Foreign investors are subject to the laws of the host economy. Hence, when the anti-competitive practices take place in the host economy, the suitable response is the development and application of national competition laws. Thus, the policymakers in Nepal should consider developing some type of a competition law to address the source of the problem directly.

Trade Policy and Strategic Alliance

The broad contours of a development-oriented trade policy for Nepal could be as follows. One, the adjustment of tariffs to modest levels seems to be within easy reach of attainment. This range of tariffs could enable Nepal, to a large extent, to satisfy its industrial protection objectives while, at the same time, limiting the relative price distortions that trade restrictions can generate and thus the damage they can do to the overall economy. Two, special mention should be made of the export component of trade policy. Good export performance is not simply a desirable aim in its own right; it is also a critical means to other important ends such as deeper import liberalization and more robust economic growth. A successful and sustainable import liberalization program demands successful exports. And for this to take place, Nepal needs to identify both potential exports and potential markets for exports. In parallel with this, the country could enhance its trade potential by coming up with products that bear specific features while retaining the marketing potential. By providing a country-specific dimension to a product that should otherwise be normally competitive by global standards, or by developing a more unique form of product on the basis of a special local feature, Nepal could enhance its competitive capacity.

Three, mechanisms must be developed that would endow the trade policy and strategy of Nepal with greater predictability and credibility, and hence ensure that whatever policy changes are made are received as being credible by the private sector. Because of the large irreversible nature of investment decisions, it is very important for the trade regime to be predictable and stable if appropriate investment and export supply responses are to be elicited from the private sector. In other words, an element of confidence in the government's policy for the exporter is crucial. A major risk for exporters is that government policies will change and export profitability will be adversely affected.

It should be reiterated that Nepal's exports prospects could be diminished if it continues to rely on limited products and limited markets. Export concentration is considered undesirable as a) it renders an economy vulnerable to external shocks related with the products on which it concentrates, b) it restricts opportunities for earning adequate foreign exchange, and c) it does not foster intersectoral linkages, and thus, militates against the emergence of a nationally integrated economy.

Against these and other perspectives, the importance of developing a trade strategy which links strategically positioned firms in Nepal, its neighboring countries, and other developing countries should be addressed. For instance, a strategic alliance between a Nepalese firm producing medium count cotton yarn, a Chinese firm producing standardized apparel and a retailers conglomerate in Singapore may be necessary for the fullest exploitation of the Nepalese textile export potential. Similarly, electronic products and components seem particularly attractive. An annual growth of 10 percent in electronics imports by developed countries is not unrealistic. Possibilities should be explored of Nepalese firms of constructing appropriate strategic alliances with suitable developed and developing country firms for penetrating electronics markets. Limited gains also exist for exploiting gains that may occur as a consequence of reduction in the escalation of tariffs, especially in the leather and paper products groups.

Rural Industrialization and Small and Medium Enterprises

A strong agriculture-industry nexus is crucial for industrial advancement. Experiences of South-east Asia divulge that continuously improved techniques for manufacture of agricultural tools as well as forward and backward linkages between agriculture and industry were a major boost for industrial growth of these countries.

Structural change in the Nepalese economy demands a strategy of simultaneous development of agriculture and industries. Rural industries form an important part of these activities. The success of rural industrialization projects is based on certain factors:

- Identifying a potential enterprise and entrepreneurs and undertaking comprehensive feasibility studies;
- probing into, and adapting, technology;
- creating production systems appropriate to local conditions;
- organizing the producers into viable groups, and imparting training to them in managing an enterprise;
- securing sufficient finance from suitable credit channels;
- setting up forward and backward linkages for finished products and raw materials;
- ensuring proper and desired infrastructure support;
- incorporating technology changes to orient production to satisfy market requirements; and

- imparting training or upgrading labor skills to develop products acceptable to markets and also to guide the adoption of appropriate technologies.

The policymakers of Nepal should also recognize that the tools and timing of competitive exposure for small and medium scale enterprises need to be selective. In this respect, there are five strategies involved that should be borne in mind by the policymakers of the country:

- support of infant industry, but for a limited period;
- promotion of activities that possess long-term learning benefits, but generate considerable external benefits;
- rapid liberalization of activities that would bring in new technologies to permit firms to utilize existing capabilities to reach competitive levels without further need for protection;
- slow liberalization of activities that need longer learning periods in order to permit firms to build up capabilities for new technologies and build up new skills for full competitiveness; and
- enhancement of supply-side measures in order to provide the necessary human capital, finance, information and extension services, while firms develop capabilities.

WTO, Poverty and Employment

Trade reforms—reducing tariffs and non-tariff barriers—have had profound effects in many developing countries and LDCs. It has been shown that a lowering of barriers to trade seems to increase the demand for relatively abundant factors of production. In case of Asia, these have been initially unskilled and semi-skilled laborers, that is, those most likely to be poor. There also exists a strong negative relationship between growth in the incidence of poverty and the rate of long-run economic growth. This is illustrated by the newly industrialized economies of South-east Asia, where the development of outward-looking, export-oriented countries led to rapid income growth and a reduction in poverty during the 1980s and 1990s.

The economic reforms required for WTO membership to move forward could boost Nepal's economic growth. This seems to be done in three ways: a) by encouraging the transfer of resources to their most productive use to optimize the gains from exploiting comparative advantage; b) by lowering policy uncertainty and instability through requiring commitments to reform to be legally binding, which raises savings rates and investor confidence and thus faster rates of capital accumulation; and c) by encouraging, through more openness to the rest of the world, the inflow of new technologies and new marketing and other business management ideas.

The more the country abolishes distortions to producer and consumer incentives and the more it provides a transparent, open and stable macroeconomic and sectoral policy environment, the faster its economy should grow, *ceteris paribus*. Moreover, the more the economy moves away from assisting import-competing industries and discriminating against actual and potential export sectors (most notably agriculture), the faster will output grow. Trade, too, will grow faster with such reform.

Also crucial in releasing the potential of the rural sector is the provision of essential infrastructure to lower the transactions costs of doing business there, plus investment in the people involved. Infrastructure includes rural roads, electricity, telecommunications and radio transmission, so that costs of transport, communications and information become more affordable. Irrigation investments also need to be facilitated. Investments in people include basic education, health services, and agricultural research and extension.

There will be more employment opportunities created, more poverty alleviated, and a more equitable income distribution will emerge over time with than without a freer and more liberal policy regime. Some urban people who have been employed in the most protected industrial sectors may lose their jobs as protection barriers are lowered; but there will be less such people, the sooner the reform measures are implemented and the more they are phased in gradually. It should be noted that many of those displaced by reform programs will have no difficulty getting another job in one of the expanding industries. That is, urban employment will still grow, but possibly somewhat at a slower rate at the beginning than otherwise owing to more employment opportunities becoming available in rural areas.

The country could build up non-agricultural employment by associating agro-enterprises and available human resources with industrial occupation in order to develop rural-urban linkages. It is also important to develop micro-enterprises and informal sector at the grassroots level, generate intermediate goods as their forward linkages, and link them to medium and large-scale industries with comparative advantages. If such a policy is framed, it could be possible to attain the defined objective of poverty alleviation to some extent, and create multiple effects in the economy by developing areas of comparative advantage.

Conclusion

Experiences of developing countries and LDCs who are already members of the WTO have revealed certain important traits. First, the Uruguay Round and its implementation process did little to improve market access for their exports of goods and services. Second, these countries were of the view that WTO rules and regulations were unbalanced in many crucial development-related areas such as the protection of intellectual property rights and the use of industrial subsidies, while the SDT, which the Uruguay Round bestowed upon them, as insufficient. Third, inadequate human and financial services and weak institutional capacities limited the ability of many developing countries and all LDCs to exploit the opportunities open to them under the WTO system, especially with regard to its dispute settlement mechanism, together with its inability to comply fully with their multilateral obligations.

Nepal, thus, has to grapple and understand these issues, and after it becomes a member, it should proactively participate in the various rounds with the goal of further integrating itself into the global economy.

The tools of industrial policy must be employed very carefully, or else they could generate large costs of their own. A major pressing policy problem in Nepal is less the establishment of new industries than of enhancing the competitiveness of existing inefficient and technologically stagnant industries. It should, therefore, address the removal of an accretion of many irrational and inefficient interventions that many governments have undertaken in the past. It should also address industrial reforms and restructuring needs with respect to various determinants of capability development such as the incentive framework, the supply of human capital, the supporting technology infrastructure, finance for technological activity, and access to foreign technologies.

In today's competitive environment, Nepal should attempt to boost its competitiveness by opting industries and products with the potential for high growth and high value added. There is a need to identify new exportable products and new markets if the country wants to survive in the long run. Immediate steps should be launched by the policymakers in this regard.

The WTO rules are ownership-neutral. Excluding the General Agreement of Trade in Services (GATS) and TRIPS, where a national treatment standard is applicable, policies such as subsidies and local content protection do not distinguish between foreign affiliates and domestic enterprise. The important point is the "trade effect" of the instrument. This implies that if Nepal wants to apply a particular policy to foreign-owned firms, it must first find a provision in the Agreement that permits the use of the policy. Then, it can apply it to a foreign firm as long as there is no "trade effect".

References

Ali, M. Shaukat (2000). *Trade and Industrial Policy in Pakistan: Post-Uruguay Round Challenges.* World Bank's WTO-2000 Project. Washington, D.C.: World Bank.

Amsden, Alice H. (2000). *Industrialization under New WTO Law.* UNCTAD X. Bangkok.

Anderson, Kym and Bishwa Nath Tiwari (1998). "Economic Reform in Nepal and WTO Accession: Implications for Agriculture and Rural Development." Government of Nepal/UNDP/UNCTAD (RAS/92/041). Kathmandu.

Asian Development Bank (2001). *Asian Development Outlook 2001.* Oxford: Oxford University Press.

Bora, Bijit, Peter J. Lloyd and Mari Pangestu (2000). *Industrial Policy and the WTO.* New York and Geneva: United Nations.

Pant, Bhubanesh (2001). *National Study on Trade in Goods.* UNDP. Kathmandu.

UNCTAD (1999). *The Developed Countries 1999 Report.* New York and Geneva: United Nations.

UNCTAD (1995). *Policy Options and Proposals for the Revitalization of the Generalized System of Preferences.* TD/B/SCP/13. Geneva: United Nations.

UNIDO (1997). *Progress and Prospects for Industrial Development in Least Developed Countries towards the 21st Century.* Fourth LDC Ministerial Symposium. Vienna.

12

Proliferation of RTAs with Special Reference to South Asia*

Introduction

The establishment of the World Trade Organization (WTO) in 1995 led to policy changes that were far-reaching and have been viewed as nothing less than a revolution in trade policy reform. However, as nations expedited their liberalization processes and integration into the world economy, imbalances and instabilities increased both among nations and within nations. It was unrealistic to assume that these revolutionary changes would keep on bringing about enhanced cooperation among countries and greater stability. In the light of this complex multilateral backdrop, regionalism has become the core component of the new international order. Presently, almost without any exception, trading countries of the world are associated with one, or more typically, two or three regional trading arrangements (RTAs), and the proliferation of RTAs is altering the world trade landscape.

Today, more than one-third of global trade occurs between countries that have some form of reciprocal RTA.[1] RTAs have often provided opportunities for comprehensive removal of trade barriers and greater harmonization of rules governing trade than can be achieved under multilateral negotiations. Trade agreements have gone beyond lowering tariffs to include measures to reduce trade hurdles related to standards, customs and border crossing, and services regulations as well as broader rules that have a positive impact on the investment climate.

---

* *Economic Integration in South Asia*, NRB (ed.), 109-124, April 2005.

The upsurge in RTAs has not only led to qualitative and quantitative changes in regional integration involving North-North and North-South countries, but it has also ignited many countries of the South to strive for free trade areas (FTAs) among themselves. It is against this background that this paper first discusses the different types of RTAs operating in the world as well as the factors that are responsible for their success. Next, their relevance in the context of the multilateral trading system is highlighted. Before concluding, three emerging RTAs, the Bangkok Agreement, the Bay of Bengal Initiative for Multi-sectoral Technical and Economic Cooperation (BIMSTEC) Free Trade Area and the South Asian Free Trade Area (SAFTA) are examined.

Forms of RTA and Ingredients for Success

Standard economic literature has classified RTA into five categories or levels of integration: preferential trade agreements involving significantly less than 100% liberalization, FTAs, customs unions, common markets and economic unions.

These five categories or stages denote a continuum of integration with the shift from a customs union to a common market representing the step up from low (or shallow) integration to high (or deep) integration. Shallow integration happens where the impact of the integration is felt solely in international trade and mainly affects border measures, such as tariffs, adopted by the state. High integration RTAs, on the other hand, are characterized by the extension of coverage to a whole range of non-tariff barriers (NTBs) and "behind-the-border" issues. Thus, their successful implementation will frequently require a greater degree of political will than is required for low integration RTAs.

At the lowest level of integration, the preferential arrangement, liberalization does not extend to the abolishment of all the trade barriers between territories nor does it cover all the varieties of economic activity within the participating countries. In such arrangements, which are also known as partial or sectoral trade agreements, two or more countries exchange preferences or liberalize trade in a selected group of product categories or in selected sectors of the economy. There are two other features that characterize such arrangements: they often extend beyond geographical regions and the liberalization engaged in can be either reciprocal or non-reciprocal in nature.

The most common type of RTA is the FTA. FTAs are the least restrictive of the RTAs, demanding member countries to dismantle only trade barriers among themselves, and permitting each member country to fix its own barriers to trade with non-members. A free trade agreement establishes an FTA where trade in goods is fully liberalized between two or more countries. This includes the elimination of tariff and non-tariff barriers to trade between signatories to the agreement. Signatories retain the ability to determine their own trade policies towards non-members. Traditionally, FTAs have only taken into account the free movement of goods but, with the realization that effective integration requires more than just the elimination of tariffs and quantitative restrictions, contemporary FTAs have expanded to include a wider range of economic sectors such as services, investment & competition regulations and government procurement. As a result of this expansion of coverage, contemporary FTAs often display some of the features of "high" integration.

In a customs union, a FTA is supplemented by the harmonization of external tariffs *vis-à-vis* non-members, that is, the creation of a common external tariff and the use of a common tariff nomenclature. Customs unions typically adopt mechanisms to redistribute tariff revenue among members. Members agree to set their external trade policy as a unified whole. The customs union represents the deepest level of shallow integration.

Simply put, a common market is a customs union with free market mobility within the grouping. It consists not only of the free movement of goods and services characteristic of a customs union, but also of the free mobility of factors of production, that is, labor and capital. Hence, "behind-the-border" issues start being addressed. The line between a customs union and a common market may often seem indistinct since the free movement of services often involves the movement of what could also be classified as factors of production.[2] The common market denotes deep integration in the sense that it involves the regulation of sectors that are traditionally considered as falling within the domestic jurisdiction of a state such as the licensing of doctors or lawyers.

Lastly, at the highest or deepest level of integration, is an economic union, which represents a common market with co-ordination of macroeconomic policies, including a common currency.

Globally, RTAs have been expanding over the second half of the 1990s, enabling many nations to seek benefit from freer trade. Depending on the level of integration, these have ranged from PTAs such as the SAARC Preferential Trading Agreement (SAPTA), FTAs such as the North American Free Trade Agreement (NAFTA) and the ASEAN Free Trade Agreement (AFTA), customs unions such as Mercosur (a Latin American regional integration mechanism with Argentina, Brazil, Paraguay and Uruguay as full members, and Bolivia and Chile as associate members), to economic union such as the European Union (EU).[3]

RTAs are beneficial and effective for developing countries when implemented with more comprehensive domestic reforms. Simultaneously, a successful RTA will contribute to the aggregate economic impact of that reform program.

For several reasons, an important determinant for the success of RTAs is the external trade regime. One, trade diversion appears to go down with the level of the external tariffs maintained by member countries after the formation of a PTA. If a country that enters into a free trade agreement increases its imports from all countries, not only its partners in the agreement, then there will be an improvement in economic welfare. Hence, countries forming PTAs need to simultaneously lower the level of external protection facing non-member countries.

Two, where there exist asymmetries in the level of external protection, the high-duty country should lower tariffs to avoid an adverse terms-of-trade shock. Three, low MFN tariffs and nonrestrictive rules of origin ensure that producers within the RTA will get access to competitively priced inputs. In today's globalized market, policies that considerably increase the input costs of producers will limit their exports to both regional and global markets. Regional integration seems to be more successful if it is attained on the basis of strong competition and ease of access to low-cost inputs.

RTAs and WTO's Multilateral Trading System

The global trading system has experienced a sharp increase in RTAs over the past two decades. The network of RTAs is becoming more and more complex and many countries are members of several agreements, sometimes with very diverse rules. As at July 2003, only three WTO members—Macau China, Mongolia and Chinese Taipei—were not associated with any RTA. The rise in the RTAs has continued unabated since the early 1990s. By May 2003, over 265 had been notified to the WTO (and its predecessor, GATT). Of these, 138 were notified after the WTO was created in January 1995. Over 190 are currently in force; another 60 are believed to be operational, though not yet notified. Based on the number of agreements reportedly planned or already under negotiations, the total number of RTAs in operations could be nearing about 300 by 2005.[4]

The boom in RTAs demonstrates changes in certain countries' trade policy objectives, the changing perceptions of the multilateral liberalization process, and the reintegration into the global economy of countries in transition from socialism. The issue is whether these regional groups help or hinder the WTO's multilateral trading system.

Often, RTAs can actually support the WTO's multilateral trading system. Regional agreements have permitted groups of countries to negotiate rules and commitments that go beyond what was possible at the time multilaterally. As a result, some of these rules have paved the way for agreement in the WTO. Services, intellectual property, environmental standards, investment and competition policies are all issues that were brought up in regional negotiations and later developed into agreements under the WTO.

The groupings that are crucial for the WTO are those that abolish or reduce barriers on trade within the group. The WTO agreements recognize that regional arrangements and closer economic integration can be beneficial to countries. It also recognizes, however, that under certain circumstances RTAs could hurt the trade interests of other countries. Generally, setting up a customs union or FTA would violate the WTO's principle of equal treatment for all trading partners ("most-favored nation"). Yet, GATT's Article 24 permits RTAs to be set up as a special exception, provided certain strict criteria are fulfilled.[5] Likewise, Article 5 of the General Agreement on Trade in Services (GATS) concerns economic integration agreements in services. Other provisions in the WTO agreements permit developing countries to enter into regional or global agreements that include the reduction or abolishing of tariffs and non-tariff barriers on trade among themselves.

It is to be noted here that while the renewed momentum for multilateral trade liberalization and rule making launched at Doha in 2001 could have assisted to reduce the risks of regionalism being pursued as a preferred course, the failed Ministerial Meeting at Cancun in 2003 may have forced many WTO members to accord more emphasis on regional initiatives. Even the United States indicated that it would double its efforts to sign bilateral agreements and RTAs that are easier to negotiate than WTO agreements.

RTAs in South Asia

In recent years, RTAs have been viewed as effective mechanisms to address the complex challenges emanating from globalization, the majority of which are beyond the capacity of individual developing countries. This has led countries of South Asia to look for opportunities both to form RTAs among themselves and to be part of the RTAs of the other regions. Accordingly, the South Asian countries have intensified regional economic integration through regional, sub-regional and bilateral approaches. It is against this light that the Bangkok Agreement, the BIMSTEC FTA Accord and the SAFTA Accord are discussed at length below.

The Bangkok Agreement: Linking South-east Asia, East Asia and South Asia

It was in July 1975 that the Bangkok Agreement, Asia's first multi-member PTA between developing countries, was signed by seven countries, namely, Bangladesh, India, Lao People's Democratic Republic, the Republic of Korea, Sri Lanka, the Philippines and Thailand after agreeing to a list of products for mutual tariff reduction.[6] The Agreement was ratified by five of the seven countries, excepting the Philippines and Thailand. The objectives of the Bangkok Agreement are to promote economic development through trade expansion among the members of the Economic and Social Commission of the Asia and the Pacific (ESCAP) and to adopt mutually beneficial trade liberalization measures.[7] The rules and regulations are designed, among others, to ensure non-discriminatory and fair trade practices and to preserve the value of the preferences including compensatory action where the value of the preference is lowered or abrogated. The other areas of cooperation include customs administration, standardization of procedures and formalities concerning mutual trade, adoption of a common tariff nomenclature and harmonization of rules of origin and of dumping.

China formally acceded to the Bangkok Agreement in April 2001 and its accession has major implications for trade in the Asia-Pacific Region. While Papua New Guinea acceded to the Agreement in December 1993, the Agreement has yet to be ratified by the Government of Papua New Guinea. Pakistan notified its intention to accede to the Agreement in February 1998, and is in the process of accession. Other countries that have demonstrated interest in joining include Bhutan, Cambodia, Fiji, the Islamic Republic of Iran, Kazakhstan, Mongolia, Nepal and Vietnam.

The Bangkok Agreement as of February 2004 encompassed only tariffs on goods. However, the members have recognized the need to ultimately widen the scope of the Agreement to deal with non-tariff barriers and trade in services.

The Bangkok Agreement has ample potential and is the only truly 'regional' trading arrangement in the Asia-Pacific region as membership covers various sub-regions. To attain its true potential in the new trading environment, the member countries realized that the Agreement was in need for change and modernization. As a result, they launched a revitalization process. The revitalization package included the revision of the text of the Agreement to address the changes in the international trading system that have occurred since the Agreement first came into force, the setting up of a Ministerial Council to take responsibility for the major decisions and the speedy conclusion of the Third Round of negotiations.

Three rounds of negotiations have been concluded under the Agreement. While the First Round of negotiations was completed in 1975, leading to the signing of the Agreement by the participating members, the Second Round of negotiations was concluded on 15 February 1991.[8] Since the conclusion of the Second Round, the national lists of concessions of the participating states have been regularly modified. Members have widened their list and China's offer list itself has witnessed a considerable rise in the number of items being granted preferential treatment.[9] The Third Round of negotiations, with the objective of widening and deepening concessions to increase intra-member trade, was completed in July 2004.[10]

The Standing Committee of the Bangkok Agreement met in Bangkok on 8-9 January 2005 for its 23rd session. The primary objective of this session was to decide on how to consolidate the second and third round concession lists as well as to continue preparations and arrangements for the first session of the

Ministerial Council. Discussions are also ongoing on deriving common rules of origin for the Bangkok Agreement members.

Membership to the Bangkok Agreement is likely to go up in the near future as China's entry has already aroused renewed interest in the Agreement from the prospective members and the results of the revitalization program are becoming more visible. Members presently have access to two large markets of the region—China and India—together with access on preferential terms to other major markets, especially the Republic of Korea.

BIMSTEC FTA: A Nexus between SAFTA and AFTA

The Bay of Bengal Initiative for Multi-sectoral Technical and Economic Cooperation (BIMSTEC), a regional trading bloc, was established in June 1997 to strengthen socio-economic cooperation among Bangladesh, India, Sri Lanka and Thailand. While Myanmar was admitted as a full member in December 1997, Bhutan and Nepal joined in February 2004. BIMSTEC's six principal areas of cooperation are agriculture, energy, fisheries, tourism, trade and transportation, among others.

At the Fourth BIMSTEC Meeting of the Trade and Economic Ministers held in Colombo on 7 March 2003, a Group of Experts (GOE) was appointed for drafting the Framework Agreement of BIMSTEC FTA. Accordingly, the Framework Agreement on BIMSTEC FTA was signed on 8 February 2004 at Bangkok during the Sixth BIMSTEC Economic Ministers' Meeting.[11] The FTA Agreement would first start on trade in goods from July 2006, while the FTA Agreement on trade in services and investment would start from July 2007.

In line with the agreement, in trade in goods, the products besides those included in the negative list would be subject to tariff cut or elimination on two tracks.[12]

In terms of the negotiations for trade in services, priority would be given to the progressive elimination of substantially all discrimination between or among the member countries and or prohibition of new or more discriminatory measures with regard to trade in services between the member countries, except for measures permitted under specific Article of the WTO General Agreement on Trade in Services.

In order to promote investments to a develop transparent and competitive environment, the members also agreed to provide for the promotion and protection of investment, strengthen co-operation in investment, facilitate investment and improve transparency of investment rules and regulations and enter into negotiations in order to progressively liberalize the investment regime through a positive list approach. The members are to develop a modality for anti-dumping measures, subsidy and countervailing measures and non-tariff measures to foster free trade in the region.

The declaration at the end of the first BIMSTEC Summit held in Bangkok in July 2004 provided significant recognition to the potentialities of multi-dimensional cooperation within the region. It expressed strong commitment of the Asian leaders to the founding objectives and principles of BIMSTEC to assess the challenges and opportunities for economic cooperation in the region and to strengthen BIMSTEC's ability to find ways and means to realize those challenges and opportunities.

A formal meeting of the Third Round of Trade Negotiation Committee (TNC) of BIMSTEC was held in Kathmandu during 8-10 March 2005. In this meeting, the preliminary framework of rules of origin and dispute settlement mechanism, the two crucial provisions of the BIMSTEC FTA Accord, was adopted. The meeting also discussed other outstanding issues concerning the FTA Accord on trade in goods.[13]

SAFTA and Regional Cooperation

The South Asia Free Trade Area (SAFTA) agreement was signed at the 12th SAARC Summit in January 2004.[14] Prior to this, the South Asian Preferential Trading Arrangement (SAPTA) had come into force in December 1995. The four rounds of SAPTA had led to the coverage of more than 5,000 tariff line items.

However, studies have demonstrated that the SAPTA process did very little in stimulating regional trade.[15]

The SAPTA framework was basically based on the "positive list" approach. The process was very lengthy and slow. Again, at least in the first two rounds of the SAPTA, NTBs were not considered for removal with the granting of tariff preferences. The other problems were that (a) the tariff cuts were not deep enough, (b) a wide range of goods was not subject to preferential tariffs, and (c) some actively traded goods were left out from preferential tariffs.

The SAFTA treaty is to come into force on 1 January 2006. Under the treaty, the non-LDCs were required to bring down their tariffs to 0-5 percent by 2013, except Sri Lanka which was required to do so by 2014. However, non-LDCs needed to bring their tariff to 0-5 percent for the products of LDCs by 2009 with regard to products of export interest to the latter. The LDCs, on the other hand, needed to bring down their tariffs to 0-5 percent by 2016.

In accordance with the SAFTA Agreement, a sensitive list, where products exempted from the Trade Liberalization Program, would be listed and then negotiated by the members and incorporated in the Agreement as an integral part. But, the number of products in the list would be subject to maximum ceiling, which are to be mutually agreed among the contracting members, with flexibility given to the LDC members to seek derogation with regard to the products of their export interest.[16] It has been agreed in the framework treaty that all the seven member states can maintain two Sensitive List of Products, in which tariff will not be reduced—one for developing countries and another for LDCs.[17] Likewise, issues such as imposition of anti-dumping duties, countervailing duties and safeguard measures are to be dealt in accordance with the WTO.[18] Rules of Origin (RoO) are to be negotiated and incorporated into the SAFTA Agreement as an integral part.

The SAFTA affirms the existing rights and obligations under the Marrakesh Agreement establishing the WTO and other treaties and agreements to which SAARC members are signatories. Trade facilitation and other measures are to be adopted. The SAFTA framework also incorporated simplification and harmonization of standards, customs clearance, import licensing, import financing by banks and transit facilities particularly for landlocked countries. It clearly stipulated the actions that contracting members can take while facing BoP difficulties, during import surges or in the case of disputes.

All in all, the SAFTA is expected to enter into force on the due date upon completion of four procedural formalities: formation of sensitive lists, rules of origin, revenue loss compensation mechanism and ratification by the all member states.

That there exist significant benefits to be reaped from the SAFTA process is clear. For example, openness to trade and investment could result in overall development and make a dent on poverty and backwardness.[19] The adoption of SAFTA would facilitate in bringing down customs duty, promote cross-border investment and, more importantly, formalize the unofficial trade that is occurring through third countries. For example, while current India-Bangladesh bilateral trade is about US$ 1.2 billion, unofficial trade is about twice that figure. According to a study, the total elimination of tariffs under SAFTA could augment intra-regional trade by 1.6 times from the existing levels.[20] The gains would mainly accrue to the smaller members of the SAARC since they would gain access to the relatively larger markets of the larger members.

However, to imagine that the engine of regional growth in South Asia will lie in the trade in goods alone is being quite optimistic. With very few exceptions, where a country's advantage lies in unique geographical or resource endowments, it is highly unlikely that an upswing in intra-regional trade can result from comparative advantages when all the economies of SAFTA are still locked into a labor-surplus and capital-scarce environment.[21] With low levels of per capita incomes in most of the member states and fewer numbers of technology driven industries, intra-industry trade based on very refined product differentiation does not seem to have a bright future either.

The Agreement in its present form also needs to be scrutinized from two other angles. First, it excludes the important services sector. It chooses to overlook the existing and potential national competitive advantage that the SAARC member states have in sectors such as tourism and hospitality (Nepal, Maldives, Sri Lanka), retailing of electricity (with Pakistan's surplus power, Nepal's and Bhutan's hydel-power capacities), transmission/ distribution of gas (Bangladesh), and health services (India), and a number of other services. In this context, it should be realized that a RTA should be both deepened and widened as well.[22]

Secondly, the Agreement does not mention anything on how SAFTA is going to integrate the existing bilateral free trade agreements (BFTAs) between some SAARC countries into the SAFTA agreement. Furthermore, rules and regulations for the effective implementation of the Trade Liberalization Program and granting of special and differential treatment to the LDCs (Bangladesh, Bhutan, Maldives and Nepal) have not been distinctly spelt out. These issues form the crux of the treaty, and until concrete and constructive negotiations are concluded on them, the future of SAFTA would remain uncertain.

Thus, for the success of SAFTA, a gamut of policy initiatives need to be undertaken by the member countries. In the first place, all the countries should have a very small negative list. Secondly, the rules of origin should be simple and transparent. Thirdly, as some of the members could dump and others may provide subsidies to exports and hence practice unfair competition, anti-dumping and countervailing measures need to be transparent. Fourthly, a priority agenda in the next summit could be the extension of SAFTA's scope to cover trade in services and investment liberalization. Because five of the SAFTA's members already signed the Framework Agreement on BIMSTEC FTA, there should not be any difficulty in building a consensus.

For evaluating the impact of SAFTA in the future, information is required on the degree to which the Agreement's provisions are being timely implemented and how they are affecting decisions by producers and consumers. As monitoring is important in this respect, an implementation scorecard would be very beneficial.[23] Besides providing crucial information, the scorecard is helpful as a disciplinary tool to disgrace governments with a record of poor implementation into action and to empower governments with good records of implementation to challenge those members who are not fulfilling their commitments.

To conclude this section on SAFTA, a comparison between BIMSTEC FTA and SAFTA is made since membership to multiple RTAs could lead to conflicting obligations.[24] For instance, in both SAFTA and BIMSTEC FTA, the target and the depth of integration differ. BIMSTEC FTA covers both trade in goods and services while SAFTA so far includes only trade in goods. Moreover, while SAFTA's aim is to bring down the tariffs to the 0-5 percent level, BIMSTEC FTA aims for total elimination. These disparities could generate complications in the implementation of these FTAs. There are also other complex issues involved with regard to the simultaneous implementation of these FTA accords. These concern the sensitive list and trade among countries that are members to both the FTAs. In the first place, there is an arrangement in both the FTA accords for maintaining the sensitive list. Due to the disparity in tariff targets, there is every possibility that the products under the sensitive list under the two FTAs would not be the same. If this happens, it is unclear as to how trade among countries that are members of both the FTAs will be conducted. Two, as each individual country would wish to protect its local market, countries that are members of both the FTAs may seek protection under the FTA that best fulfils their demands. In this circumstance, it would be difficult to determine which FTA would prevail when trade is carried out among members of both the FTAs. Again, Pakistan and Maldives are not members of BIMSTEC while Thailand and Myanmar are not part of SAARC. All in all, as membership to multiple RTAs could create conflicting obligations, negotiations under SAFTA and BIMSTEC FTA need to be carried out by ensuring that such contradictions do not come about.

Conclusions

To sum up, the RTAs that augment national income normally consist of the following components: a) low external MFN tariffs, b) some sectoral and product exemptions, c) nonrestrictive rules-of-origin tests that build toward a framework common to many agreements, c) measures for facilitating trade, d) measures to enhance new cross-border competition, especially in services, and e) rules on investment and intellectual property that are suitable to the development context.

Depending on their design and implementation, RTAs can generate positive or negative impact on trade. In this context, the broader policy context in which an RTA is designed and implemented is of prime importance. Agreements that have been framed to complement a general program of economic reform have been very effective in augmenting trade.

RTAs provide a second-best means of promoting trade liberalization in a context where multilateral negotiations progress slowly. In such an atmosphere, openness through RTAs can build up some of the same institutional and competitive pressures as increased openness *via* multilateral negotiations.[25]

The Bangkok Agreement is the oldest RTA of the Asia Pacific region that currently includes countries from South Asia (Bangladesh, India and Sri Lanka), South East Asia (Lao People's Democratic Republic) and East Asia (China and Republic of Korea) and whose aim is to continuously reduce tariff, non-tariff barriers and forge trade-related cooperation. With a combined population of about 2.5 billion people, this PTA has the potential to become the world's largest RTA with respect to population coverage. Expansion of membership is expected to boost the trade linkages between East and South Asia, and also serve as a bridge linking these sub-regions with other sub-regions.

BIMSTEC has emerged as an important regional entity and indicates a major stride by South Asia towards free trade. BIMSTEC FTA could act as a bridge between the ASEAN Free Trade Area (AFTA) and the SAFTA. It is necessary for the TNC to finalize the FTA Accord on trade in goods by the end of 2005 since it is to be enforced from July 2006. Moreover, the BIMSTEC Summit also endorsed enforcement of FTA on trade in services and investment promotion from July 2007.

The proliferation of RTAs have also inspired the South Asian countries to create a SAFTA which is to be launched beginning 2006 upon completion of formalities, including ratification by all contracting states and issuance of notification by the SAARC Secretariat. The SAFTA Accord marks a movement away from the mere tinkering with tariffs under SAPTA for establishing a FTA in the region. It has the potentiality of going beyond its stated objective of liberalization of trade in goods. Through a successful integration, the South Asian region can attract significant foreign investment; this integration could also lead to restructuring of the economies while making the region a competitive economic block.

However, as South Asian countries are still marginal players in world trade, the benefits to be procured from multilateral agreements should not be undermined. Hence, the countries should follow the two-track approach, giving priority to promoting multilateral trade negotiations under the WTO as well as strive for meaningful RTAs which they are currently pursuing. Moreover, as the current wave of regionalism has embraced almost all the WTO members, South Asian nations cannot afford to move against the stream.

Notes

1. Details are provided in World Bank (2005).

2. An example is consulting.
3. A list of the prevalent RTAs is presented in World Bank (2005).
4. These data are taken from the WTO website.
5. Article 24 states that if a free trade area or customs union is formed, duties and other trade barriers should be lowered or removed on substantially all sectors of trade in the group. Non-members should not find trade with the group any more restrictive than before the group was formed.
6. The Bangkok Agreement will formally come to be known as the Asia-Pacific Trade Agreement (APTA) by Ministers at the first session of the Ministerial Council in 2005.
7. The Agreement was not formulated to divert or restrict trade from countries, but to expand mutual trade through fuller exploitation of their trade potential, expansion of productive capacities and higher economic growth.
8. Under the First Round, the total number of products for which tariff preferences were given was 104, in addition to 15 items on which special concessions were granted to Lao PDR. But, tariff preferences were renegotiated and revised in 1979. The total number of product items for which tariff preferences were prolonged for renegotiations was 93 items. Of the 93 products, the *ad valorem* duties of 80 products were lowered by an average of 23 percent, and the tariff of 9 products was bound at the existing tariff levels. With regard to the other 4 products, specific duties were lowered, varying from 10 percent to 67 percent. The Second Round of negotiations led to tariff concessions being exchanged on 438 items in addition to 63 items for which special concessions were granted to Bangladesh. The extent of tariff concessions among the participating members varied between 13 to 30 percent.
9. The number of products in China's list of concessions is 739, in addition to 18 items for which special concessions have been given to the LDCs.

10. As member countries are currently consolidating the third round and second round list of concessions, the exact number of concessions arising from the third round is not known. However, preliminary data indicate that the number of items for which tariff concessions were given have risen from 1,721 to 4,279 (from 112 to 609 in the case of special concessions to the LDCs). Details are given in ESCAP (2004a).
11. Although initially Bangladesh was not a signatory to this Framework Agreement as the three developing countries (India, Thailand and Sri Lanka) objected to the move to compensate the loss of revenues for the LDCs, it joined the Framework Agreement on 25 June 2004.
12. In the fast track, products listed by a Party on its own accord shall have their respective applied MFN tariff rates slowly reduced/eliminated in accordance with specified rates to be mutually agreed by the Parties within the following timeframe:

Countries	**For Developing Country Parties**	**For LDC Parties**
India, Sri Lanka and Thailand	1 July 2006 to 30 June 2009	1 July 2006 to 30 June 2007
Bangladesh, Bhutan, Myanmar, and Nepal	1 July 2006 to 30 June 2011	1 July 2006 to 30 June 2009

Under the normal track, on the other hand, products listed by a Party on its own accord shall have their respective applied MFN tariff rates slowly lowered/abolished in accordance with specified rates to be mutually agreed by the Parties, within the following time frame:

Countries	For Developing Country Parties	For LDC Parties
India, Sri Lanka and Thailand	1 July 2007 to 30 June 2012	1 July 2007 to 30 June 2010
Bangladesh, Bhutan, Myanmar and Nepal	1 July 2007 to 30 June 2017	1 July 2007 to 30 June 2015

13. Moreover at this meeting, Thailand submitted a new framework on technical barriers to trade (TBT) to the respective technical teams for study. The discussion on the TBT framework would be held in the next meeting of the TNC in Myanmar in April, 2005. In that meeting, the TNC is expected to deliberate on various issues such as tariff and customs harmonization, sensitive list, tariff liberalization program, protection during the transition period and safeguard measures, which are very important for the success of the FTA. For details, please refer to *The Kathmandu Post*, 12 March 2005.

14. It was at the 8th SAARC Summit in New Delhi in 1995 that the SAFTA was initially mooted. At that time, it was proposed that it should come into operation in 2005. The effective date of SAFTA was changed to 2001 together with the formation of a Group of Eminent Persons (GEP) to draw up a roadmap for SAFTA at the 9th SAARC Summit in Male in 1997. At the 10th SAARC Summit in Colombo in 1998, the GEP report was submitted which suggested that a more practical timetable for SAFTA was 2008. It also recommended the effective date for the LDCs of the region should be 2010. Accordingly, the date for the launching of SAFTA was postponed but without indicating any time-frame. However, it was decided to have a 'Framework Treaty' by 2001. The preparation of SAFTA got delayed owing to regional politics. It was only in January 2004 that the SAFTA finally came into shape. For a detailed historical background on the SAFTA, please refer to Kelegama (2004).

15. This is illustrated in Mukherji (2002) and Kemal (2004).

16. Moreover, the sensitive list is to be reviewed every four years or earlier, as decided by the SAFTA Ministerial Council, with the aim of reducing the number of items in the list. Again, since a large part of gain come from resources for production being allocated in a more efficient manner, it

is crucial that the number of products on the sensitive list is kept to a minimum, and that industrial restructuring is allowed to take place. Furthermore, suitable measures need to be undertaken to address the difficulties in the protected sectors with the aim of removing the products from the list as soon as possible.

17. This list is to be finalized between now and the date it enters into force.
18. It was also agreed to accord special regard to the situation of LDCs with respect to anti-dumping and/or countervailing measures, to consider more flexibility for the LDCs in continuation of quantitative restrictions as well as to take direct trade measures with the objective of enhancing sustainable exports from the LDCs, and to set up a suitable mechanism to compensate the LDCs for their loss of customs revenue until alternative domestic arrangements are developed to address this situation.
19. The benefits from SAFTA are discussed in Dadwal (2004).
20. This estimation is given in RIS (2004).
21. As illustrated in Mehta and Kumar (2004), there are other factors, both economic and non-economic, responsible for the low level of intra-regional trade in South Asia which stood at 4.9 percent in 2001, as compared to 22.4 percent for intra-ASEAN trade and 20.8 percent for trade among the Mercosur group. One, since the majority of the South Asian economies are dependent on agriculture and their technological advances with regard to production processes are not very different, the goods produced by them are quite similar. Secondly, the countries of the region possess an almost identical pattern of comparative advantage in a relatively narrow range of products. Analogously, their bilateral trade structures hardly reveal any complementarities in the trade structure. Again, owing to the lower quality of products produced within

the region, some countries import goods from outside the region, despite the prices being higher. Finally, geography limits the markets for Nepal and Bhutan owing to land-lockedness, and these countries have to trade basically with India. On the other hand, political issues are responsible for the low level of trade between India and Pakistan.

22. For example, the Indo-Sri Lanka BFTA has been developed into an Indo-Lanka Comprehensive Economic Partnership Agreement where liberalization of services has been included. Moreover, in the agreement on the BIMSTEC FTA, liberalization of services under a GATS-plus framework has been incorporated. For details, please see Kelegama (2004).
23. An example is the 'Single Market Scoreboard' employed by the EU Commission. The details are given in World Bank (2005).
24. It should be pointed out that BIMSTEC evolved an FTA within seven years of its establishment at its 1st Summit while it took SAARC two decades and twelve summits.
25. ADB (2002) compares RTAs with multilateral trading arrangement.

References

Adhikari, Ratnakar (2004). "Dangerous Fast Track." *The Kathmandu Post*. 20 February. Available at: http://www.sawtee.org/art3.html#22

Asian Development Bank (ADB) (2002). *Asian Development Outlook 2002*. New York: Oxford University Press.

Dadwal, Shebonti Ray (2004). "SAFTA is on Track, But FTA?" *The Financial Express*. 10 April.

Economic and Social Commission for Asia and the Pacific (ESCAP) (2003). "Facts about the Bangkok Agreement." Bangkok: ESCAP. Available at: http://www.unescap.org/ tid/BAfacts.pdf

ESCAP (2004). 'SAARC Summit Meeting: Regional Cooperation in South Asia Moving Forward." *Regional Rapid Response Trade Bulletin*. Flier No. 1/2004. Available at: http://www.unescap.org/tid/news/flier/04.pdf.

ESCAP (2004a). "Multilateralism and Free Trade Areas in Asia and the Pacific: Progress, Challenges and Prospects." E/ESCAP/SCITI/1. September. Available at: http://www.unescap. org/ about/CMG/ TI/English/SCITI

Harrison, Glenn W. and David G. Tarr (2003). "Rules of Thumb for Evaluating Preferential Trading Arrangements: Evidence from Computable General Equilibrium Assessments." *The Policy Research Working Paper 3142*. Washington, D.C.: World Bank.

Joe, Thomas K. (2004). "A Subcontinental Free Trade Utopia." *Himal South Asian*. January. Available at: http://www.himalmag.com/2004/ january/perspective.htm

Kelegama, Saman (2004). "SAFTA: A Critique." *South Asian Journal*. No. 4. April–June. Available at: http://www.southasianmedia.net/ Magazine/Journal/safta_critique.

Kelegama, Saman and Ratnakar Adhikari (2002). *Regional Integration in the WTO Era: South Asia at Crossroads*. Kathmandu and Jaipur: South Asia Watch on Trade, Economics and Environment and Consumer Unity and Trust Society.

Kemal, A. R. (2004). "SAFTA and Economic Cooperation." *South Asian Journal*. No. 6. October-December. Available at: http://www. southasianmedia.net/Magazine/ Journal/ 6_safta.

Mahhub ul Haq Human Development Centre (2002). *Human Development in South Asia 2001*. Oxford: Oxford University Press.

Mehta, Pradeep and Pranav Kumar (2004). "RTAs and South Asia: Options in the Wake of Cancun Fiasco." Available at: http://rspas.anu.edu. au/paper/asarc2004_11.pdf

Mehta, Rajesh (2002). "Establishment of Free Trade Arrangement among BIMSTEC Countries: Some Issues." Research and Information System for the Non-Aligned and Other Developing Countries. January. Available at: http://www.ris.org.in/dp23_pap.pdf

Mukherji, I. N. (2002). "Charting a Free Trade Area in South Asia: Instruments and Modalities," in T.N. Srinivasan, ed., *Trade, Finance and Investment in South Asia*. New Delhi: Social Science Press.

Mutai, Henri (2003). "Legal Implications for the Conduct of Trade Negotiations." Available at: http://www.tralac.org/scripts/content. php?id=1914

Research and Information System for the Non-aligned and Other Developing Countries (RIS) (2004). "South Asia Development & Cooperation Report 2004." Available at: http://www.ris.org.in/sadcr2004

South Asia Watch on Trade, Economics and Environment (2004). "Revitalizing the Bangkok Agreement." *PROACT Monthly*

E-Newsletter. 1:6. April. Available at: http://www.sawtee.org/PROACT-E-newsletter_Apr_04.html

Suleri, Abid Qaiyum and Bhaskar Sharma (2004) "The SAFTA Mirage." *Himal South Asian*. February. Available at: http://www.sawtee.org/art3.html#22

World Bank (2005). *Global Economic Prospects: Trade, Regionalism and Development*. Washington, D.C.: World Bank.

WTO. "Regionalism: Friends or Rivals?" Available at: http://www.wto.org/english/thewto_e/ whatis_e/tif_e/ bey1_e.htm

WTO. "Regional Trade Agreements." Available at: http://www.wto.org/english/tratop e/region e.

The Kathmandu Post, 13 December 2004.

The Kathmandu Post, 8 February 2005.

The Kathmandu Post, 12 March 2005.

13

Nepal's Trade Sector: Review, Repercussions and Recommendations*

Introduction

Trade is crucial to developing and least-developed countries (LDCs) for a variety of reasons. Firstly, it is often the principal mechanism for achieving the benefits of globalization. Countries win when they gain market access for their exports and new technology through international transfers, and when heightened competitive pressure improves the allocation of resources.

Secondly, the continuing reallocation of manufacturing activities from industrial to developing and LDCs provides many opportunities for expanding trade both in goods and in services. And finally, the growth of trade is firmly buttressed by international institutions. The World Trade Organization (WTO), established in 1995, is the primary institution in generating a commercial environment suitable to the multilateral exchange of goods and services.

The dynamism of international trade during the past two decades in particular, and its growing influence on international economic relations, has increased attention, especially in LDCs, on its contribution to economic growth. The link between trade, development and growth is a symbiotic one. Trade allows specialization based on comparative advantage, and assists countries to upgrade production processes and increase value-added through a more efficient use of resources. Increased

---

* *Economic Review*, 17: 86-112, April 2005.

competition that accompanies specialization and productivity growth has been instrumental in cementing the linkages between trade and growth. Also notable has been the process of market liberalization that has opened up trading avenues for new countries and products.

With the undertaking of market-oriented economic reforms in the early 1990s, Nepal increased its integration into the world economy. The principal components of the reform programs included liberalization of trade and industrial policies and rationalization of the foreign exchange regime. The core elements included reduction and restructuring of import duties, dismantling of most quantitative restrictions (QRs) and import licensing requirements, and introduction of full convertibility for current account transactions.

Although Nepal is one of South Asia's most open and trade dependent economies, the country cannot fully exploit the potential for export growth since its exports are focused in a few products and markets. Against this foreground, this paper is organized as follows. The next section assesses the role of the trade sector and its contribution to the Nepalese economy during the last decade. The major policies linked to this sector and other pertinent issues are also evaluated. Next, the overriding problems of the external sector together with some suggestions for its revival are highlighted. The final section concludes the study.

Trade Sector Review

Trade Liberalization

Acknowledging the significance of trade in the economic development process, Nepal has been shifting towards liberal and market-oriented trade reforms since the mid-1980s that was accompanied by various reform programs. The policymakers in Nepal have based their trade liberalization policies on a set of two hypotheses: a) liberalization of industrial and trade policies will boost industrial efficiency by providing greater access to imported intermediate inputs, capital goods, and technology, exposing local producers to both internal and international competition, thereby forcing them to lower costs, and removing curbs on the growth and size of firms so as to exploit the scale economies; and b) improvement in efficiency and the subsequent reduction in costs will stimulate domestic demand and enable Nepal's industrial goods to compete abroad, thereby relaxing demand-side constraints on industrial growth.

It was after the balance of payments (BoP) crisis in mid-1980s that Nepal initiated the trade liberalization program under the Economic Stabilization Program supported by the 18–month stand–by arrangement reached with the IMF in 1985.[1] The system of import quotas from third countries was dismantled and the import license auction system was introduced in July 1986. Then, with the completion of Economic Stabilization Program, the country undertook the three-year Structural Adjustment Program supported by the IMF and the World Bank in 1987.

Trade reforms were expedited in the early 1990s with the introduction of the partial convertibility in the current account on March 1992. This replaced the system of administrative control over import by the market mechanism. The partial convertibility system attempted to provide a built-in device to bring about a favorable impact on the current account and the BoP position. It also assisted in loosening the grip of bureaucracy on economic activities and promoting open competition in the market.

In order to achieve the full benefits of integrating the Nepalese economy with the world economic system, the government announced the full convertibility of current account transaction on February 1993. This automatically implied that the entire volume of trade would be conducted on the basis of the market exchange rate. The number of items put under the import auction was cut down to six. Later on July 1993, the new budget abolished the import auction license system altogether. Keeping only a few items under licensing, the government put all the items under the

OGL. With this, the government completely did away with QRs on import.

In the past, long and open border with India restricted the country's flexibility in framing and implementing independent economic policies. Consequently, Nepal had been subjected to negative spillover effects of inward looking and inefficient industrial system in India. But this gradually changed in the early 1990s when India embarked upon bold trade liberalization programs, including the drastic lowering of barriers to imports of capital goods and other inputs into production. Subsequently, Nepal also started to capitalize on the opportunity to open up as carried out by India.

One point is clear. The speed of Nepalese liberalization is guided by the pace of liberalization in India and the geo–political realities of the country. Hence, full liberalization of the Nepalese trade regime in a short period may neither be attainable nor be desirable. Nonetheless, policy commitments need to be realized, and for this substantial improvements may be warranted in the bureaucratic and administrative sectors, including removal of impediments and barriers such as procedural delays.

Plan Objectives and Trade Patterns

Although the Ninth Plan (1997-2002) had laid down certain objectives such as a) maximum utilization of the trade sector for the overall economic development of the country and expanding the benefits of foreign trade to the rural areas and b) diversification of trade and strengthening of backward linkages to make the export trade stable, these objectives were hardly met.

According to the Tenth Plan (2002-2007), the two-fold objectives with regard to foreign trade were a) to make the trade sector liberal, competitive and market-oriented for the overall growth of the country by extending returns accomplished from external and domestic trade up to the people's level through excessive participation of the private sector and b) to increase contribution of trade sector to the GDP progressively through import substitution and export promotion. The main strategies for attaining these dual objectives were through making the export trade competitive and market-oriented, the diversification of both country-wise and commodity-wise trade and the strengthening of the interlinkages between industry, trade, agriculture and other economic sectors. The core policies were to generate competitiveness in the trade sector in line with global and regional trade agreements, to ensure easy market access for Nepalese manufactured products, to expand transit facilities, to set up an export processing zone (EPZ) and to accord priority to exports of hydropower, software, labor and other services.

The Tenth Plan identified the following problems with regard to Nepal's trade sector: a) dependence on a few commodities and markets; b) reliance on import of raw and semi-finished materials; c) weak backward and forward linkages of the production of exportable products; and d) rising trend in the volume of trade deficit. To tackle these problems, the Plan laid down the following policy measures:

- ❖ Exports will be augmented by commodity-wise and country-wise diversification through the identification of exportable commodities of comparative advantages.
- ❖ For generating employment opportunities and raising income of the rural people, stress will be accorded on increasing the production and export of agro-based industrial products and on enhancing their qualities.
- ❖ There will be special arrangements for market, information dissemination, technology, financial support and transport facility. Standardization of the exportable commodities will be made at the international level and their competitiveness in the world market will be enhanced.
- ❖ The Government will provide ample support to the private sector by disseminating information concerning present and prospective export markets, flowing of trade information and intensifying the monitoring and evaluation process.

- ❖ The arrangement of tax-free EPZs together with the provision of necessary acts and laws will be made for promoting the export sector.
- ❖ To make the country's external trade more simplified, economical, reliable, and business-oriented, the existing acts, laws, institutional processes and coordinating system will be assessed and reformed.
- ❖ Export of hydropower, computer software and labor and other services will be given due thrust in addition to commodities listed as exportable.
- ❖ In order to acquire advantages from the membership of the WTO, the trade sector will be made competitive in such a way so as to be consistent with various trade agreements.
- ❖ Nepal's trade will be integrated with the global trade regime by developing a multi-modal transport system.

During the ten-year period from FY 1994/95 to FY 2003/04, total trade increased from Rs. 81.3 billion to Rs. 190.2 billion. During this period India's share in total trade of Nepal increased from 28.0 percent to 57.6 percent, while the share of overseas countries plummeted from 72.0 percent to 42.4 percent. If just the last two years are compared, that is, FY 2002/03 and FY 2003/04, there was a growth of 9.1 percent in total foreign trade. Moreover, total trade with India soared by 12.5 percent while trade with other countries rose by just 4.9 percent in FY 2003/04 compared to FY 2002/03. These are all depicted in Table 1.

Table 1: Direction of Trade

(Rs. in million)

Fiscal Year	Total Trade					Export					Import				
	India		Overseas		Grand Total	India		Overseas		Total Exports	India		Overseas		Total Imports
	Amount	% Share	Amount	% Share		Amount	% Share	Amount	% Share		Amount	% Share	Amount	% Share	
1994/95	22740.2	28.0	58578.5	72.0	81318.7	3124.3	17.7	14514.9	82.3	17639.2	19615.9	30.8	44063.6	69.2	63679.5
1995/96	28081.2	28.8	69254.4	71.2	97335.6	3682.6	16.1	19198.5	83.9	22881.1	24398.6	32.8	50055.9	67.2	74454.5
1996/97	30079.5	25.9	86110.4	74.1	116189.9	5226.2	23.1	17410.3	76.9	22636.5	24853.3	26.6	68700.1	73.4	93553.4
1997/98	36125.4	31.0	80390.1	69.0	116515.5	8794.4	32.0	18719.1	68.0	27513.5	27331.0	30.7	61671.0	69.3	89002.0
1998/99	44650.4	36.2	78551.2	63.8	123201.6	12530.7	35.1	23145.6	64.9	35676.3	32119.7	36.7	55405.6	63.3	87525.3
1999/00	63546.8	39.4	97849.1	60.6	161395.9	22618.7	43.8	29004.3	56.2	51623.0	40928.1	37.3	68844.8	62.7	109772.9
2000/01	81055.6	47.3	90285.7	52.7	171341.3	26030.2	46.8	29623.9	53.2	55654.1	55025.4	47.6	60661.8	52.4	115687.2
2001/02	84578.3	54.8	69755.5	45.2	154333.8	27956.2	59.6	18988.6	40.4	46944.8	56622.1	52.7	50766.9	47.3	107389.0
2002/03	97354.2	55.9	76928.5	44.1	174282.7	26430.0	52.9	23500.6	47.1	49930.6	70924.2	57.0	53427.9	43.0	124352.1
2003/04*	109516.6	57.6	80671.2	42.4	190187.8	30777.1	57.1	23133.6	42.9	53910.7	78739.5	57.8	57537.6	42.2	136277.1

* Provisional

Source: NRB (2004a).

Total exports increased from Rs. 17.6 billion in FY 1994/95 to Rs. 53.9 billion in FY 2003/04. Between FY 2002/03 and FY 2003/04, exports rose by 8.0 percent. Exports to India went up by 16.4 percent while exports to other countries fell by 1.6 percent. Still, the share of India in total exports remained at 57.1 percent in FY 2003/04 compared to 52.9 percent in FY 2002/03, while the share of other countries in total exports stood at 42.9 percent in FY 2003/04 compared to 47.1 percent in FY 2002/03. In FY 1994/95, the contributions of India and other countries to total exports were 17.7 percent and 82.3 percent, respectively.

Total imports, on the other hand, went up to Rs. 136.3 billion in FY 2003/04 from Rs. 63.7 billion in FY 1994/95. While total imports catapulted by 9.6 percent in FY 2003/04 in comparison to FY 2002/03, imports from India and third countries soared by 11.0 percent and 7.7 percent respectively. Similarly, as illustrated in Table 1, the share of India in total imports stood at 57.8 percent while that of other countries remained at 42.2 percent in FY 2003/04, compared to their shares of 30.8 percent and 69.2 percent, respectively, in FY 1994/95.

Between 1994/95 and 2003/04, trade deficit soared by 79 percent. However, when comparing FY 2002/03 and FY 2003/04, trade deficit went up by 10.7 percent and reached Rs. 86.4 billion. This was ascribed to the 7.8 percent rise in trade deficit with India and 15.0 percent rise in trade deficit with other countries.

An assessment of commodities according to SITC grouping does not display any noteworthy changes in the composition of goods exported between FY 1994/95 and FY 2003/04 as illustrated in Table 2. Accordingly, as in FY1994/95 manufactured goods classified chiefly by materials, miscellaneous manufactured articles and food and live animals are the major exportable items in descending order even in FY 2003/04. The shares of these items in total exports stood at 43.8 percent, 28.5 percent, and 11.6 percent, respectively in FY 2003/04 compared to 52.5 percent, 32.7 percent and 8.9 percent, respectively, in FY 1994/95. Similarly, in terms of imports, the major contributors are manufactured goods

Table 2: Trade by SITC Grouping

(Rs. in million)

SITC Group	1994/95	1995/96	1996/97	1997/98	1998/99	1999/2000	2000/01	2001/02	2002/03	2003/04*
Food & live animals	1562.7	1946.6	2661.7	3123.2	3724.5	4240.5	4776.6	5094.2	6100.9	6276.9
Tobacco & beverage	11.3	9.7	14.9	22.8	50.0	117.2	75.6	145.7	138.7	55.2
Crude materials, inedibles except fuel	485.5	768.7	663.5	487.1	469.9	561.3	751.1	624.5	800.1	714.3
Mineral fuels & lubricants	0.0	1.3	1.4	20.9	0.5	2.2	1.3	1.6	5.5	14.5
Animals & vegetable oil & fats	214.1	251.3	312.6	2136.3	3597.2	3229.7	4104.0	7421.4	4278.7	3375.7
Chemicals & drugs	302.3	640.4	1353.4	1968.5	2804.0	3933.2	4041.7	3308.3	3279.0	3865.9
Manufactured goods classified chiefly by materials	9260.3	10455.7	11028.6	11637.1	13539.6	15838.7	18909.3	17394.9	17794.7	23601.7
Machinery & transport equipment	37.1	35.2	59.6	58.0	97.8	390.8	343.6	364.9	208.2	619.5
Miscellaneous manufactured articles	5765.8	5772.2	6540.3	8059.6	11392.8	21509.2	22650.9	12589.3	17281.5	15380.1
Commodity and transactions not classified according to kind	0.1	0.0	0.5	0.0	0.0	0.0	0.0	0.0	43.3	6.9
Total Exports	**17639.2**	**19881.1**	**22636.5**	**27513.5**	**35676.3**	**49822.7**	**55654.1**	**46944.8**	**49930.6**	**53910.7**
Food & live animals	4464.0	4785.8	5400.5	4929.0	7619.5	10839.0	5994.4	6333.2	9370.5	8554.0
Tobacco & beverages	500.9	508.6	590.7	799.5	846.1	906.5	906.1	717.1	792.2	1026.8
Crude materials, inedibles except fuel	3347.9	4865.9	5487.1	6976.2	6246.7	7012.4	7559.6	6712.7	8479.3	10550.6
Mineral fuels & lubricants	4717.1	5549.3	7160.3	9537.3	8737.5	9097.9	11269.2	15222.3	19944.2	21904.1
Animals & vegetable oil & fats	2056.0	2830.9	2327.6	2025.8	3329.0	4446.0	5589.2	7887.5	7750.5	8634.4
Chemicals & drugs	7193.2	8686.8	8504.2	11077.3	12476.4	14474.2	12941.9	12380.9	14319.5	16544.9
Manufactured goods classified chiefly by materials	25300.6	28129.7	44741.9	32601.6	25638.0	34420.0	41188.0	32889.1	34888.2	36510.5
Machinery & transport equipment	13027.6	15301.1	13794.9	16734.7	18063.7	20547.9	23027.8	19513.8	20702.1	25694.2
Miscellaneous manufactured articles	3057.2	3794.6	4016.4	3974.0	4302.4	6682.8	7210.2	5670.3	6582.7	5103.8
Commodity and transactions not classified according to kind	15.0	1.8	1529.8	346.6	266.0	78.2	0.8	62.1	1523.0	1753.8
Total Imports	**63679.5**	**74454.5**	**93553.4**	**89002.0**	**87525.3**	**108504.9**	**115687.2**	**107389.0**	**124352.1**	**136277.1**

* Provisional

Source: NRB (2004a).

classified chiefly by materials, machinery & transport equipment, and mineral fuels & lubricants that accounted for 26.8 percent, 18.9 percent, and 16.1 percent of total imports, respectively, in FY 2003/04. Their respective shares in FY 1994/95 were 39.7 percent, 20.5 percent and 7.4 percent.

In terms of product diversification, while comparing FY 2003/04 to FY 2002/03, the principal commodities that were responsible for the increase in exports to India included soap, toothpaste, polyester yarn thread, M.S. pipe and plastic utensils. However, exports of vegetable ghee, pulses, cardamom, copper wire rod, pashmina and ayurvedic medicine to India fell. On the other hand, the major commodities that contributed to the decline in the exports to other countries were readymade garments and pashmina. There was an increase in the exports of woolen carpets, handicrafts, tanned skin, pulses and silverware and jewelleries to other countries. It should be noted that between FY 1994/95 and FY 2003/04 some uniformity have been maintained in the export intensity with regard to the goods exported to India although some fluctuations in the annual export of various commodities existed.

With regard to exports to other countries, Nepal's export to other countries till recently was dependent primarily on exports of carpets and readymade garments. While carpets and readymade garments formed 88.6 percent of total exports to other countries in FY 1994/95, these two items accounted for 65.8 percent in FY 2003/04.[2] In between FY 1994/95 and FY 2003/04, there has not been much significant change in the commodity composition of exports to overseas countries. One major exportable commodity that emerged during this period was pashmina whose export value amounted to Rs. 1.1 billion in FY 2003/04.

The annual import requirements of Nepal are quite volatile in nature, and primarily consist of development goods, machinery and equipment, consumer items, petroleum products and industrial raw materials. The import of gold has been declining since FY 1997/98 and considerably after FY 2000/01 following the liberalization of gold imports in India.[3] Compared to exports, imports are diversified and several commodities possess similar shares of total imports in the top rung, especially with regard to imports from overseas.

While comparing FY 2003/04 and FY 2002/03, the major imports from India that witnessed an increase included chemicals, chemical fertilizer, medicine, other machinery & parts, vehicles & spare parts, electrical equipments, petroleum products, M.S. wire rod, M.S. billet, and cold rolled sheet in coil. On the other hand, imports of textiles, cement, rice, agricultural equipment and parts, hot rolled sheet in coil and thread from India dropped. With regard to imports from third countries, the principal items that posted an increase included betel nut, crude palm oil, crude soybean oil, chemical fertilizer, writing and printing paper, copper wire rod & scrapes, steel rod & sheet, telecommunication equipment & parts, raw wool, zinc ingot, aircraft & spare-parts, other machinery & parts, and thread. Likewise, the following items disclosed a fall in imports from other countries: raw silk, textiles, readymade garments, transport equipment and parts, video television & parts, computer parts, medical equipment & tools, and medicine.

There exists a geographical concentration in Nepal's exports, the top four major trading partners in FY 2003/04 being India, USA, Germany and United Kingdom. Analogously, the country's imports have been primarily from India, Singapore, China and Thailand.

In aggregate, the following conclusions may be derived relating to the foreign trade position of the country:

- No significant change has been recorded with regard to the composition of exports, especially with regard to overseas countries.
- No noticeable change has been observed with respect to the diversification of export markets.

- The export/import ratios, which indicate the degree of trade-off between exports and imports, have been slightly going down after FY 2000/01 as shown in Table 3.
- Table 3 indicates that there have been some fluctuations in the contribution of exports to the GDP. While exports/ GDP stood at 8.0 percent in FY 1994/95, it rose to 13.6 percent in FY 1999/2000 before going down to 10.9 percent in FY 2003/04. Similarly, while the contribution of imports in GDP was 29.1 percent in FY 1994/95, it rose to 33.4 percent in FY 1996/97 before dropping to 27.5 percent in FY 2003/04.
- The share of manufactured good exports in total exports has gone down from 87.1 percent in FY 1994/95 to 80.1 percent in FY 2003/04. Conversely, the share of primary good exports has climbed up from 12.9 percent in FY 1994/95 to 19.9 percent in FY 2003/04.

Table 3: Trade Indicators

(in percent)

Fiscal Year	Export/ Import	Exports/ GDP	Imports/ GDP	Trade Deficit/ GDP	Manufactured Exports/Total exports	Primary Exports/ Total exports
1994/95	27.7	8.0	29.1	-21.0	87.1	12.9
1995/96	26.7	8.0	29.9	-21.9	85.0	15.0
1996/97	24.2	8.1	33.4	-25.3	83.9	16.1
1997/98	30.9	9.1	29.6	-20.4	79.0	21.1
1998/99	40.8	10.4	25.6	-15.2	78.0	22.0
1999/00	47.6	13.6	28.6	-15.0	83.6	16.4
2000/01	48.1	13.5	28.1	-14.6	82.6	14.4
2001/02	43.7	11.1	25.4	-14.3	71.7	28.3
2002/03	40.2	10.9	27.3	-16.3	77.3	22.7
2003/04	39.6	10.9	27.5	-16.6	80.1	19.9

Source: NRB (2004a).

Trade Policy of 1992

The Trade Policy of 1992 focused on promoting sustainable trade to enhance the economy by undertaking open and liberal policies, and by allowing wider participation of the private sector. It also accorded priority to new product development, trade diversification, reduction in imbalances and coordination with other sectors of the economy. These objectives highlighted outward orientation with particular stress on export development. The role and importance of the private sector were also clearly recognized. The salient features of the policy were: a) minimal role of public sector; b) undertaking of liberal and dynamic trade policy and procedures; c) stress on production and export of quality goods and services; d) simplification of tax procedures; and d) strengthening of institutional development.

The export policy acknowledged the need for a conducive formulation of macroeconomic policies. The strategies included, among others, the following: a) making the Nepalese currency partially convertible ultimately leading to its full convertibility; b) delicensing of exports except those banned or under QRs; c) implementation of duty drawback system by devising suitable mechanisms; d) setting up of the EPZ; e) exemption from all charges and income tax on exports; f) simplification of procedures; and g) strengthening of export capability through proper development of infrastructure, backward and forward linkages, and institutional and manpower development, as well as improvement in product marketing and promotion activities.

On the import front, the major strategies consisted of the following: a) linking imports with exports; b) delicensing of imports, except for those on the quantitatively restricted list or in the auction system; c) reducing transit costs; and e) simplification of procedures.

However, the majority of the measures announced in the Trade Policy of 1992 have not been implemented to the desired extent. For instance, neither the EPZ nor the Nepal Trade Promotion Organization has been set up.

Nepal-India Trade and Transit Treaty and Trade Integration in South Asia

Trade between Nepal and India is guided by the Nepal-India Trade

Treaty first signed in 1991 and later modified in 1996. The treaty was further renewed on 3 March 2002. Unlike the Treaty signed in 1996, several new restrictions were introduced such as stricter Rules of Origin and incorporation of safeguard clauses. The new Rules of Origin (RoO) encompass: (a) value addition (domestic content) requirements of 30 percent of ex-factory prices (from March 2003), and changes in tariff heading (CTH) at four-digit level of the harmonized system code. For manufactured exports of Nepal, that cannot satisfy the CTH criteria, the new Rules of Origin (RoO) demand that these products have undergone a sufficient manufacturing process within Nepal, determined on a case-by-case basis. Moreover, four Nepalese items would now be permitted to enter free of basic customs duty into the Indian market on a fixed quota basis.[4]

The ten-year trade figures in Table 1 depict that India's share in Nepal's trade has been gradually rising, especially during the last four years, but overseas trade still accounts for more than 40 percent of both imports and exports. Herein lies the significance of transit facilities for Nepal. With regard to the Nepal-India Transit Treaty signed between the two countries on 5 January 1999, there is a provision of the automatic renewal of the transit treaty every seven years. Under this Treaty, India provides port facilities at Calcutta and Haldia for the country's trade with overseas countries. Fifteen transit routes to Calcutta/Haldia are specified. Nepal can also utilize the facilities at Mumbai Port (including the Jawaharlal Nehru Port Trust) and Kandla Port for third-country trade. Moreover, import insurance is needed only for the sensitive goods. The godown facility at Calcutta airport and the provisions permitting Nepali importers to hand over the original copy of Custom Transit Declaration at the Indian customs should ease the import and export of goods.

While the South Asian Association for Regional Cooperation (SAARC) was set up when its Charter was formally adopted on 8 December 1985 by the Heads of State or Government of Bangladesh, Bhutan, India, Maldives, Nepal, Pakistan and

Sri Lanka, the agreement on South Asian Preferential Trading Arrangement (SAPTA) took off only in December 1995. The SAPTA accord attempted to reduce tariffs and non-tariff barriers among the SAARC member countries. SAPTA was envisaged primarily as the first step towards the transition to the South Asia Free Trade Area (SAFTA), leading subsequently, towards a Customs Union, Common Market and Economic Union. The four rounds of SAPTA had led to the coverage of more than 5,000 tariff line items. However, studies have demonstrated that the SAPTA process did very little in stimulating regional trade.[5] The process was very lengthy and slow. Again, at least in the first two rounds of the SAPTA, non-tariff barriers (NTBs) were not considered for removal with the granting of tariff preferences. The other problems were that a) the tariff cuts were not deep enough, b) a wide range of goods was not subject to preferential tariffs and (c) some actively traded goods were left out from preferential tariffs.

The SAFTA agreement was signed at the 12th SAARC Summit in January 2004.[6] It is to come into force on 1 January 2006. The SAFTA aims at a) enhancing mutual trade and economic cooperation, b) eliminating trade barriers, c) promoting conditions of fair competition, d) building effective mechanism for implementation and resolution of disputes, and e) furthering regional cooperation.

The SAFTA calls for free movement of goods in the region *via* elimination of tariffs, para-tariffs that include border charges and fees and non-tariff restrictions on movement of goods and any other equivalent measures.

During the fifth Meeting of the Committee of Experts (CoE) in October 2004, an agreement was reached in principle to evolve a common RoO for the SAFTA. The RoO would be based on the value addition approach. This is a major change from what the SAARC countries agreed to earlier on, that is, to evolve RoO on product-to-product basis adopting all applicable approaches. It also agreed to lower the sensitive lists, which incorporate commodities that will not be subjected to trade liberalization program, considerably from the proposed level of 20 percent of the total tradable items. The CoE needs to conclude its SAFTA negotiations by June 2005 and proceed on to make preparations for its enforcement from 1 January 2006.

All in all, the SAFTA is expected to enter into force on the due date upon completion of four procedural formalities: formation of sensitive lists; rules of origin, revenue loss compensation mechanism and ratification by the all member states.

Nepal's Entry into the WTO and the BIMSTEC

Nepal officially became the 147th member of the World Trade Organization (WTO) on 23 April 2004. By joining the WTO, Nepal can fully enjoy the rights that all members have under the WTO agreements, such as non-discrimination by other WTO members and the ability to use the WTO's dispute settlement procedure. Broad commitments were made in 11 services sectors and 70 sub-sectors out of a total of 170 classified by the WTO. Nepal accepted an average tariff binding of 42 per cent in agricultural products and about 24 per cent in industrial goods.

Among the commitments on legislation with respect to the trade regime, Nepal agreed to amend or enact 38 various acts and regulations to become compatible with WTO provisions. For instance, the country is required to implement fully the provisions of the Agreement on Sanitary and Phytosanitary Measures and Agreement of Technical Barriers to Trade (TBT) by 1 January 2007. With respect to the Agreement on Trade-Related Intellectual Property Rights (TRIPs), as an LDC, Nepal needs to develop a new Industrial Property Act, which will include all the substantive provisions of the TRIPs agreement. It would encompass all categories of industrial property and would incorporate the basis for an adequate enforcement and be promulgated no later than 1 January 2006. The country has to introduce legislation on anti-dumping, countervailing duties and safeguard measures within one year from the date of accession, in order to safeguard its local industries against unfair trading practices such as dumping and subsidies by exporting countries.

Thus, there are various challenges that Nepal will face. The country needs to seek alternative revenue avenues to finance development gradually, changing laws and regulations to make laws compatible with WTO commitments and obligations, developing transparent mechanisms and creating institutions as well as financing the cost of negotiations coupled with recourse to legal measures and implementation.

Nepal became a member to the Bay of Bengal Initiative for Multi-sectoral Technical and Economic Cooperation (BIMSTEC) together with Bhutan in February 2004. The other members of this regional trading group are Bangladesh, India, Myanmar, Sri Lanka and Thailand. BIMSTEC's six core areas of cooperation, *inter alia*, are agriculture, energy, fisheries, tourism, trade and transportation.

On 8 February 2004, the Framework Agreement on BIMSTEC FTA was signed in Bangkok during the Sixth BIMSTEC Economic Ministers' Meeting. The FTA agreement would first start on trade in goods from 2006, while the FTA on trade in services and investment would begin from 2007.

The draft agreement consists of 27 articles and encompasses areas such as RoO, trade liberalization program, customs and trading procedures, sensitive list, global safeguard and BIMSTEC's transitional safeguard, among others. The members are to develop a modality for dispute settlement arrangement, anti-dumping measures, subsidy and countervailing measures and non-tariff measures to foster free trade in the region.

A meeting of the Third Round of Trade Negotiation Committee (TNC) of BIMSTEC took place in Kathmandu during 8-10 March 2005. An agreement was made relating to the preliminary framework of RoO and dispute settlement mechanism. The detailed rules and regulations relating to this framework would be finalized through negotiations at the future meetings.

BIMSTEC FTA is a step to free trade among countries in two of the fastest growing sub-regions of Asia, South-east Asia and South Asia. This FTA could act as a link between the ASEAN Free Trade Area and the SAFTA.

Trade-related Bottlenecks and Remedies

This section of the paper makes an attempt to spell out the major problems, both structural and policy-related, of the trade sector and provide suggestions to resolve them.

Technological Mastery

Technological mastery is an essential condition for industrial upgrading, sustaining competitiveness and entering markets for high-valued goods. Technological weaknesses in Nepal include the low level of technology deployed in productive activities, almost total absence of local technological capability, including the inability to adapt and utilize new technologies, and a lack of resources to procure new technologies.

Due to weak technical and management capabilities, the Nepalese exporters are not able to adhere to the complex and detailed specifications, required by importers from other countries in terms of quality, size, delivery time and packaging, among others. In view of the competitiveness in the international markets, the exporters need a better understanding of elements of their production cost to be able to conduct realistic and crucial price negotiations with buyers. Their almost total lack of such capacities is aggravated by differences in "business culture". The business culture in the international market involves quick and timely deliveries, with minimal space for flexibility in fulfilling contracts.

It is crucial for Nepal to initiate measures to improve productive capacities and make significant gains in productivity and competitiveness through technological upgrading, especially as many of its productive activities utilize sub-optimal technologies at present. The implementation of a successful technology policy, however, depends on a skilled and educated labor force to tackle the many issues relevant to acquisition, utilization, absorption and generation of technology. It also depends on the country's capacity to invest in research and development (R&D) especially to promote locally developed technologies that have an effect on productivity growth, and to establish a link between R&D and production units.

Quality Standardization and Investment in Infrastructure

Quality control is integral to competitiveness. Problems of quality in Nepal include precision, grading, and standardization. The current low number of industrial firms having ISO-9000 Certification is a glaring demonstration of these problems, which in turn are restricting the ability of local firms to penetrate in principal export markets such as the EU, USA, and Japan.

In the backdrop of the rising competitiveness in the international market for quality standard and the likely negative impact of low quality Nepalese export products on their reliability and the consequent deterioration in the competitiveness, there is a need to undertake quality standardization and improvement programs to maintain the quality of export products. It is also important to define minimum export quality and a system of compulsory quality inspection and standardization through which each export product has to pass.

Nepal is landlocked and geographically situated away from the major world economic centres; hence, emphasis must be accorded to improve infrastructure and thereby lower business transaction costs. It is therefore crucial that the country makes every attempt to attract investment in sound infrastructure development to enhance export competitiveness. More efforts are required for building and maintaining world-class telecommunications, roads and airports. Electricity and energy supply should be consistent and affordable.

Competitive Ability and Development of Human Resources

In this age of global competition, it is not just enough for the Nepalese firms to be competitive at the domestic level. They need to be competitive in the global context for which they should hold some competitive advantage such as economies of scale, cutting-edge technology, marketing strengths, efficient production and distribution systems, and/or cheap labor.[7] The country does not possess comparative advantage in any one of the areas excluding the availability of cheap labor.

Building up skilled human resources is the key for grabbing opportunities for market opening. The priority accorded by the East Asian countries on this area of social development provides a good example of success story, which seems worth replicating by Nepal. In the recent past, human resource has become the key to success in international trade. Three areas could be identified in the context of Nepal. One, capacities should be developed in product innovation. Two, promotion of marketing skills should be emphasized. The third area is the personnel in the public sector, particularly institutions relating to trade and commerce. Limitations in trade-related expertise, analytical skills and negotiating skills are the result of the small staff, lack of resources for hiring and training and insufficient experience.

Coordination of Trade with Development Strategies and Safeguard Arrangements

Despite the fact that Nepal has done utmost to open up its economy, the expected beneficial results could not be generated owing to lack of coherence between trade policies and other development policies. Thus, there is a need to coordinate trade and development strategies and process.

Although openness in general is preferable to protectionism, free trade without any safeguards could lead to disaster, as has been demonstrated by the East Asian and the Latin American crises. It is thus crucial to create space for policy maneuvers, particularly in the economically sensitive sectors. It is in this context that safeguard arrangements are suggested.

Commodity and Market Diversification

Too much reliance on few low-value export items such as readymade garments and carpets has acted as obstacles in enhancing trading opportunities. The export concentration ratio (denoted as the share of the principal export products [carpets and garments] in the total export value) is quite high.[8] On top of that, while exports of readymade garments and carpets form a large share of the country's export basket, they are insignificant in terms of the international supply, so that the country has no influence whatsoever on the world prices that is advantageous to it. Moreover, hardly any efforts have been made either to reduce the export concentration ratio or to develop into new areas of products or services that could be exported into the international market.[9]

Another problem is the absence of market diversification for the development of the trade sector. For instance, in FY 2003/04, about 70 percent of total foreign exchange earnings have been contributed from exports to the USA, Germany and Switzerland.

Thus, Nepal has not seriously taken efforts to develop products, identify product market and establish a link between the two, although the objective of product and market diversification has been adumbrated in all the Plan documents as well as the various policies announced by the Government from time to time. Hence, this is an area where immediate steps should be taken particularly as Nepal has become a member for the WTO and will be bound to face global competition.

Remedies for the Post-MFA Phase-out

Starting 1 January 2005, trade in textile and clothing products is no longer subject to quotas under a special regime outside normal WTO/GATT rules but is based on the general rules and disciplines specified in the multilateral trading system. It has been contended that under either free trade or a global quota system, the new and smaller suppliers would be squeezed out of international markets because of the size and greater productivity of established exporters. Thus, to the extent it is true that, with the elimination of the MFA, trade in textiles and clothing products would tend to be drawn back to the larger exporters like India and China, a small LDC like Nepal might encounter major problems unless proper steps are undertaken.

To become competitive in the global market, focus should be given to areas such as upgradation of technology as well as establishment of a training institute to improve skill, product specialization for updated fashion and quality, among others. The Government of Nepal could play a pivotal role in the development of technical services by permitting the provision of consultancy services through foreign investment.

There is also a need for more investment in productivity enhancement by applying modern technology. Labor laws also need to be made compatible with the garment industry. While formulating the labor policy, issues such as job security, labor strikes and export delivery should also be considered.

Nepal enjoys the GSP facility in EU under the Everything but Arms (EBA) initiative introduced in 2001, which has abolished quotas and tariffs on all imports, including textiles and apparels. The EBA initiative has a significant value to Nepal as it can gain zero duty access to the EU market only under this scheme. Moreover with the extension of the derogation facility to the country by the EU for another two years, garment exports from Nepal to the EU would continue to enjoy exemption from its stricter rules of origin requirement and yet obtain the duty- and quota-free market access.[10] Hence, the EU market could be more valuable for sustainability in the post-MFA era at least in the short run.[11]

As IMF's Trade Integration Mechanism has assured that assistance from the international community will be provided to LDCs with adjustment difficulties owing to the expiry of the Agreement on Textiles and Clothing (ATC) and the restoration of more liberal trade in textiles and clothing, Nepal should take advantage of this facility.

The proposal relating to the creation of a garment processing zone (GPZ) in Nepal appears quite pragmatic.[12] The objective of the GPZ would be to facilitate government strategies for effective implementation of incentives and institution of trade support services within the zone. This would also lower the different types of procedural hassles. A recent study has also suggested the concept of industrial cluster under the GPZ.[13] Under this, a large-scale production with greater control over the management of sourcing and supply chain to lower production cost would take place. For facilitating the mass production with economies of scale, ancillary industries of basic materials for manufacturing of garments need to be developed within the industrial cluster. All the facilities would be located in proximity to the manufacturing zone and to the transit point to reduce delivery time.

Tariff Determination and Valuation

The tariff rates on some imported commodities can be different based on how the good is categorized under the different headings of the harmonized codes. These lead to opportunities for arbitrary decisions, delays and corruption. For instance, when a company imports equipment the duty varies depending on whether it is a "main manufacturing machinery" or not. The same equipment can imply 'main manufacturing company' for one company while not for a firm in another company leading to an opportunity for making arbitrary decisions.

The valuation of imported products at customs for determining the import duties is another hurdle for many firms. Customs officials are concerned that firms underinvoice their imports to lower their duties. Hence, these officials make use of "reference value" which refer to the values that commodities are believed to have, instead of the actual invoice value of the goods. These reference values are normally based on the highest import price historically declared on an invoice, and may overvalue goods significantly when the price of the goods has fallen over time. This is particularly problematic as the reference values are not revised often. To mitigate this problem, proper training should be provided to the custom officials in line with the WTO system of inspection.

Strong Legal Framework and New Trade Policy

The country does not possess a strong, flexible and legal framework for regulating trade. *The Export-Import Control Act, 1957* was undertaken primarily with the objective of controlling or prohibiting the export or import of restricted items and those announced by the government from time to time through publication. Moreover, this Act, in the present context, seems to have lost its significance as hardly anything has been mentioned about the process of registration of export-import agencies or houses, export promotion, sharing of information, finance, export incentives, institutional arrangements, and dispute settlement, among others. Hence, this Act should be amended, taking into consideration its compatibility with the WTO provisions. Or else, a separate foreign trade act should be formulated and enacted, for making foreign trade systematic by assessing and consolidating existing acts and regulations.

Moreover, the Trade Policy of 1992 has been outdated. In the present context of globalization and liberalization and as Nepal has joined the WTO, the SAFTA and the BIMSTEC FTA, and is in the process of becoming a member to the Bangkok Agreement, it is exigent that a New Trade Policy be formulated.[14]

Effective Trade Institution

The Ministry of Commerce, Industries and Supplies and the Department of Commerce are the major bodies responsible for governing trade in Nepal. There is also the Export Promotion Committee whose primary objective is the formulation of national policies for export development, monitoring of the export trends and operating the Export Development Fund for export promotion programs, that is, product development and export promotion activities. Then, there is the Trade Promotion Centre (TPC), which focuses primarily on enhancing and strengthening of foreign trade through export promotion programs.

However, these institutions have been ineffective in meeting their objectives. The institutional capabilities to monitor activities and assist in trade information and other services are quite limited. Hence, with the increasing role of the private sector and the rapid development and application of information technology, it appears that the TPC should be reconstituted as adumbrated by the Trade Policy of 1992, and a new Nepal Trade Promotion Organization should be established. One of the tasks of this Organization should be to launch an effective communication campaign to convince importing countries that the goods generated in the country reflect competitiveness and that competitiveness is based on genuine comparative advantage.

Development of Export Processing Zones

It was in December 1990 when the government constituted a high-level working committee under the chairmanship of the Industry Minister to set up an EPZ in Kathmandu to promote export-oriented industries. An EPZ is an industrial area especially designed for export-oriented industries and it provides the facility of tax exemption on imports of raw materials needed by the manufacturers inside the region. However, the manufactured goods are not allowed to be sold in the country. Even in 1990, some products were identified which could be produced by the industries inside the EPZ: carpets, garments, leather-based products, electric and electronic goods, products based on herbs, and jewellery. However, fifteen years have passed, and there is no sign of the creation of an EPZ yet. It is crucial for the Government to take necessary steps immediately to formulate relevant laws for establishment of EPZs, and measures should be initiated to set up EPZs at appropriate locations.[15]

Reliable Trade Data and Periodic Reviews

There is scarcity of data on market information, pricing, quality, and level of competition, among others. Similarly, reliable data on trade are lacking as the figures published from one institution could be different from another institution. The proposed Nepal Trade Promotion Organization could be entrusted with this task, including creating commodity-wise database relating to investment, production, imports and exports, among others.

Periodic reviews of performance of the country in both regional and international markets need to be undertaken in order to maintain the country's export thrust. Periodic policy analysis should be conducted by all relevant stakeholders in order to minimize the inherent gap between policy formulation and implementation with agreed time frames. This will enable the adoption of the corrective measures to be timely executed. Reviews thus call for capacity in the various institutions to deal with issues such as a) target-setting, b) collection of timely and relevant data, c) analytical skills, and d) information dissemination.

Lessons from SAARC Countries

A comparison of Nepal's export policy with the export policy of both India and Bangladesh reveals that both India and Bangladesh have accorded priority to the growth of specific product-wise exports and exports to new market by giving special incentives, which is missing in Nepal and which is very crucial in this competitive era for sustainability.[16] India has also given special considerations for the development of backward regions. Both India and Bangladesh have accorded special protection to the products of small scale and cottage industries to enhance such industries towards exports by giving double weightage in incentives. So far, Nepal has done hardly anything to uplift the backward regions towards export business; it has provided little protection and incentives to the small scale and cottage industries. Again, there exist no policies in allowing foreign trading houses in export business as well as encouragement to these exporters who improve the quality of product for exports. Hence, reviews of export policies of India and Bangladesh shows that in Nepal there is a need for substantial improvement in its existing export policy.

Policy Credibility

Clear goals in trade must be systemically implemented in order to revive and build business confidence and remove in-built skepticism. In order to remove uncertainty and aid exporters in planning, the Government's policies must be perceived to be real, predictable and likely to be sustained within a given timeframe. Trade policy measures targeted to promote exporters must thus be compatible with other measures on the fiscal side and BoP, among others. The drive to export must not encounter frequent policy reversals and must not be compromised by other policies that have an adverse impact on the exporters to deliver.

Conclusions

Although trade is considered as an engine of growth in economic development of a country, in Nepal there prevails a big gap between the objectives and vision and the current state of affairs in the trade sector. Though Nepal is already a member of the WTO, the institutional and legal structures to implement the WTO agreement have not been properly developed. Market and product concentrations of exports have led to volatile export proceedings. Structural difficulties of trade-related services and infrastructures have obstructed to materialize potential comparative advantages.

The country still relies on a relatively small basket of export and a few destination markets in spite of structural change in its merchandise exports. A large proportion of its exports encounter dwindling world demand, demanding an urgent restructuring of its export basket. Similar to other LDCs of South Asia, Nepal has difficulties relating to lack of competitive ability, supply side limitations, high export concentration, and implementation problems that inhibit its ability to seek gains from international trade.

Integration of Nepal into the global economy is an insufficient but necessary precondition for long-term sustainability of poverty eradication. This can only be attained through an integrated approach, including trade and macroeconomic policy, private sector development and participation, finance, infrastructure, education and other supply-side measures. Regional integration, compatible with multilateral trade rules, can be a paramount stepping stone for Nepal to integrate itself into the world economy and can aid in making liberalization work by enhancing the credibility and transparency of policy reforms.

Notes

1. Even before the liberalization era, measures such as the bonus system, dual exchange rate system and export subsidy were introduced to boost exports. However, as they failed to generate intended impact on exports, they were removed. In 1987, export duty drawback system was introduced under which exporters could get a refund on duties, which included both import taxes and sales tax paid on imported inputs. The bonded warehouse scheme, introduced in October 1988, was an alternative scheme to the duty drawback system and assisted the carpet industry to get a refund on taxes paid on its imported raw materials.
2. With regard to carpets, weak demand, problems relating to quality as well concerns over child labor in importing countries had an adverse impact on export of carpets leading to a deceleration in the second half of the 1990s. Although many problems have been tackled, the growth of carpet exports has not picked up as in the late 1990s. With respect to readymade garments, export growth initially can be attributed to the spillover of Indian exports, owing to quota limitations on India. Moreover, a rise in profitability and willingness of local producers to enter the industry was also responsible for the growth of Nepalese garments exports. However, exports of readymade garments that

benefited from preferential treatment under the MFA encountered problems as international trade regulations underwent modifications. The decline in garment exports could be ascribed to the supply bottlenecks and the industry's inability to compete with other South Asian countries. Beginning 1 January 2005, trade in textile and clothing products is no longer subject to quotas under a special regime outside normal WTO/GATT rules, but is governed by the general rules and disciplines laid down in the multilateral trading system. This will lead to a further decline in garment exports as the country has now to compete with China, India and Southeast Asian countries, among others, in the textiles and clothing market. A clearer explanation is provided in Ministry of Industry, Commerce and Supplies (2004).

3. In terms of imports from India, a provision was introduced in FY 1992/93 whereby certain items could be imported from India through the payment of convertible currency. This list has included 39 items as of mid-July 2004 and more are likely to be added to the list based on the basis of the structure of foreign currency reserves of the country, the effect on value addition and competitiveness of the industries as well as the prospect of export promotion. Details are given in NRB (2004).
4. While 100,000 tons of vegetable ghee would be permitted to enter India each year free of basic customs duty, 10,000 tons of acrylic yarn, 7,500 tons of copper products, and 2,500 tons of zinc oxide would also be allowed.
5. This is illustrated in Mukherji (2002) and Kemal (2004).
6. The SAFTA was initially mooted at the 8th SAARC Summit in New Delhi in 1995 when it was proposed that it should be effective by 2005. The effective date of SAFTA was changed to 2001 together with the formation of a Group of Eminent Persons (GEP) to draw up a roadmap for SAFTA

at the 9th SAARC Summit in Male in 1997. At the 10th SAARC Summit in Colombo in 1998, the GEP report was submitted which suggested that a more practical timetable for SAFTA was 2008. It was decided to have a "Framework Treaty" by 2001. Due to regional politics, the preparation works for SAFTA got delayed. Finally, in January 2004 the SAFTA accord was signed.

7. Details are provided in Adhikari and Ghimire (2001).
8. This is elaborated in Ministry of Industry, Commerce and Supplies (2004).
9. The growth of exports of readymade garments, for instance, was due to the quota system under the MFA and have already started to go down in the post-MFA era.
10. The derogation facility had expired on 31 December 2004.
11. The Government of Canada also agreed to grant duty-free access to Nepalese readymade garments from 1 January 2003, allowing duty-free export of Nepalese textiles and apparels into Canada. As the garment industry is passing through a difficult phase, attempts could also be made to penetrate into the Canadian market which could provide some kind of a breathing space for the time being.
12. The framework of a GPZ is provided in Shakya (2001).
13. This concept of industrial cluster is elaborated in Shakya (2004).
14. In this context, India announced a detailed Foreign Trade Policy (2004-09), covering a period of five years in September 2004. The twin objectives include: a) to double India's percentage share of global merchandize trade by 2009; and b) to act as an effective tool of economic growth by according priority to employment generation, particularly in semi-urban and rural areas. Nepal could also follow this path by announcing a New Trade Policy valid for a specific number of years.

15. In this context, it is relevant to mention here that in order to address the poor infrastructural services and administrative inefficiencies emanating from lengthy bureaucratic procedures, Bangladesh developed specially designed EPZs and has been giving support services to industries. The EPZs could be emulated by Nepal since improving the infrastructure in the specified areas can be much faster and cheaper than doing it on a larger geographical area.
16. The export policies of India and Bangladesh are highlighted in Research & Study Centre Pte. Ltd. (2000).

References

Adhikari, Ratnakar and Hiramani Ghimire (2001). *Integrating LDCs into the Multilateral Trading System: Rhetoric Galore.* Kathmandu: South Asia Watch on Trade, Economics and Environment.

Kemal, A. R. (2004). "SAFTA and Economic Cooperation." *South Asian Journal.* No. 6, October-December. Available at: Available at: http://www.southasianmedia.net/ Magazine/Journal/6_safta.

Ministry of Industry, Commerce and Supplies (2004). *Nepal: Trade and Competitiveness Study.* Kathmandu.

Mukherji, I. N. (2002). "Charting a Free Trade Area in South Asia: Instruments and Modalities." In T.N. Srinivasan (ed.), *Trade, Finance and Investment in South Asia.* New Delhi: Social Science Press.

National Planning Commission (NPC) (1998). *The Ninth Plan (1997-2002).* Kathmandu: NPC.

NPC (2003). *The Tenth Plan (2002-2007).* Available at: http://www.npc.gov.np/tenthplan/ english/ Chapter_6-Macro_economic_Sector.pdf

Nepal Rastra Bank (NRB) (2004). *Monetary Policy for FY 2003/04.* Kathmandu: NRB.

NRB (2004a). *Quarterly Economic Bulletin.* Kathmandu: NRB.

Organization for Economic Cooperation and Development (2001). *The DAC Guidelines: Strengthening Capacity for Development.* Paris: OECD.

Pant, Bhubanesh (2002). *Nepal' Accession the WTO: National Study on Trade in Goods.* A UNCTAD/UNDP Research Report.

Pant, Bhubanesh (1994). *Trade and Development: Nepal's Experiences.* New Delhi: Oxford & IBH Publishing Co. Pvt. Ltd.

Research and Information System for the Non-aligned and Other Developing Countries (RIS) (2004). "South Asia Development & Cooperation Report 2004." Available at: http://www.ris.org.in/sadcr2004

Research & Study Centre Pvt. Ltd. (2000). *A Study on the Preparation of the Long Term Export Promotion Plan & Strategies*. Kathmandu.

Shakya, Bijendra. (2001). "Implications of MFA Phase Out under the WTO System, and the Impact of the US African and Caribbean Bills on Nepalese Garment Industry." A theme paper presented at the National Seminar on 'Nepalese Garment Industry under Changing Global Trading Environment." 26 December. Kathmandu.

Shakya, Bijendra (2004). "Nepal's Apparel Sector at Crossroads: Assessment of Adjustment Problems and Preparation for Quota Free Trade." A theme paper presented at the Workshop organized by GAN and co-sponsored by International Trade Centre (UNCTAD/WTO). December. Kathmandu.

South Asia Watch on Trade, Economics and Environment (2004). "BIMSTEC: More than just a radar 'blip.'" *PROACT E-Newsletter*. 1:10. August.

South Asia Watch on Trade, Economics and Environment (2004). 'SAFTA Accord: Challenges,' *PROACT E-Newsletter*. 1:3. January.

The Kathmandu Post, 12 March 2005.

The Kathmandu Post, 3 November 2004.

The Kathmandu Post, 9 October 2004.

The Himalayan Times, 28 October 2004.

14

Export Diversification for Reducing Trade Deficit*

It has been more than six decades since export diversification has been given utmost focus on the list of priorities for development policy as it was observed that dependence on a few exportable commodities by developing countries expose them to commodity shocks, price fluctuations and declining terms of trade. As a result, a country's foreign exchange reserves and the ability to have funds for imported inputs become subject to instability and uncertainty. However, a number of developing countries are still constrained by the export structure that relies on a few export products and markets.

There are a number of responsible factors that have inspired countries to undertake export diversification that has the potential to positively contribute to growth and development. First, increased investment in a broad range of activities and sectors enhance the sources of income and contributes to mitigating the adverse effects of export instability and fluctuations in the terms of trade. Second, the diversification of exports is also associated with reduced fluctuations in foreign exchange earnings, increases in employment, higher value addition and improvements in the quality of manufactured products. Third, diversification is linked to economic growth *via* externalities of learning-by-doing and learning-by-exporting fostered by competition in world markets. Other industries can benefit through knowledge spillovers from new techniques of production, management or marketing practices. Fourth, export diversification allows the government to achieve some of its macroeconomic objectives such as sustainable

* *The Himalayan Times,* 22 January 2019.

economic growth, favorable balance of payments (BoP) situation and redistribution of income, among others.

In recent years, three developments have intensified the focus on diversification opportunities in this era of globalization: a) the increasing spread and importance of global production chains; b) rapid growth of new sources of demand in large emerging economies, such as Brazil, China and India; and c) the growing significance of services trade propelled by rising incomes and the outsourcing of more and more services activities.

Even though Nepal is one of South Asia's most open and trade dependent economies, it has not been able to fully exploit the potential for export growth since its exports are focused in a few products (such as carpets, cardamom, juice, jute goods and readymade garments) and markets (with India's share in Nepal's total exports being about 57 percent in 2017/18). Though trade is considered to be an engine of growth for economic development, market and product concentrations of exports have led to volatile export growth in the country.

In 2017/18, merchandise exports increased 11.1 percent to Rs. 81.19 billion compared to an increase of 4.2 percent in 2016/17. Merchandise imports, on the other hand, increased 28.0 percent to Rs.1242.83 billion in 2017/18 compared to a rise of 25.5 percent a year earlier. Country-wise, exports to India, China and other countries went up by 12.4 percent, 43.3 percent and 7.5 percent respectively in 2017/18. Likewise, imports from India, China and other countries surged by 27.8 percent, 25.5 percent and 19.3 percent. Consequently, total trade deficit expanded by 26.7 percent to Rs. 1161.62 billion in 2017/18 from Rs. 917.06 billion in the previous year. Similarly, the export-import ratio plummeted to 6.5 percent from 7.4 percent in 2016/17. It further went down to 6.2 percent during the first five months of 2018/19.

The foregoing data divulges that the country's export earnings seem quite volatile and have adversely affected the economy that has been specializing in the production of a narrow range of goods and services. It also needs to be recalled that to promote competitiveness and increase production capacity to meet domestic and international demand, the Government of Nepal had streamlined the Nepal Trade Integration Strategy's (NTIS) list of high value goods and services with export potential, reducing the items from 19 in 2010 to 12 in 2016. Products and services in the revised NTIS included a) large cardamom; ginger; tea; herbs; fabrics, textile, yarn, and rope; leather; footwear; chyangra pashmina; and knotted carpets; and b) skilled and semi-skilled professionals; IT services and business process outsourcing; and tourism. However, the majority of these products have not been performing well.

For enhancing export diversification, export growth, including diversification of markets and higher-valued products, should be a major thrust of trade policy. Trade and industrial policies need to be targeted at promoting structural reforms to improve Nepal's efficiency and international competitiveness and reduce its vulnerability to external shocks. Secondly, an export-friendly enabling environment should be generated which comprises sound domestic policies, sufficient infrastructure, and provision of effective trade support services. Thirdly, the drive to export must not encounter frequent policy reversals and must not be compromised by other policies that have an adverse impact on the capacity of exporters to deliver.

To conclude, export diversification (both destination-wise and commodity-wise) which has long been a stated policy goal for Nepal, can play an instrumental role in reducing the country's trade deficit. This is also vital for improving growth and mitigating instability. So far, however, no serious endeavors have been undertaken to develop new products, identify product markets and set up the linkage between the two.

Section II: Foreign Direct Investment

15

FDI: Benefits, Costs and Determinants*

Introduction

Over the last more than two decades, attitudes toward foreign direct investment (FDI) have changed significantly. During the 1970s, many developing country governments discouraged such investment on the grounds that foreign firms would reap "rents" (that is, unearned profits) at the expense of the local economy. At the same time, the abundant supply of commercial bank credit crowded out FDI inflows. But, then along came the debt crisis, drying up the flow of bank credit to developing countries.

Consequently, during the 1980s, many countries were compelled to ease their restrictions of FDI and alter their policies to attract FDI. Over and above the lack of alternative financing, governments acknowledged that FDI could generate benefits that were crucial in an era of international competition and that could not be acquired in any other way as technology, new management methods, and access to export markets were becoming better plugged into the global market place.

FDI could be defined as equity investment of multinational corporations (MNCs) in host countries. About 35,000 MNCs are operating around the world, with 150,000 foreign affiliates. They manage FDIs and have become the driving force of the international economy.

From 1985 to 1990, global FDI grew four times faster than GDP and twice as fast as domestic investment. During 1991, 25 countries made 82 changes in FDI policy. Nearly all of these

* *The Economic Journal of Nepal*, 17(3): 167-177, July-September 1994.

changes were in the direction of greater liberalization of FDI. These flows to developing countries totaled about US$ 38 billion in 1992, a four-fold increase since the mid-1980s.

FDI has appeared attractive to developing countries that are encountering declining domestic investment and high costs of foreign borrowing as well as those that are restructuring their economies to promote greater private sector participation. Unlike foreign borrowing, FDI involves a risk-sharing relationship with the investors. It can take place even in the absence of well-developed domestic financial markets.

The next section examines the advantages and disadvantages of FDI. This is followed by an analysis of the main determinants of FDI. Next, the experiences of Nepal are discussed, followed by a scrutiny of other important issues. The last section concludes the study.

Benefits and Costs

Foreign-owned firms may stimulate local productivity through backward linkages to service suppliers and the labor force and by serving as a paragon of working practices and management techniques. It has been contended that the best measure of FDI's impact is not just the initial balance of payments (BoP) transaction but also the foreign firm's local purchases from suppliers and sales to customers in the host market since these are analogous to exports and imports.

The contribution which FDI can make to economic development is related to its ability to lower specific scarcities in the countries which receive it. On the one hand, it supplies capital which might not otherwise be available due to a low level of domestic saving and because access to bond and other portfolio finance from developed countries has been limited. On the other hand, FDI carries with it a complementary package of inputs. These include managerial and marketing expertise, knowledge of technical processes not easily obtainable by other means, scarce labor skills and, in some cases, facilities for training local workers in a variety of skills.

FDI is preferred to other types of flows. One convincing argument is that it consists of a package of capital, technology and market access which tends to go to manufacturing sectors which possess actual or potential comparative advantage. On the other hand, official flows and even commercial loans are often tied with social overheads and sectors which do not enjoy comparative advantage in the developing recipient countries. In manufacturing sectors which enjoy comparative advantage, the inflow of FDI would give rise to economies of scale and higher productivity, and create linkage effects. Moreover, there are a number of financial advantages of FDI over other types of flows for the developing recipient countries. For FDI, repayment is required only if the productive activity is profit-making and repayment can, to a large extent, be regulated through tax policies and legislations. Incentives can be created to encourage reinvestment to minimize repatriation of profits. There is also a closer match between the maturing structures of earnings and repayments. For other types of flows, there is often the case of using short-term loans to finance long-term projects.

Since FDI involves capital flows into the host country, it is sometimes viewed as an alternative to other forms of capital inflows, such as foreign aid or foreign borrowing. This argument is correct, as far as it goes, but is not the complete story. First, because the additional capital associated with FDI is committed to a particular investment in productive facilities, it demands complementary expenditure on infrastructure services and education, among others. Second, FDI almost always brings more than just financial resources with it. It usually involves the following: (a) the transfer of some production technology; (b) some management and organizational know-how that includes the production process and such other aspects of the business as organization, accounting, and marketing, among others; and (c) export marketing channels or other aspects of access to export markets. For all these reasons, FDI is only in small measure an alternative to increased foreign borrowing or to increased domestic saving.

Nonetheless, FDI also possesses some limitations. One, it has been concentrated, historically, in a few countries and in a few sectors. About three-fourths of all FDI takes place between developed countries; two-thirds of the remaining flows to developing countries have gone to only ten countries. With regard to sectors, in Bangladesh, for instance, FDI is responsible for a significant share of manufactures for the domestic market, such as pharmaceuticals, cigarettes and electrical goods, and export-oriented readymade garments.

Two, it is claimed that foreign firms create enclaves which have little relations with the rest of the economy and do not give rise to any significant spillover effects on the local economy. Three, remittances of profits and capital could bring about severe BoP difficulties for the host countries. Four, it is argued that foreign firms often stultify the development of local enterprise. This could be because they borrow on the domestic capital market and shift funds away from domestic firms. Five, it is contended that foreign enterprises typically do not allow local participation in ownership. Finally, a host of criticism concern the oligopolistic nature of such foreign enterprise from which a number of disadvantages can emanate. For instance, the parent firm may not allow a subsidiary operating abroad to export and prices may be maintained much above the competitive level.

Determinants

For attracting FDI, political and economic stability are indispensable. Excluding the primary determinants—sound macroeconomic environment and growth potential, credit worthiness, export market access, and an adequate and transparent regulatory regime—there are a number of other factors that could attract or deter FDI flows. One set gives due importance to relative rates of return and portfolios choice. Still another set emphasizes market imperfections and suggests that FDI is the result of some firms posing particular skills such as technological and managerial advantages. Yet, another set emphasizes important complementary variables, such as political stability, government regulations, and tax policy.

The chief determinants of FDI seem to be the firm-specific attributes that underline the competitive advantages of MNCs, the ability of MNCs to gain from internalizing market relationship, the strengths of particular host countries as locations for foreign production by MNCs, and the policies of both the host and home countries.

Among these factors, certain firm-specific assets may be the principal determinants of whether FDI takes place, whereas locational factors—such as market size and the prospects for increased sales, labor cost, and tariffs—are crucial in determining where the FDI takes place. Host country policies provide a necessary precondition for attracting FDI, although effective policies by themselves may not be adequate to stimulate large inflows of FDI.

Traditional factors that were responsible for FDI flows to developing countries in the 1970s and early 1980s, such as labor cost, product life cycle, and the servicing of a protected market have weakened. In many industries, the proportion of labor cost to total manufacturing cost has fallen, and new patterns of the international product life cycle have emerged. Changes in technologies in some sectors have altered the economic scale of production, weakening the case for offshore production in low labor-cost countries. In this new environment, FDI flows generally have been attracted to developing countries possessing an efficient and dynamic private sector, followed by responsive institutions and a motivated skilled labor force. Over the past two decades, the pattern of incentives and the degree to which various incentives are employed to encourage FDI have undergone significant changes. Generally, in recent years there has been less frequent uses of micro-incentive measures. There has also been a realignment of investment incentives, with top priority accorded to protective measures. A shift away from horizontal, sector-wise schemes to vertical ones, for instance, promoting the use of new technologies, has been perceived.

As indicated earlier, a good macroeconomic environment is a key factor to attract FDI since macroeconomic policies play an important part in shaping and changing the economic environment. For developing countries, where economic conditions are less favorable than those in developed countries, microeconomic policies become a major tool to compete for foreign investment. Moreover, since there is no guarantee that FDI must benefit host countries, government policies play a crucial role in ensuring that foreign investment contributes satisfactorily to economic development and the benefits are maximized. Also important is a foreign exchange regime that affords ready access to foreign exchange for imported inputs and freedom to remit dividends and profits. Moreover, foreign investors are influenced by the quality of infrastructure, the level of industrialization and the size of the existing stock.

FDI could be facilitated by a legal framework that advocates open admission policies, subject to certain clearly defined and permissible restrictions (for example, national security), recommends equal treatment of foreign and domestic investors, permit the free transfer of profits, other payments due from the investors to external creditors, and repatriation of capital, and legitimizes expropriation only in accordance with legal procedures in pursuance of public purpose, without discrimination, and against payment of appropriate compensation defined under detailed criteria to reflect market value. These principles would imply, for example, easing restrictions on the freedom to employ expatriates and on the number of prohibited sectors in the host economy.

Nepal's Experiences

Until the early 1980s Nepalese officials tended to regard FDI investment as exploitative and coercive. During the last couple of years, however, the Government has approached FDI in a pragmatic and experimental manner.

Foreign investments in Nepal are normally in the form of foreign currency or capital assets. Reinvestment of earnings from foreign investments also constitutes foreign investment. Together with this direct form of foreign investment, foreign loans, use of rights, specialization, patents relating to technology of foreign origin, use of foreign-owned trademarks and use of foreign technical, consultancy, management and marketing services also constitute foreign investment.

Nepal has liberalized its investment codes to provide a more hospitable environment for foreign companies. The Government enacted a *Foreign Investment and Technology Transfer Act* and the Foreign Investment and One Window Policy in 1992. The salient features were the following: (a) opening up of foreign investment for all industries with a fixed investment of more than Rs. 20 million, except those related to defence, tobacco and alcohol and all cottage industries; (b) specification of terms and conditions for repatriation of profits by foreign investors; (c) provision of assurances against expropriation of foreign investment by the government; and (d) simplification of authorization procedures and institutional arrangements to provide one window services to foreign investors.

Various facilities have been provided under the Foreign Investment and One Window Policy, 1992: (a) interest income on foreign loans would be taxed at a rate of 15 percent; (b) royalties, technical and management fees would be taxed at a rate of 15 percent; (c) income received from exports would be free from income tax; (d) industries set up with foreign investment would receive all the facilities and incentives including income tax facilities given to domestic industries under the *Industrial Enterprises Act, 1992*; (e) customs duty, excise duty and sales taxes levied on raw materials and auxiliary raw materials of export-oriented industry would be reimbursed to the exporters depending on the volume of exports within 60 days from the date of the receipt of an application for such reimbursement; (f) industries that export 90 percent or more of their total production would be provided with the same facilities as those industries set up in the export processing zone (EPZ); (g) government land and land within the industrial districts would be handed over to industries for the setting up of industries on a priority basis; and (h) there would be no interference from the government on the fixation of prices of the products of any industry.

A foreign investor making investment in foreign currency could repatriate the following amount outside the country: (a) the amount obtained from the sale of the share of foreign investment as a whole or any part thereof; (b) the amount acquired as the payment of the principal of, and interest on, any foreign loan; (c) the amount received under an agreement for the transfer of technology; and (d) the amount received as compensation for the acquisition of any property.

However, such measures are not sufficient; complementary actions such as bilateral information and promotion services, safeguard instruments (such as bilateral investment treaties and investment guarantee schemes), as well as trade measures, are necessary.

FDI in small economies normally concentrates on production for export. However, in Nepal's case, this is hampered by a lack of natural and human resources (as regards the latter, a scarcity of educated manpower and acute shortages of advanced managerial, accounting and technical skills). With regard to infrastructure, Nepal compares unfavorably with many other developing countries in terms of power and water supply, telecommunications and transportation. Moreover, the country is geographically disadvantaged, being land-locked and cannot offer the cheap and efficient transportation links with other countries required by foreign companies. Institutional infrastructure is also less developed, for instance, with respect to financial services. As regards the level of industrialization, the share of industry in GDP is less than one fifth.

Various objectives have been vital in shaping Nepal's dealings with FDI. One could be the transfer of technology in order to modernize the economy and make it more efficient. Moreover, the economic reforms begun in the early 1990s accorded top priority to increasing exports. FDI ventures were seen as a way to do this, both through producing products of exportable quality and price, and because of skill or access in marketing such products overseas.

Nepal recently became a member of Multilateral Investment Guarantee Agency (MIGA), and has enhanced its access to FDI. The MIGA, which was established in April 1998 as the new member of World Bank group by 42 World Bank member countries that subscribed 53 percent of the agency's authorized capital of US$ 1.08 billion, has the objective to stimulate private investment through insuring investment against non-commercial risk, such as political risk, provides promotional and advisory services to help members and creates an attractive investment climate. As of April 1994, licences we granted for the setting up of 240 industrial projects on a joint-venture basis, or 100 percent foreign investment and/or for the transfer to technology to these industrial projects.

Related Issues and Policies

The Nepalese rupee is currently valued above the exchange rate that would prevail if there were no barriers, taxes, or subsidies on Nepalese imports or exports. This implies that exports are less profitable than they would be if trade were freer and, combined with other policies, results in economic policy discriminating against exports.

Another adverse impact of the overvaluation of the rupee is the devaluation risk that may be associated with foreign equity investment. Potential investors may feel that if the ongoing economic reforms are successfully pursued to their logical end, the reduction of trade restrictions and export subsidies may demand a significant compensating devaluation of the currency. This would lower the foreign currency value of equity investment in Nepal. Worries about such a future could lead potential investors to reduce the value of their equity investment, or even to delay investment.

In the initial stages of investigation, information on how a project should be structured, what its market would be, and what are the qualifications of possible Nepalese partners are prerequisites, but many potential foreign investors have faced difficulties in getting timely access to these important facts.

To attract FDI that is focused on producing manufactured goods primarily for exports, Nepal must compete with other countries that are able to attract the same investments. For some products, the competition is regional (for instance, South Asia), and for some it is global.

To obtain the maximum benefits from FDI, Nepal must implement policies to maximize the linkage effects created by foreign firms. This is to ensure a full integration of local firms into the FDI sector in the course of time to prevent the formation of a foreign enclave leading to an increasing degree of foreign dependency.

Conclusions

FDI policy cannot be developed in isolation, but should be regarded as an integral part of the overall economic policy if foreign participation is to be in line with national development goals and objectives.

Nepal should create a stable macroeconomic environment with prudent and reasonable consistent macroeconomic policies. This is important if foreign investors are to take a long-term view in investing in Nepal. Facing a stable macroeconomic environment, the foreign investors will be more willing to compromise their own global objectives with the needs of Nepal.

Although economic conditions, resource endowment and other indicators conducive to FDI are, generally speaking, less favorable in Nepal, this does not imply that there are no investment opportunities. However, their exploitation will require special efforts to create the conditions propitious for an increased inflow of FDI.

References

Alworth, Julian (1988). *The Financial Decisions of Multinationals.* Oxford: Basil Blackwell.

Bhagwati, Jagdish (1985). "Protectionism: Old Wine in New Bottles." *Journal of Policy Modelling.* 7: 23-33.

Culpeper, Roy and Michel Hardy (1990). *Private Foreign Investment and Development: A Partnership for the* 1990s. Ottawa: North South Institute.

Dervis, Kemal and Peter A. Peter (1987). *The Macroeconomics of Successful Development: What Are the Lessons?* Cambridge: MIT Press.

French, Kenneth and John Poterba (1991). "Investor Diversification and International Equity Markets." *American Economic Review.* 81: 221-26.

Howell, Michael and Angela Coazzini (1991). *International Equity Flows.* New York: Salomon Brothers.

Julius, Deanne S. (1991). *Foreign Direct Investment: The Neglected Twin of Trade.* Washington, D.C.: Group of Thirty.

McCulloch, Rachel (1992). "Foreign Direct Investment in the United States." *Finance and Development.* 30 (1): 13-15.

Ministry of Industry (MOI) (1994). *Procedural Manual for Foreign Investment in Nepal.* Kathmandu: MOI.

MOI (1992). *Foreign Investment and One Window Policy, 1992.* Kathmandu: MOI.

MOI (1992). *Foreign Investment and Technology Transfer Act, 1992.* Kathmandu: MOI.

MOI (1992). *Industrial Enterprises Act, 1992.* Kathmandu: MOI.

Shah, Anwar and Joel Slemrod (1991). "Do Taxes Matter for Foreign Direct Investment?" *World Bank Economic Review.* 5 (3): 473-491.

United Nations Centre on Transnational Corporations (1991). *World Investment Report 1991: The Triad in Direct Foreign Investment.* New York: United Nations.

16

Enhancing FDI Flows to Nepal during the Period of Post-conflict Transition and Global Recession*

Background

Foreign direct investment (FDI) in developing countries has a long history. It has fluctuated over time, as investors have responded to changes in the environment for investment, including government policies toward FDI and the broader economic policy framework. Hence, trends in FDI have reflected changes in policy stances by developing countries, from import substitution in the 1950s and 1960s through natural resource-led development in the 1970s, structural adjustment and transition to market economies in the 1980s, and an increased role for the private sector in the 1990s.

Sudden and sharp capital inflow reversals have been a salient feature of recent emerging market crises. Among the different types of capital flows, short-term bank flows and portfolio flows, especially, have been most volatile. Longer-term capital flows such as FDI, on the other hand, have generally been more stable. Thus, FDI is viewed as a "desirable" form of capital inflow compared with other more volatile flows. Again, beyond providing additional financial resources (when not financed locally), FDI can facilitate the transfer of intangible assets such as technology, skills, and management know-how, thus helping to directly raise productivity and growth; in addition, FDI could assist in securing foreign market access. In short, FDI seems to offer a bundle of "good" characteristics ranging from a high degree of stability,

* *Economic Review*, 22: 19-39, April 2010.

financial resource augmentation, positive productivity effects, and access to foreign markets.

Analogous to other economic activities, FDI has been going through dramatic changes since the end of 2008. The atypical magnitude of the ongoing economic and financial crisis—the worst in the last 60 years—provokes major apprehensions about the propensity and capability of multinational corporations (MNCs) to continue investing and expanding abroad. Faltering profits, reduced access to financial resources, declining market opportunities, coupled with the risk of a possible worsening of the current global economic downturn are some of the factors responsible for a fall in FDI flows.

The global crisis has largely affected FDI flows, after their steady upward trend between 2003 and 2007, with FDI inflows touching a historic figure of $1.9 trillion in 2007. Because of the financial crisis, global FDI inflows are estimated to go down from $1.7 trillion in 2008 to below $1.2 trillion in 2009, with a slow recovery in 2010 (to a level up to $1.4 trillion) and gaining momentum in 2011 (approaching $1.8 trillion). The crisis has altered the FDI landscape: investments to developing and transition economies soared, increasing their share in global FDI flows to 43 percent in 2008. This was partly attributed to a concurrent large decline in FDI flows to developed countries (29 percent) (UNCTAD, 2009). However, in 2009 FDI flows to all regions will experience a setback.

The decrease in FDI flows, together with a surge in corporate restructurings and divestments, emanates from two main factors. One, the capability of firms to invest has been lessened by a reduction in access to financial resources, both internally—owing to a decline in corporate profits—and externally—owing to lower availability and higher costs of finance. Two, the propensity to invest has been diminished by negative economic prospects, especially in developed countries that have been the worst affected (UNCTAD, 2009a).

With respect to Nepal, so far the country does not seem to have witnessed an adverse impact in terms of FDI inflows due to the global recession. Nepal's foreign investment rules and regulations are based on the *Foreign Investment and Technology Transfer Act 1992,* which was amended in 1996 in line with open and liberal economic policies. One of the major policies of the Three-Year Interim Plan (2007/8-2009/10) is the promotion of domestic and foreign investment for the development of the economic sector of the country. Again, in the case of Nepal, as a conflict-stricken economy, FDI is more sought since it has an even more instrumental role in buttressing the building-up process. Though many attempts were made in the past to boost FDI flows to the country, they did not have any noteworthy impact.

On the basis of the above background, this paper first discusses the definition along with the determining factors and benefits of attracting more FDI followed by a review of some theories of FDI. The problems encountered by post-conflict economies in promoting FDI as well as Nepal's experiences in attracting FDI are then highlighted. Before concluding, some policy measures are suggested.

Definition, Determinants and Benefits

Definition

FDI occurs when an investor based in one country (the home country) acquires an asset in another country (the host country) with the intent to manage that asset. The management dimension is what distinguishes FDI from portfolio investment in foreign stocks, bonds and other financial instruments. In most instances, both the investor and the asset it manages abroad are business firms. In such cases, the investor is typically referred to as the "parent firm" and the asset as the "affiliate" or "subsidiary".

There are three main categories of FDI as given below:

- ❖ Equity capital is the value of the MNC's investment in shares of an enterprise in a foreign country. An equity capital stake of 10 percent or more of the ordinary shares or voting power in an incorporated enterprise, or its equivalent in an unincorporated enterprise, is normally considered as a threshold for the control of assets. This category includes both mergers and acquisitions and "greenfield" investments (the creation of new facilities).

- Reinvested earnings are the MNC's share of affiliate earnings not distributed as dividends or remitted to the MNC. Such retained profits by affiliate are assumed to be reinvested in the affiliate.
- Other capital refers to short or long-term borrowing and lending of funds between the MNC and the affiliate.

These three main categories of FDI described above are those used in balance-of-payments (BoP) statistics.

The available statistics on FDI, which are far from ideal, come mainly from three sources. First, there are statistics from the records of ministries and agencies that administer the country's laws and regulations on FDI. The request for a license or the fulfillment of notification requirements allows these agencies to record data on FDI flows. Typically, re-invested earnings, intra-company loans, and liquidations of investment are not recorded, and not all notified investments are fully realized in the period covered by notification. Second, there are the FDI data taken from government and other surveys, which evaluate financial and operating data of companies. While these data provide information on sales (domestic and foreign), earnings, employment and the share of value added of foreign affiliates in domestic output, they often are not comparable across countries because of differences in definitions and coverage. Third, there are the data taken from national BoP, for which internationally agreed guidelines exist in the fifth edition of the IMF's *Balance of Payments Manual* (IMF, 1993).

Determinants

How FDI impacts growth and development depends, to a large

degree, on the type and volume of FDI. Hence, it is crucial to understand what attracts FDI, how this has changed over time, and what these changes in determinants and types of FDI mean for differential growth prospects.

The major determinants of inward FDI can be divided into many categories, and link to the following: a) general policy factors (political stability and privatization); b) specific FDI policies (incentives, performance requirements, and investment promotion), c) macro economic factors (human resources, infrastructure, market size, and growth); and d) firm specific factors (technology).[1]

General Policy Factors

Theory indicates that long-term investment benefits from stability as it lowers the risks for the long-term investor. This has been supported by investor surveys and evidences. Politically unstable countries appear to attract relatively small amount of FDI.[2]

Countries that provide a welcoming "investment climate" attract more investment. A welcoming investment climate is governed by many factors determining investment. Stricter regulation of business entry is associated with higher corruption and thus weaker governance, deterring investment. Even though countries have begun to understand what a welcoming investment climate involves, with some reductions in red tape, there is still a wide variation in administrative and regulatory practices.

FDI Policies

Renewed confidence in the advantages of FDI has led many countries that were restricting FDI in the 1960s, 1970s and 1980s to be more open towards FDI in the 1990s and beyond (Lall, 2000).

Much of the FDI potential in developing countries was not acknowledged a few decades ago as many countries had stringent restrictions on foreign ownership, and many of what are now regarded as conducive factors (for instance, a competitive environment and good quality local capabilities) were not in order. This is slowly changing. Almost all countries are now actively and aggressively welcoming FDI.

Investment liberalization has coincided with an increased focus on FDI protection and promotion. Countries now actively try to attract FDI and have set up FDI promotion agencies. Tools included for FDI promotion comprise incentives, export processing zones (EPZs) and science parks, among others.

Macro-economic Factors

General and specific FDI policies have become less restrictive to inward FDI. With fewer policy barriers, other factors have become more crucial as determinants. Among these are basic economic pull factors like good quality and appropriate human resources and infrastructure on the supply side, and market size and market potential on the demand side. Macro-economic policies that shape the underlying fundamentals of cost-competitiveness have become more crucial over time in attracting FDI. Lall (2000a) argues that FDI location decisions will, to a large extent, depend on economic factors, and not on temporary policy interventions.

Firm Specific Factors

Since the 1950s, researchers have attempted to understand the evolution of FDI through micro-economic factors. International business studies have had a long tradition studying MNCs and use an eclectic paradigm for FDI, the Ownership-Location-Internalization (OLI) framework (Dunning, 1993).[3] Economists such as Caves (1974) and Dunning (1979) have emphasized that MNCs need to possess some firm-specific asset that differentiates them from domestic firms to compensate for the extra costs in terms of local knowledge that a foreign firm must incur to operate in foreign markets. The firm-specific asset is called an ownership (O) advantage. As the firm-specific asset is often related to access to some superior technology or to specific knowledge of production processes, foreign affiliates require the right skill-mix to use the specific technology and to undertake a complex production process in usually large-sized plants. MNCs should also have an internalization (I) advantage to internalize business contacts, and not to outsource. Finally, the reason why a multinational invests in one country, but not in another, depends on the country's locational advantage (L).

It is suggested by Markusen (1995) that technology or the firm-specific asset (ownership advantage) is the primary reason for FDI. The claim that technology rather than different factor endowments and prices underpin FDI can also explain why trade and FDI can be complements rather than substitutes.

Benefits

In general, FDI inflows can contribute to the growth and development of the economy in host countries by generating employment and expanding the supply of goods. FDI associated with MNCs can create spillover effects, providing new skills, technologies, and marketing networks for local producers. Foreign firms also can provide training for workers—not only in manufacturing processes, but also in management. Such training can make local workers more productive, particularly when technology transfer is involved, and increase their wages (ADB, 2004).

FDI can help earn foreign currencies for host countries by increasing the manufacture of goods and services that are exported. The earning of foreign currencies is critical for developing countries to generate a current account surplus to finance the import of necessary inputs, among other things. If a current account surplus is not available to finance imports, the country's capital account must be relied upon, which can lead to debt accumulation. FDI focused on export-oriented industries can positively affect the volume of trade in the host country, and stimulate economic growth. In addition, the global marketing network of MNCs that invest in export-oriented industries can be used to market products of local affiliates and other worthy local firms in the host country.[4]

If the domestic market of a prospective host country is expected to be large in the future, especially in countries with large populations, MNCs may use FDI to establish large domestic production bases in those markets. Purchasing power and consumption can rise quickly in developing economies with rapidly expanding economies. Countries with large populations can thus provide rich business opportunities for MNCs for the production of goods for domestic markets at local production bases. Such production can replace imports and reduce the burden of foreign borrowing. This type of FDI can also expand consumer welfare in the host country if local consumers are provided a wider range of products of better quality at lower prices.

Technology transfer and knowledge spillovers often can be expected from FDI inflows. Spillovers are indirect effects of FDI, and can be defined as circumstances where FDI improves the technology or productivity of domestic firms. Spillover effects can have both vertical and horizontal impacts on host economies. Vertical spillovers refer to inter-industry impacts.[5] Horizontal spillovers occur when FDI promotes intra-industry competition in local markets through imitation effects and positive effects on human capital, industrial relations, market competition, and technology transfer. Vertical and horizontal effects can help local firms raise productivity as a result of improvements in human capital and industrial management skills, competition and efficiency, production processes, technological capabilities, and research and development (R&D). Through these linkages, FDI can help diversify local industries and thus diminish the economic vulnerability of host economies to external shocks that result from a narrowly based industrial structure.

FDI can play an important role in the overall development process, and in meeting the MDGs (Addison and Mavrotas, 2004). First, FDI is a source of capital accumulation, both physical capital and human capital. Provided that the FDI projects are well-designed, their rate of return will raise economic growth, thereby adding to the growth of employment, an indirect effect which is additional to the jobs created by FDI projects themselves. Second, FDI can generate much-needed revenues for governments to spend on MDG-focused infrastructure and services. These revenue effects are both direct (through corporate taxes paid by the enterprises themselves as well as revenue from FDI in the natural resource sectors) and indirect (when FDI raises economic growth and therefore the economy's total tax base).

To sum up this section, FDI's development benefits are potentially strong, but whether this potential is realized or not largely depends on the host country having a clear vision of how FDI fits into its overall development strategy. FDI can be used to diversify the economy thereby reducing over-dependence on a few commodity-based sectors, for example by creating new manufacturing and service-sectors, particularly in exports and in services which use the new information and communication technologies (ICTs).

Theories

Market Imperfections

One of the earliest attempts to introduce market imperfections in the theory of FDI was made by Hymer (1976). He argued that the investing firm must have some advantages specific to its ownership which are sufficient to outweigh the disadvantages they faced in competing with indigenous firms in the host country. These exclusive advantages imply the existence of some kind of market failure. This is because in a perfectly competitive world, all firms are competing equally and have no advantage over others. FDI cannot take place in such a world.

However, as other writers (Hood and Trijuens, 1993; Dunning, 1988, 1993) have pointed out, the existence of ownership advantages does not necessitate production abroad, for the foreign firm can exploit its advantage through licensing or through producing at home and exporting. To explain the choice of FDI over producing at home and exporting, it is necessary to take into account local-specific factors such as trade barriers and market characteristics.

Internalization Theory

Internalization theory also focuses on market imperfections. But these imperfections are in the markets for intermediate inputs and technology. Intermediate inputs in this context are not just semi-processed materials, but more often are types of knowledge incorporated in patents and human capital, among others (Hood and Young, 1984). Imperfections in markets for intermediate inputs create difficulties and uncertainty for the firm to fully exploit its advantages. A profit-maximizing firm faced with such imperfections will try to overcome these in the external market by internalizing them in their operation, either through backward or forward integration.

There are a number of such imperfections that are considered important in stimulating internalization. An example is government intervention in the form of tariff, taxation, and exchange rate policies that create difficulties in the firm's sourcing activities and in exploiting location-specific advantages. All these factors stimulate firms to internalize.

Product Cycle Hypothesis

The above explanations of FDI have been based upon static advantages, either specific to firms or specific to a location. However, the relative importance of these advantages will change over time as the product develops through its life cycle. As a consequence, the firm's choice between export, FDI and licensing might also change. Vernon (1966) developed the product cycle model to deal with such dynamic aspects of FDI activities. Initially, Vernon attempted to explain US investment in Europe during the post-war period by answering two questions. The first related to why innovations occur in developed countries and the second concerned why they are transferred abroad. Vernon tried to answer these questions by relating the product life cycle, which is divided into three stages progressing from the "new" to the "mature" and ultimately the "standardized" product, to the location decisions made by firms and the choice between exports and overseas production.[6]

Although the product cycle hypothesis has several weaknesses and might be an oversimplification of reality, it has provided an explanation of why innovations occur mostly in developed countries, while at the same time it explains both trade and investment flows.

Eclectic Paradigm

According to Dunning (1979), the product cycle hypothesis is only a partial explanation. He developed an eclectic approach to the problem. The principal hypothesis of this eclectic theory is that a firm will engage in FDI if three conditions are met.

1. It possesses ownership advantages over firms of other nationalities in serving particular markets. These advantages are specific to the firm.
2. Given (1) is satisfied, it must be more beneficial to the firm to exploit the advantages itself rather than to sell or lease or license them to foreign firms, that is, to internalize its advantages through an extension of its activities rather than externalizing them.
3. Given (1) and (2) are satisfied, it must be profitable for the firm to combine these advantages with some factors in the foreign country.

The key point of the eclectic theory is that any one of these advantages may be necessary but not sufficient to give rise to FDI. It is necessary to consider all three conditions together. Dunning (1993) concludes that all forms of FDI can be explained by the above three conditions.

Investment Development Path Theory

The Investment Development Path (IDP) theory was introduced by Dunning (1981) as an extension of Eclectic Paradigm to explain the net outward investment position of countries in relation to their development stages. The Eclectic Paradigm suggests that the direct investment stock of countries is determined by three factors, namely, ownership, location and internalization (OLI) advantages.

According to the IDP theory, the country passes through five main development stages determined by the changes in the OLI parameters of domestic firms of the country (Dunning and Narula, 1996).[7] These changes affect the international investment position of the country with respect to its development.

Recent Empirical Studies

According to Blomström & Kokko (2003) and Borenzstein, De Gregorio, and Lee (1998), the contributions of FDI to the development of a country are widely recognized as filling the gap between desired investment and domestically mobilized saving, increasing tax revenues, and improving management and technology, as well as labor skills in host countries. These could help the country to fight its way out of poverty.

Empirical studies suggest that FDI provides a source of capital and complements domestic private investment. Some studies (Blomström & Kokko, 2003, and Chen & Démurger, 2002) conclude that FDI contributes to total factor productivity and income growth in host economies, over and above what domestic investment would trigger. Further, these studies find that policies that promote indigenous technological capability, such as education, technical training, and R&D, increase the aggregate rate of technology transfer from FDI and that export promoting trade regimes are also important prerequisites for positive FDI impact. For instance, the study by Borenzstein, De Gregorio, and Lee (1998) using data on FDI received by developing countries tested the effect of FDI on economic growth in a cross-country regression framework. They found some indications that FDI has a positive effect on economic growth, but this impact was dependent on the human capital stock in the host economy.

However, there is growing empirical evidence suggesting that the impact of FDI on economic growth is not automatic. Borenzstein, De Gregorio, and Lee (1998) show that for FDI to contribute to economic growth, the host country must have achieved a minimum threshold level of development in education, technology, infrastructure, financial markets, and health. Thus, FDI contributes to economic growth only when the host country has reached a developmental level capable of absorbing the advanced technology that it brings.

Excessive FDI may not be beneficial. Through ownership and control of domestic companies, foreign firms know more about the host country's productivity, and they could overinvest, at the expense of domestic producers. Possibility exists that the most solid firms will be financed through FDI, leaving domestic investors stuck with low-productivity firms. Such "adverse selection" is not the best economic outcome.[8]

FDI in Post-conflict Economies

Post conflict transition countries cannot be considered as normal economies. The majority of them are burdened by substantial market failures, relative small market size, severe economic constraints and weak institutions necessary for a well-functioning economy. Many of them fall into the category of countries described as least developed; some of them are landlocked, such as Nepal. These countries are also afflicted by a number of risks and capacity deficits including political instability and security problems. Physical infrastructure is often destroyed or unavailable, including electricity, water, transport and access to land. Corruption is often rife, while transparency and the rule of law are very weak. These economies are also normally deprived of skilled labor as they struggle to cope with the effects of brain drain and capital flight.

In the process of post-conflict recovery, reconstruction and development of physical and institutional infrastructure are the prime goals. The two major avenues of such development are foreign aid and FDI. Development aid alone cannot transform devastated economies into vibrant, self-sufficient systems while FDI can bring added advantages, and can eventually even abolish the need for foreign aid (Turner *et al.*, 2008). FDI generates employment opportunities, which are crucial in the attainment of long-term economic stability. It provides capital to raise the productive capacity of the host economy, access to international markets, helping countries to shift from aid-dependent to investment-driven post-conflict reconstruction. The presence of foreign investment can also provide a type of "peace dividend", instilling the people with a stronger sense of hope and providing incentives to consolidate peace.

Attracting a form of FDI that is beneficial to post-conflict countries depends upon prioritizing quality of investment, rather than focusing solely on the size of investment flows. FDI can only be justified if it is high value and makes a genuine contribution to the host economy, with respect to employment generation and spillover of knowledge or technology. Any investment regime must acknowledge that foreign investment is part of economic development within a reconstruction and peace-building process, and not an end in itself.

Hence, in order for FDI to transform post-conflict transition countries, some positive and proactive steps need to be initiated to ensure that FDI fits into some domestic investment demand systems, such that it creates the necessary spill-over effects and internal linkages with the local economy.

With regard to the impact of internal conflict in FDI in conflict-ridden countries, limited literature exists in both theoretical and research form. Vadlamannati (2007) showed how internal state conflict affected FDI inflows in Sri Lanka from 1980 to 2006.[9] The claims brought forward by Vadlamannati's study are that foreign investors, while choosing an investment destination keenly observe whether the investment destination is war free or not and do not take into account the issues like number of terror events. However, once the investment is made in the country, foreign investors are likely to react to the extremities of the civil war in the form of the number of terror events. Besides, this study also shows that ongoing civil war in the country coupled with poor economic performance in the past are the prime reasons for volatility in FDI inflows.

Overall, experiences demonstrate clearly that investors will often invest in locations with suboptimal investment climates, as long as there is a clear business case and as long as they believe that the location satisfies certain minimum business environment standards. They often also invest when things are moving in the right path and the government is committed to reform. Hence, once reform is perceived to be underway, it would become more feasible to consider promoting selective investment in key sectors. In this perspective, experiences from a number of post-conflict countries show that investment promotion agencies (IPAs) have a number of responsibilities to fulfill in building credibility (Box 1).

Box 1

Experience from Post-Conflict Countries

Experiences in post-conflict countries such as the Balkans, Sub-Saharan Africa and Indonesia (Aceh) suggest that investment promotion agencies (IPAs) face three key challenges in building credibility:

- ❖ Building the country's image as a stable and peaceful place for investors to locate their businesses.
- ❖ Building the country's "promotional product", in other words the IPA needs to build effective "arguments" to sell the country as location for investment. These include being able to point to a good investment environment, strong business-related infrastructure, labor skills, power and water supply, among others.
- ❖ Building a targeted marketing strategy and creating a network of business contacts that will get the country back on to investors' "radar screens"; in other words, IPAs face a real challenge in letting potential investors know that the country is open and ready to do business with them.

Source: IFC (2007).

Nepal's Experiences

Background

Development priorities of Nepal include achieving sustained economic and human development to reduce poverty by strengthening technological capacities and skills, improving access to world markets, and creating more and better employment opportunities. To pursue these strategies, the country needs significantly increased flow of investment capital, especially FDI. However, globalization has led to an increase in competition for FDI among developing countries, thereby making it even more difficult for Nepal to attract new investment flows. Hence, one of the development challenges facing Nepal is how to attract and retain FDI on a sustainable basis. It is true that in the present context of global economic recession, it could be difficult for the country to attract FDI inflows as most developing countries are competing for similar types of FDI. Still, FDI is highly preferred in this post-conflict economy as it can play a key role in facilitating the building-up process.

A direct investment enterprise is defined as "an incorporated or unincorporated enterprise in which a direct investor, who is resident in another economy, owns 10 percent or more of the ordinary shares or voting power (for an incorporated enterprise) or the equivalent (for an unincorporated enterprise)" (IMF, 1993, p. 86). However, Nepal does not apply the current 10 percent rule. According to the *Foreign Investment and Technology Transfer Act 1992*, foreign investment means the following investment made by a foreign investor in any industry: a) investment in share (equity); b) reinvestment of the earnings derived from the investment in share (equity); and c) investment made in the form of loan or loan facilities. The minimum investment needs to be equivalent to US$ 20,000.

FDI in Policy-making

A policy for utilizing foreign capital and technology as a valuable supplement for large-scale industries and mineral industries was introduced for the first time in the Sixth Plan (1980/81-1984/85). As an upshot, the *Foreign Investment and Technology Transfer Act 1982* was introduced. Presently, however, Nepal's foreign investment rules and regulations have been formulated on the basis of the *Foreign Investment and Technology Transfer Act 1992* that was amended in 1996 in line with open and liberal economic policies.

According to *Foreign Investment and Technology Transfer Act, 1992*, foreign investors are equally treated as local investors and the same Act prevails regarding incentives and facilities to foreign investors. Incentives and facilities are designed to make investment viable and products competitive. Some of them include the following: a) foreign investors are allowed to hold 100 percent ownership in industries, except the cottage scale enterprises and a few restricted activities such as security-related ones; b) technology transfer is allowed in all types of industries even in the areas where foreign investment is not allowed; c) full repatriation of the amount received from the sale of equity, profits, or dividends and interest on foreign loan and the repatriation of the amount received under an agreement for the transfer of technology is permitted; d) foreign investors will be granted a business visa until their investment is retained; e) the resident visa will be provided to foreign investors, who at a time, makes an investment in excess of US$ 100,000 or equivalent; and f) only nominal import duty is levied on raw materials. Despite the implementation of most of the policy measures of the *Foreign Investment and Technology Transfer Act, 1992*, the country has not been able to attract FDI for its development benefits.

One of the major policies of the Three-Year Interim Plan (2007/8-2009/10) is the promotion of domestic and foreign investment for the country's economic development (NPC, 2008). The main objectives of foreign investment include raising of the foreign investment level by broadening the industrial base, seeking foreign aid to supplement resources needed for a sustainable high economic growth and employment generation, and augmenting technology and management skill transfer.

Some policies pertaining to FDI in the Three-Year Interim Plan are spelled out below:

- Foreign investment in the form of joint ventures would be encouraged in the following: hydropower production;

components of tourism development such as airport construction and its management as well as airlines, star hotels and construction of recreational facilities; agriculture and non-timber based high value products; and development of education and health-related facilities. Financial services, information technology, and biotechnology related industries, would also be incorporated in the field of such investments.

- ❖ With respect to the medium and large-scale production industries, 100 percent share-based investment would be permitted. Similarly, that list would also comprise export-oriented industries, natural resources excavation, construction of toll roads and construction of goods management terminal.
- ❖ Suitable policy would be formulated to attract capital, skills, efficiency and technology of the non-resident Nepalese.
- ❖ Nepalese diplomatic missions abroad would be mobilized for the promotion of foreign investment.
- ❖ A high-level investment promotion board would be set up to facilitate foreign investment. This board would operate as a "one window" shop for satisfying the requirement of project approval, licensing, tax facilities and infrastructure management as necessary, for the large-scale investors.

One of the objectives of the *Budget Speech for 2008/09* is investment promotion (MOF, 2008). A policy has been initiated to guarantee industrial and investment security, reform in legal and organization structure for creation of investment climate, procedural simplification, additional provision for sick industry rehabilitation, and opportunities for foreign, non-resident Nepalis and private sector investment. A law related to Special Economic Zone is to be enacted for development and management of industrial estates, EPZs and special commercial areas. A Garment Processing Centre is to be set up in Simara. An Investment Board with full authority would be established for industrial investment promotion.

Institutional Arrangements

As per *the Industrial Enterprises Act, 1992*, there existed a provision to establish the One Window Service (OWS) whose aim was to provide all services required by foreign investors under one roof. Specifically, the policy listed two types of services to be provided by the OWS: a) permission, facilities, and other administrative services under the *Foreign Investment and Technology Transfer Act, 1992*, and b) other infrastructural facilities (such as registration, land, electricity, telecommunication, water) and other services as required by the investors. However, the One Window Committee set up to provide infrastructure facilities under the one-window system was not successful in addressing the true needs of the investors.

An Industrial Promotion Board was formed under the chairmanship of the Minister of Industries on the basis of the *Industrial Enterprises Act, 1992*. The principal objectives of the Board were a) providing necessary co-operation in developing and implementing policies, laws and regulations pertaining to industrial development of the country, b) developing guidelines in meeting the aims of liberal, open and competitive economic policies undertaken by the country in order to make the industrial sector competitive, c) coordinating between the policy level and the implementation level of the industrial policy, and d) suggesting to the Government for including any other industry in the classification of industries. An evaluation of the functions, duties and powers of the Industrial Promotion Board depicts that it is confined to a large extent to policy-related matters.

Nepal formed a Board of Investment (BOI) under the chairmanship of the Prime Minister in December 2001. The BOI was established for promoting investment and making it more transparent and reliable. The other objectives of the Board were, among others, a) formulating new policies by reviewing the existing investment policy, b) maintaining coordination between various government and non-government organizations for the promotion of investment, c) pinpointing the areas of priority sector for investment promotion, d) monitoring the activities associated with investment promotion, and e) providing directives to the concerned department to boost up investment. However, it is disappointing to note that the BOI has not been functioning smoothly as per its objectives. Though the announcement of the formation of an Investment Board in *Budget Speech for 2008/09* with full authority for promoting industrial investment seems to be a positive step, just simply the formation of the BOI is not adequate. It needs to accord priority to implementation of a focused and targeted investment promotion and facilitation policy.

Experiences indicate that most successful investment regimes in a number of countries have been driven with a single-minded goal at the highest level of Government. A powerful institutional arrangement with all necessary powers will command respect and authority and enable the country to put foreign investment at the top of the development agenda. This type of arrangement is essential in promoting and attracting FDI and also in facilitating the post-approval process. In this respect, as the Board of Investment kind of institutional arrangement in Sri Lanka and Bangladesh have been found quite successful in carrying out its functions, Nepal could draw many lessons from the experiences of these two countries (Pant and Sigdel, 2004).[10]

Data Limitations

In Nepal, the *Foreign Investment and Technology Transfer Act, 1992* empowers the Department of Industries (DOI) to administer, implement and evaluate all foreign investment projects. The compilation, maintenance and publishing of statistical data related to the industrial sector of Nepal (including FDI) are generally made by the DOI. The DOI approves direct investment applications and the Foreign Exchange Management Department of the NRB approves principal and interest repayments by these enterprises.

The FDI figures for Nepal are based on data provided by the DOI and are linked to the number of projects approved. There are often significant time lags between approval and actual investment; the actual investment may not take place at all. For instance, in 2008/09, the number of approved FDI projects was 230. The foreign investment tied with these projects amounted to Rs. 6.25 billion. However, it is believed that the actual disbursement of FDI in Nepal is much lower than the approvals.[11] Information on reinvested earnings and on withdrawals of investment (disinvestments) is generally not captured. Although the DOI requires all FDI-related enterprises to submit their financial statements every three months, this practice has not been followed.

In 2002 and 2003, a survey was undertaken by the NRB in an attempt to improve the recording of FDI data. Direct investment surveys forms were provided to 158 previously-identified direct investment enterprises. However, completed survey forms were received from just 78 enterprises. A number of problems were encountered: a) some enterprises had ceased operations and/or changed their locations with no known forwarding address; b) data reported by the enterprises did not relate to the requested period; and c) most of the responding enterprises reported net losses from operations in Nepal.

To resolve the problem pertaining to the compilation and monitoring of FDI data, the formation of a Foreign Direct Investment Supervision Committee is being initiated comprising members from the Department of Industries, the Federation of the Nepalese Chamber of Commerce and Industry, and the Foreign Exchange Management Department and Research Department of the NRB. The proposed Committee would regulate the data reporting by direct investment enterprises and the systematic compilation of such data.

Again, for proper recording of FDI data, Nepal is participating in the Coordinated Direct Investment Survey (CDIS) that is being conducted by the IMF.[12] In a country where data on FDI has not been properly recorded, participation in this Survey would greatly facilitate in the improvement of the country's recording system.

Other Impediments

Nepal faces multiple challenges such as inadequate development of macroeconomic environment, unsatisfactory physical and economic infrastructure development, low level of technological development, disadvantaged geographical situation and lack of entrepreneurship and managerial capacity in its efforts for attracting FDI. Administrative instability, lack of consistent planning, insufficient institutional capacity, reliance on unsolicited proposals and a lack of government support arrangements are other obstacles.

The absence of supporting infrastructures such as telecommunication, transport, power & water supply as well as skilled labor discourage foreign investors since it increases transaction costs. Investment comes along with the need to communicate with clients at ease and operate efficiently under reliable utilities. Such factors include proper infrastructure and utilities that would make investing in Nepal a pleasure with no hassles.

Political instability denotes that Nepal presents mainstream foreign investors with an unacceptably high level of political risk. Significant prospective investors will delay the identification and implementation of projects until the risk profile becomes acceptable.

Plausible Measures

The current global environment is characterized by an intense "global race" for foreign investment. No doubt, FDI is drawn to different countries for different reasons. Nonetheless, at a general level, in order for a country to be more attractive to investors, there is a need to put in place measures to ensure the existence of an enabling environment, that is, one that is conducive to doing business. In this respect, some measures that could facilitate in the promotion of FDI in Nepal in this post-conflict era are provided below:

- Regional integration could be used as a strategy to overcome the limitations of market size of Nepal. Furthermore, since all countries in the South Asian region are trying to attract FDI, a great deal of competitive overbidding and unnecessary loss of resources could be avoided through some harmonization of FDI policies among different governments.
- Policies and strategies for the promotion and attraction of FDI should clearly delineate areas in which FDI is desired; FDI should not be attracted indiscriminately but should be geared to the country's needs and requirements while taking investor concerns into full account.[13] At the same time, countries and regions from which foreign companies are to be attracted, as well as the foreign companies themselves, need to be carefully screened on their suitability and targeted on the basis of solid research and superior marketing techniques. In this context, particular attention could be paid to attracting investment from nationals living abroad as experience shows that in many countries the diaspora has been the pioneer of foreign investment.
- Nepal should strive to improve, in particular: (a) a well-disciplined, relatively cheap, but reasonably well-educated labor force; (b) access to adequate infrastructural and institutional facilities, including ICT facilities; (c) a stable legal and financial framework and environment; and (d) a stable political environment with a government committed to economic development and reform and absence of excessive red tape and corruption in the FDI approval and implementation process.
- The country needs to accord priority to improving the rule of law, including transparency in the formulation of the laws and regulations, consistency among them, and due implementation, enforcement as well as proper

dissemination and communication of laws and regulations and any changes therein and consistent interpretation by all concerned official entities. Laws and regulations should not change too often while incentives for investors need to be carefully evaluated on their net benefits. All in all, there is a need of a substantial revision of the *Foreign Investment and Technology Transfer Act, 1992* in the context of Nepal's entry into the WTO, SAFTA and BIMSTEC.

- ❖ Without accurate and reliable FDI data, policymakers in Nepal face difficulties in the formulation of appropriate investment policies. In this context, the formation of a Foreign Direct Investment Supervision Committee that is being initiated for regulating the FDI data reporting by direct investment enterprises and the country's participation in the CDIS are steps in the right direction.
- ❖ The issue of peace and stability must be addressed with increased urgency. The extra costs of security for firms that wish to invest in Nepal and those who are already present are high. The extra cost from the view of many prospective investors makes such investment efforts not worth it. Hence, they stay away.
- ❖ Effective FDI promotion involves image building, investment generation and investor servicing to influence investment decisions.
    - Image-building activities comprise effective communication about the location and include producing and distributing fact sheets, videos, brochures and newsletters, holding briefings and engaging in media relations, public relations and advertising. Image-building techniques must be accompanied by removing administrative obstacles and managerial impediments, investment-generation and investor-servicing activities.
    - Investment-generating activities are necessary where the flow of new investments falls short of national

objectives and where the country wants to expand into new areas of investment for reasons of resource availability, comparative advantage or long-term development. To attract new investment, Nepal should engage in in-bound and out-bound overseas missions and seminars, communications (advertising, mail and telephone), campaigns and direct contact with individual investors.

- Servicing investors usually entails a range of pre-approval, approval and post-approval activities. These entail providing information on doing business, granting approvals and clearances quickly and efficiently, assisting in the implementation of projects, helping with access to essential infrastructure, and supporting and monitoring investor performance.

❖ The close partnership between the private and public sector is essential to build confidence. In this respect, it is recommended that a forum be established where the private and public sectors could sit together to discuss business promotion-related issues. The forum needs to be composed of the prime minister, relevant ministries' ministers and secretaries, all the presidents of the national chambers, top businessmen/industrialists, and top bankers, among others. The forum may meet regularly to review the economic situation of the country. The problem faced by the business community can be discussed and decisions could be taken immediately. This kind of partnership between the government and private sector will help restore market confidence.

Conclusions

Economic development is essential for every country, but it is especially crucial for post-conflict transition countries such as Nepal, requiring peace-building, recovery and reconstruction. Development aid *per se* cannot transform a post-conflict economy, and it is here that FDI can be an effective technique for revitalizing industries and rebuilding infrastructure.

The country needs to remain attractive for FDI in the current context of global recession, especially for such investment that serves its long-term development goals and enhances competitiveness (for instance, investment in areas such as infrastructure and hydropower). Retaining existing investment is equally important, particularly in the present deteriorating security conditions where MNCs may consider closing foreign affiliates or transferring them to other safe locations. Moreover, as the recent political trends are very disturbing, the country must make every possible effort to ensure that the trend of FDI inflows is not jeopardized by such negative images.

Finally, though some measures have been spelled out in this paper for boosting FDI flows into Nepal, there are certain issues pertaining to FDI that demand further research. In the first place, should Nepal try to influence the mix of FDI by pursuing to draw in only export-oriented FDI and smaller firms and exclude MNCs in order to limit the risks of monopoly? Secondly, how can the country be successful in directing FDI into specific locations or socially preferred sectors? Thirdly, how can Nepal satisfy the particular challenges posed by its small domestic market size, by the shortage of skilled labor and by the weakness of physical infrastructure? And, lastly, how can the country move ahead with the appropriate sequencing in tackling the different policy requirements?

Notes

1. For instance, ICT developments have had a significant impact on the way companies structure their international activities. Most importantly, it has facilitated a more specialized production attracted to those locations that can offer the most competitive environment for any given activity. Details are given in Velde (2006).
2. The major exception to this rule are countries rich in natural

resources which have managed to attract a huge amount of FDI despite an often unstable environment.

3. This is further discussed in the next section.
4. In India, for instance, FDI from the US has been observed to positively and significantly affect the export intensities of domestic firms operating in the nontraditional export market. See Banga (2003) for further elaboration.
5. For example, when foreign manufacturing firms tap local suppliers for procurement of inputs, the demand for local inputs expands production possibilities in the host country through backward linkages.
6. In the first stage, market conditions in developed countries, particularly in the US, facilitate the innovation of new products. The second stage is when the product is maturing, and potential competitors appear. Some degree of standardization has been introduced in the design and production process. Faced with the resultant competition, producers are more concerned with the cost of production. In the final stage of this model, namely the standardized product, developing countries are at a comparative advantage as a production location. At this stage, market knowledge and information are less important; therefore, the priority is for the least-cost location. The net result is that the production facility or assembly is moved to developing countries to take advantage of low labor costs.
7. In the first stage of IDP, outward FDI of the country is at a negligible level or zero because of insufficient ownership advantages of domestic firms. In the second stage of IDP, outward direct investments remain still at a negligible level, but inward FDI begins to rise as the location advantages of the country improves, particularly with the help of government policies. Eventually, the rate of outward FDI begins to increase in the third stage of IDP. In the fourth stage, outward FDI of the country becomes equal to or

greater than its inward FDI. Finally, the net outward investment level of a country fluctuates at the zero level in the fifth stage of IDP while the growth rate of both inward and outward FDI continues to rise.

8. The impact of excessive FDI is discussed in Kumar (2007).
9. The methodology included generating econometric models based on linear approach which takes into account both FDI presence and actual FDI inflows into the country to estimate the impact of civil war. Also examined are the role of internal conflict and economic performance on volatility in FDI inflows and intensity of volatility in FDI inflows. Vadlamannati's paper brought into play these empirical models using conflict variables and other key macroeconomic variables, which would allow obtaining some general characterization of the effects of internal state conflict on FDI inflows in Sri Lanka.
10. In the case of Sri Lanka, for instance, investor friendly policies, simplified systems and procedures and business-like attitudes adopted by the BOI over the last few years led to phenomenal growth of FDI inflows. The country has achieved the highest ever growth of FDI inflow in 2008, which reached US$ 889 million. This was achieved in a year when worldwide FDI inflows were down by 15 percent. Sri Lanka was able to attract such FDI inflows introducing innovative measures such as simplified application and approval procedures where the investment approval could be granted within a day. The investor was freed of the burden of filing and lodging a large number of documents. In addition there was a reduction of bureaucracy, of cumbersome practices, a reduction of waiting time, and a simplification of the process of company formation and registration. The long-term effect was an improvement of the doing business index of Sri Lanka. The setting up of the Cabinet Sub-Committee on Investment Facilitation (CSIF) headed by the President to resolve the major

policy issues faced by the investors is further proof of the importance Sri Lankan authorities accord to and of their commitment to the promotion, facilitation and retention of FDI (*The Colombo Times*, 11 May 2009). These measures are worth emulating by Nepal in pursuit of attracting FDI under severe competitive conditions.

11. According to the BoP data, however, FDI amounting to only Rs. 1.83 billion flowed into the country in 2008/09. It should be noted that this figure is an underestimation since not all the FDI that came into the country has been captured in this data.

12. The major objectives of the CDIS include the following: a) collecting comprehensive and harmonized information, with geographic detail, on the stock of inward FDI as at end 2009; b) for the major investing countries, also gathering comprehensive and harmonized information, with geographic detail, on the stock of outward FDI; and c) exchanging bilateral data among the participating countries.

13. In this context, an example from India seems worth-mentioning. India's FDI inflows reached US$ 42 billion in 2008-09, an 11 percent jump from the previous year. It is being seen among the top five investors' destinations during the next two years, according to UNCTAD's *World Investment Prospects Survey 2009-2011*. The Government has turned pro-active and is instituting measures to attract inflows. Ministries are coordinating with investor countries and enterprises to present investment opportunities across sectors. The Government, for the first time, has established a non-profit company, Invest India, in collaboration with industry body FICCI and state governments for attracting foreign investment focusing on small and medium companies. Invest India is all set to bridge the information gap for small and medium foreign investors *via* its website

with comprehensive knowledge about the policy framework that they seek. For details, see Mukherjee (2009)

References

Addison, Tony and George Mavrotas (2004). "Foreign Direct Investment, Innovative Sources of Development Finance and Domestic Resource Mobilization." Available at: http://www.helsinkiprocess.fi/nettcom/ImgLib/24/89

Asian Development Bank (2004). *Asian Development Outlook 2004*. Manila: ADB

Banga, R. (2003). "The Differential Impact of Japanese and U.S. Foreign Direct Investments on Exports of Indian Manufacturing." New Delhi: Indian Council for Research on International Economic Relations. Available at: http://econopapers.repec.org/ RAS/pba255.htm

Blomström, Magnus and Ari Kokko (2003). "Economics of Foreign Direct Investment Incentives." *EIJS Working Paper Series*. No. 168. Available at: http://www.hhs.se/eijs

Borenzstein, Eduardo, Jose De Gregorio, and Jong-Wha Lee (1998). "How does Foreign Direct Investment Affect Economic Growth?" *Journal of International Economics*. 45: 115-135.

Caves, R.E. (1974). "Multinational Firms, Competition and Productivity in Host-Country Markets." *Economica*. 41(162): 176-193.

Chen, Yu and Sylvie Dermurger (2002). "Foreign Direct Investment and Manufacturing Productivity in China." Available at: http://www.bm.ust.hk

Dunning J.H. (1993). *Multinational Enterprises and the Global Economy*. Wokingham: Addison-Wesley.

Dunning J.H. (1988). *Explaining International Production*. London: Unwin Hyman.

Dunning, J.H. (1981). "Explaining the International Position of Countries towards a Dynamic or Developmental Approach." *Weltwirtschaftliches Archiv*. 117:30-64.

Dunning J.H. (1979). "Explaining Changing Patterns of International Production: In Defence of the Eclectic Theory." *Oxford Bulletin of Economics and Statistics*. 41: 269-93.

Dunning, J.H. and R. Narula. (1996). "The Investment Development Path Revisited—Some Emerging Issues." In J. Dunning and R. Narula, eds., *Foreign Direct investment and Governments*. London: Routledge.

Hood, N. and T. Truijens (1993). "European Locational Decisions of Japanese Manufacturers: Survey Evidence on the Case of the UK." *International Business Review*. 2 (1): 39-63.

Hood, N. and S. Young (1984). *The Economics of Multinational Enterprise.* London: Longman.

Hymer, S. H. (1976). "The International Corporations of National Firms: A Study of Direct Investment." MIT Monographs in Economics. Cambridge, Massachusetts.

International Finance Corporation (IFC) (2007). "Nepal: Mini-Diagnostic of the Investment Climate." March. Available at: http://www.ifc.org/ifcext/fias.nsf/ attachments

International Monetary Fund (IMF) (1993). *Balance of Payments Manual Fifth Edition*. Washington, D.C: IMF.

Kumar, Anil (2007). "Does Foreign Direct Investment Help Emerging Economies?" *Economic Letter*. 2(1). January.

Lall, S. (2000). "FDI and Development: Research Issues in the Emerging Context." *Policy Discussion Paper*. No. 20. University of Adelaide: Centre for International Economic Studies.

Lall, S. (2000a). "Evaluation of Promotion and Incentive Strategies for FDI in Sub-Saharan Africa." Oxford University.

Markusen, J.R. (1995). "The Boundaries of Multinational Enterprises and the Theory of International Trade." *Journal of Economic Perspectives.* 9: 169-189.

Ministry of Finance (MOF). 2008. *Budget Speech of Fiscal Year 2008/09.* Kathmandu: MOF.

Mukherjee, Nivedita. 2009. "Defying the Slowdown." *India Today*. 1 October.

National Planning Commission (NPC) (2008). *The Three-Year Interim Plan (2007/08-2009/10)*. Kathmandu: NPC.

Nepal Rastra Bank (2009). "Challenges of Attracting FDI in the Globalization and Changed Context: Case of Nepal." Unpublished Report. January.

Pant, Bhubanesh and Bama Dev Sigdel (2004). "Attracting Foreign Direct Investment: Experiences and Challenges." *NRB Working Paper*. NRB/WP/1. April.

Turner, Nicholas, Obigiofor Aginan and Vesselin Popovski (2008). "Post Conflict Countries and Foreign Investment." *Policy Brief.* United Nations University. Available at: http://www.ciaonet.org/pbei/unup

United Nations Conference on Trade and Development (UNCTAD) (2009). *World Investment Report: Transnational Corporations, Agricultural Production and Development.* Geneva: UNCTAD.

UNCTAD (2009a). "Assessing the Impact of Current Financial and Economic Financial Crisis on Global FDI Flows." April. Available at: http://www.unctad.org/en/docs//diaeia20093_3en.pdf

UNCTAD (2009b). *World Investment Prospects Survey 2009-2011*. Geneva: UNCTAD.

Vadlamannati, Krishna Chaitanya (2007). "Effects of Internal State Conflicts on FDI Presence, Actual FDI, Volatility in FDI & Intensity of Volatility in FDI: Evidences from Sri Lanka." June.

Velde, Dirk Willem (2006). "Foreign Direct Investment and Development: A Historical Perspective." Overseas Development Institute.

Vernon R. (1966). "International Investment and International Trade in the Product Cycle." *Quarterly Journal of Economics.* 80: 190-207.

WTO. "Defining and Measuring Foreign Direct Investment." Available at: http://www.wto.org/english/news_e/ pres96_e/pr057_e.htm

The Colombo Times, 11 May 2009.

17

FDI for Reconstruction*

Earthquake-affected economies cannot be considered as normal economies. The majority of them fall under the least-developed category and are saddled with relative small market size, severe economic constraints and weak institutions necessary for a well-functioning economy. Economic impacts are witnessed through the damages or destruction to assets or 'stocks', arising from the earthquake itself, or from events in the aftermath of an earthquake. In the household sector, the major loss is the damage to houses and apartments and building contents. In the business sector, there are damages to buildings, but most crucial is the loss of machinery and other productive capital. Physical infrastructure is often destroyed, including electricity, water, transport and access to land. Development aid alone cannot transform these earthquake-affected economies, and it is here that foreign direct investment (FDI) can be an instrumental tool to revitalize industries and rebuild infrastructures. However, the impact of FDI varies with the ability of local stakeholders to take advantage of the potential benefits. In particular, the local regulatory framework has to provide for competitive conditions that are conducive to local entrepreneurship. Moreover, local individuals and firms need to have the ability to learn from foreign partners.

In Nepal the devastating earthquake of 25 April 2015, measuring 7.8 on the Richter scale, and the subsequent aftershocks led to economic and institutional devastation of vital infrastructure such as schools, factories, roads, and water systems. According to National Planning Commission's *Post Disaster Needs Assessment*, the earthquake is estimated to push an additional 2.5 to 3.5 percent Nepalis into poverty in FY 2015/2016. Prior to the earthquake,

---

* *The Himalayan Times*, 8 October 2015.

the situation was such that the country had only come out from a decade-long conflict and was laying the foundation for stability and growth. It was on track for the MDGs' targets and the poverty level was taking a downward trend. However, the earthquake has posed daunting challenges to the policymakers with the task of creating an integrated and comprehensive approach to post-earthquake reconstruction with a view to sustainable economic development. In attempting to meet these objectives, FDI can complement internally generated revenue and foreign aid and generate added advantages, both tangible and intangible. FDI assists in creating employment opportunities, which are urgently needed to attain long-term economic stability. It transfers new skills and technologies, provides private capital to increase the productive capacity of the host economy, and facilitates access to international markets—facilitating the country to move from aid-dependent to investment-driven reconstruction.

However, so far, Nepal has not been able to draw on the potential technological and other contributions that FDI can make to the process of development. In this respect, a healthy enabling environment for business is paramount. The country should focus on infrastructure investment which is critical for economic growth and welfare. Infrastructure investment has the potential for increasing efficiency and competitiveness, and to promote both international linkages and domestic integration. However, obtaining the required financing on adequate terms is often a challenge, reflecting in part issues pertaining to the returns to infrastructure investment, government finance constraints, and long gestation periods. Likewise, policymakers need also to pay due attention in minimizing risks through good governance and capable institutions, high absorptive capacity and an effective regulatory framework. Although infrastructure is an area in which foreign investors used to shy away from investing in the past due to various risks associated with such projects resulting from long gestation and pay back periods, in the present context of Nepal, seeking FDI has become imperative.

Although Nepal has one of the most liberal investment regimes in the region, it has lagged behind many other developing countries in attracting FDI. There is urgent need for projecting a positive image of the country to prospective foreign investors highlighting measures undertaken for strengthening the legal framework, lowering transaction cost and improving investment climate. However, it should be noted that presently Nepal, affected by the great earthquake, is not an ideal location for foreign investors to undertake projects as there are destroyed infrastructure and serious disruptions in economic activities, resulting in falling production and GDP—all factors that deter FDI. Nevertheless, the country can take steps to actively pursue FDI, and to benefit from its potential contributions to investment, employment, public finances, macroeconomic stability, infrastructure, business development and economic growth in general. Yet, achieving these outcomes requires a balance between, on the one hand, providing a competitive policy environment to compensate for the increased risks facing investors and, on the other, maximizing FDI's positive impact on the national economy.

To conclude, for 2015/16, the country's urgent priority is to rebuild in a better way the areas devastated by the earthquake. In this respect, more FDI is needed to sustain the growth momentum. The Budget of 2015/16 has stated that the *Foreign Investment and Technology Transfer Act* would be revised to attract foreign investment and that an Investment Forum would be organized for encouraging more investment. Still, various investment obstacles must be resolved and possible reform measures must be implemented soon.

18

FDI: Creating an Investment-friendly Climate*

Foreign direct investment (FDI) is a principal avenue of development finance. Since it can contribute to economic development, governments want to attract it. Indeed, the global demand for such investment is highly competitive, and developing countries are making significant improvements in their investment regimes, including the granting of non-discriminatory treatment to foreign investors and the elimination of most restrictions on capital movements. According to UNCTAD's *World Investment Report 2016*, FDI inflows to developing economies reached a new high of $765 billion in 2015, 9 per cent higher than in 2014.

The economic determinants of FDI are vital, the major ones being market size and per capita income, access to regional and global markets, market growth, raw materials, skilled labor, physical infrastructure, and technology. Likewise, broader economic policies including corporate taxes, trade openness and other business climate issues such as regulations are also crucial. Similarly, a transparent and dependable legal framework and a simple investment approval process are also crucial. However, political instability and violence makes a country less appealing for FDI, since they make the economic and political environment less predictable. For instance, political instability in Thailand in 2008 led to a massive drop in FDI inflow, with effects being felt in 2009.

FDI is regarded as one of the prime transmission vehicles of advanced technology from developed to developing countries. Generally speaking, poor developing economies are short of

---

* *The Himalayan Times*, 23 January 2017.

the major necessary conditions in order to be able to innovate and spawn new discoveries and designs. Accordingly, they have to benefit from the diffusion of technology that stems from elsewhere and it is through FDI from advanced economies that the technological diffusion can take place.

FDI can also assist developing countries to convert their comparative advantages into competitive advantages. Moreover, evidence illustrates that FDI increases the productivity of host firms and the wider economy, as well as contributing to increased job numbers and other broader spillovers.

In Nepal, it was the Sixth Plan (1980/81-1984/85) that for the first time incorporated a policy for utilizing foreign capital and technology stating that foreign investment and technology were primarily required in large-scale industries and mineral industries. Currently, the country's major foreign investment laws include the *Foreign Investment and Technology Transfer Act, 1992* (since amended), the Foreign Investment Policy of 2015, the *Foreign Exchange Regulation Act of 1962*, and the annual budget, which summarizes customs, duties, export service charges, sales, airfreight and income taxes, and other excise taxes that impact foreign investment. Likewise, the recently passed *Industrial Enterprises Act, 2016* and *Special Economic Zone Act, 2016* encompass a number of clauses pertaining to FDI.

The Foreign Investment Policy 2015 aims at facilitating the development and expansion of infrastructure, bringing in modern technology and managerial and technical skills, and generating employment opportunities by attaining higher rate of economic growth, among others. Priority sectors, as defined by the Policy, include a) hydroelectricity, b) transport infrastructures, (c) agricultural industries, food and herb processing, d) tourism, and e) mining and manufacturing. The Policy states that foreign investors will be treated at par with domestic investors, and industries operated by foreign investors would not be nationalized.

So far, however, Nepal has not been able to attract a significant amount of FDI. This has been attributed to a number of factors, some of which stand out prominently. In the first place, the political instability and ensuing policy and legal uncertainty implies that foreign investors would contemplate twice prior to investing in Nepal. Secondly, poor infrastructure, especially power and transportation network, which escalate the cost of doing business in Nepal, acts as a strong disincentive for foreign investors to invest in Nepal. In this respect, the World Bank's *Doing Business 2017* shows that out of 190 countries, Nepal's rank in "Ease of Doing Business" fell from 99th position in 2016 to 107th in 2017. Third, the different trade unions with sometimes inconceivable demands have hampered the business climate of the country. Fourth, overlapping laws and institutional arrangements, differing priorities of different agencies of the government, together with critical gaps between policies and their actual implementation have also acted as hindrances in the creation of an investment friendly environment in the country.

Yet, the country is pursuing strategies and aggressively seeking FDI which is critical for economic growth. For instance, the Ministry of Industry together with the Investment Board of Nepal is organizing Nepal Investment Summit on the theme "Harnessing Investment Opportunities in Nepal" during 2-3 March 2017 with the aim of encouraging foreign investment and promoting linkages between domestic and foreign investors. FDI commitment of at least $1 billion is targeted.

To conclude, both economic theory and empirical evidence generally indicate that FDI has a beneficial impact on the host country. It can enhance enterprise and human capital development, create jobs, and stimulate technology spillovers. While political and economic stability as well as continuity and predictability of policy are essential, it is primarily the government's responsibility to make sure that these and other conditions are in place so that FDI can contribute to development goals.

19

Current Issues and Manifold Challenges of FDI*

Ample evidences exist showing that foreign direct investment (FDI) is a core ingredient to sustainable economic growth. Beyond simple financing, FDI is instrumental in the rapid and efficient cross-border transfer and implementation of best practices—ranging from technological, managerial, to environmental and social standards.

However, FDI comes with certain pre-conditions. In the first place, political and macroeconomic stabilities are a pre-requisite for FDI. Many studies have revealed that political and economic stabilities are the major determinants for FDI.

Two, a sound policy and regulatory framework and efficient supporting institutions to enforce the relevant laws and regulations are essential for FDI to come in and prosper. The disparity between countries in how favorable their investment climate may be, including how many administrative and regulatory hindrances an investor has to overcome, and how commercial disputes are handled through the judiciary system have a vast impact on where the investor will go.

Three, an adequate physical and social infrastructure supplements an effective policy and regulatory framework to generate the necessary climate for attracting FDI. These include the quantity and quality of roads and communication systems, skilled labor, as well as the efficiency with which public services are delivered.

According to the latest UNCTAD's *Global Investment Trends Monitor*, global flows of FDI plummeted 13 percent in 2016 to an

* *The Himalayan Times*, 16 June 2017.

estimated $1.52 trillion owing to weak world economic growth and world trade volumes. Inflows to developing economies fell 20 percent to an estimated $600 billion arising from slowing economic growth and falling commodity prices. However, in 2017 global flows are estimated to rise by 10 percent due to sound economic fundamentals. Still, in the short run, uncertainties regarding the shape of future economic policy developments could limit FDI.

Despite this gloomy picture in 2016, developing countries have been competing for FDI since quite some time, primarily induced by the liberalization of investment policies such as by providing investment guarantees and fiscal incentives, guaranteeing national treatment, allowing profit repatriation and simplifying administrative procedures, as well as the lowering or removal of capital controls. The promotion of these policies was triggered by a host of factors, including (a) speedy improvements in technology, (b) the initiation of global and regional production networks, (c) the building up of bilateral investment agreements, and (d) increasing recognition of the benefits of FDI.

A member of WTO and Multilateral Investment Guarantee Agency (MIGA), Nepal has already signed the *Bilateral Investment Protection and Promotion Act* (BIPPA) with six countries, including India, to encourage FDI in Nepal. The country's location between two large economies ensures access to potential markets.

To promote FDI, Nepal introduced fairly liberal *Industrial Enterprises Act*, 2016 which offers tax rebate and exemption to certain industries and *Special Economic Zone Act, 2016* which facilitates export promotion through special economic zones. Similarly, the "Foreign Investment and Technology Transfer Bill" which encompasses a number of provisions such as income tax rebate, credit facility, and foreign exchange facility is at the final stages of being endorsed by Parliament. Likewise, the "Industrial Property Rights Bill" is also to be introduced soon.

In recent months, FDI commitments to Nepal has been taking an upward trend, registering a 30 percent increase in the first half of the current fiscal year in comparison to the previous year.

Likewise, foreign investors pledged a total of US$ 13.5 billion as foreign investment during the Nepal Investment Summit held in Kathmandu in early March 2017. However, these figures do not connote anything unless these commitments are actually realized.

At the same time, it should be realized that globalization is leading to an increase in competition for FDI among developing countries thereby making it tougher for Nepal to attract new investment flows. Similarly, disincentives to foreign investors in Nepal include paucity of skilled labor, administrative instability, lack of a good functioning infrastructure, poor governance, weak institutional capacity for the implementation of economic policies, and lack of coordination between different government agencies. Most importantly, political instability implies that Nepal presents mainstream foreign investors with a high degree of political risk. Prospective investors will defer the identification and implementation of projects until the risk profile becomes acceptable. Overall, a perception exists among foreign investors that the pro-investment policies and incentives for attracting prospective new investors are somehow lost in the reality they confront when they actually begin to set up and operate their business.

To conclude, FDI is now perceived in Nepal as a vital source of capital, advanced technology, and managerial skills. However, the challenges ahead in attracting it are manifold. The Government has an important task to create the pre-conditions for beneficial FDI to enter and play its catalyst role in the country's economic development.

20

FDI: Making It Easy for Investors*

The focus of foreign direct investment (FDI) policies has generally been towards the economic dimension of development. During the 1980s, such policies often encompassed economic and investment liberalization as well as the deregulation measures. While such liberalization often improves the economy's efficiency, a number of crises, including the 1997 South-east Asian financial crisis and the 2008-2009 global financial crisis, validated the need for prudent regulation and supervision for improving the stability of the economy and investment climate. Moreover, according to World Bank's *Global Investment Competitiveness Report 2017/18*, the two major factors influencing multinational corporations' investment decisions in developing countries include political stability and a business-friendly regulatory environment. These two factors outweigh other country characteristics, including infrastructure, access to land and low tax rates.

The overall benefits of FDI for developing country economies have been extensively documented. FDI prompts technology spillovers, assists human capital formation, contributes to trade integration, helps generate a more competitive business climate and enhances enterprise development. It can also boost productivity, raise investment in research and development and lead to better-paying and more stable jobs in host countries. Among all its benefits, however, it is FDI's spillover potential—the productivity gain resulting from the diffusion of knowledge and technology from foreign investors to local firms and workers—that is perhaps the most valuable input to long-run growth and development. Moreover, beyond the strictly economic benefits, FDI can also

---

* *The Himalayan Times*, 15 January 2018.

support in the improvement of environment and social condition in the host country by relocating "cleaner" technology and directing to more socially responsible corporate policies.

Though the benefits of FDI are real, they do not come about automatically. For garnering the optimal benefits, the host governments must formulate and implement the right policies and create an investment-friendly climate which encourages domestic as well as foreign investment, provides incentives for innovation and improvements of skills and contributes to a competitive business climate.

Still, when inviting FDI, governments often downplay the value of the business climate and tend to accord more priority to market size, availability of natural resources and costs. Nonetheless, the challenge for policy makers is not about securing substantial amounts of FDI activity *per se*, but rather in maximizing the linkages and positive spillovers that can be derived from foreign investors.

In Nepal's case, foreign investors are skeptical of the quality of the domestic institutions and the enforceability of the law. Again, poor infrastructure, which escalate the cost of doing business in Nepal, has been a major disincentive for foreign investors. Moreover, overlapping laws and institutional arrangements, differing priorities of various agencies of the government have also been obstacles to the generation of an investment-friendly climate in the country.

Likewise, investor aftercare services in Nepal have often been an overlooked element of investment promotion. These include administrative services that facilitate the operations of foreign firms (such as obtaining business licenses and work permits), operational services that support the effective and efficient operations of foreign firms (such as support for training, identifying local suppliers and cluster development to improve productivity and competitiveness) and strategic services that influence the future direction of the firm and the development of capabilities.

For attracting FDI and optimizing it, greater policy transparency, especially through increasing information flows, is essential for boosting investor confidence. Nepal also needs to undertake positive image building activities aggressively in order to induce investors that it has an attractive and competitive environment for business and to dismiss possible negative images of its location.

Similarly, lessening investor risk through upgrading quality and effectiveness of laws, and predictability and efficiency of their implementation, are preconditions for attracting, retaining and expanding FDI. Regulatory simplification, dismantling barriers to investment entry and addressing infrastructure constraints are crucial confidence-building gestures for the investors.

Finally, policies to attract FDI should not be prepared in isolation. They need to be well-integrated and mainstreamed in national plans and strategies as FDI cuts across nearly all aspects of development. This will require active cooperation and proper coordination of all concerned government agencies, ministries and the private sector. Ultimately, investment promotion, in the end, is just about marketing a specific location to foreign investors. This together with practical policies is bound to bring in technical know-how, enhance work force skills, raise productivity, generate business for local firms and create employment opportunities.

21

Overcoming the Obstacles of FDI*

In development literature, foreign direct investment (FDI) is regarded as being instrumental for the economic growth of all countries, particularly the developing ones. It serves as a panacea for breaking out of the vicious circle of low savings/low income and assists in the import of capital goods and modern technical knowhow. While FDI impacts the efficiency of domestic producers through technological dispersion and spill-over effects, it also impinges on the labor market, affecting unemployment levels, human capital formation, and poverty.

The outlook towards inward FDI has changed significantly over the last few decades, with most countries undertaking liberal policies to attract investments from foreign multinational corporations (MNCs). On the expectation that MNCs will augment employment, exports, or tax revenue, or that some of the knowledge brought by the foreign companies may spill over to the host country's domestic firms, governments have slashed a host of entry barriers and opened up new sectors to foreign investment. A number of host governments also provide different types of investment incentives to persuade MNCs to invest in their jurisdiction, including fiscal incentives such as tax holidays and lower taxes for foreign investors, financial incentives such as grants and preferential loans, as well as measures like market preferences and infrastructure, among others.

FDI is viewed as one of the most development-friendly avenues of private investment because of its stable nature. In comparison to portfolio investment which can enter and exit a host country quickly and easily, FDI is generally long term and can

---

* *The Kathmandu Post*, 9 April 2018.

create structural improvements in the host country. Thus, while portfolio investments escalate the vulnerability of a host country if they abruptly leave during periods of economic uncertainty or difficulties, FDI usually remains stable during short-term economic disruptions.

FDI can have a number of beneficial impacts on the host nation. It can accelerate productivity gains in host countries. By successfully absorbing frontier knowledge brought in by FDI, local firms can enhance their productivity. Technological advances implemented by MNCs may spill over to the rest of the economy, giving rise to positive externalities and promoting domestic private activity. FDI can also boost competition among firms in the local market *via* reallocation of resources away from less productive to more productive enterprises, thus increasing total productivity in the long run.

Many factors affect FDI decisions. While macroeconomic factors are always crucial, the size and growth rate of a domestic or regional market for the goods or services produced in FDI-based operations are also important. The different costs of doing business in the host country also stand out prominently, including the tax rates, the availability and price of skilled and unskilled labor, and the state of a country's energy network. The quality and extent of a country's transportation and telecommunications infrastructure are critical as well. Further, a range of other factors often termed as a country's "business and investment environment" are equally important. For instance, countries where it takes relatively little time and cost to open a new business attract more FDI, relative to GDP, than places where forming a new business is more lingering and onerous.

There is also an array of political factors which sharply affects MNCs' locational decisions. A country's political stability and the degree of corruption involved in government decisions affecting businesses are important issues for MNCs. In that perspective, the reliability and consistency of the rule of law in a developing economy, and how strictly and reliably the government enforces contracts, protects property rights, and expedites the fair settlement of business disputes are threshold issues for MNCs mulling over new FDI commitments.

In Nepal's case, the development aims comprise attaining sustained economic development to lower poverty by bolstering technological capacities and skills as well as providing employment opportunities, among others. Increased flow of FDI is necessary to pursue these strategies. However, the country has not been ensuring a favorable investment-friendly climate for ensuring that foreign capital keep flowing into the country. According to *World Bank's Doing Business 2018*, Nepal has been ranked 105 among 190 economies in the ease of doing business.

Until recently, Nepal was also portrayed as a destination with a high degree of political risk for foreign investors. However, due to the successful completion of the recent polls and expectations of political stability, foreign investors have, in recent days, been eyeing to make investments in Nepal.

For investors, the expected relative risk/return ratio is the driving force of investment decisions. They tend to invest in countries and projects where they expect the maximum returns and the minimum risks. Hence, Nepal's success in attracting foreign investment thus depends on its competitiveness as an investment location relative to other countries.

To conclude, FDI is a desirable form of capital inflow to Nepal as it is less susceptible to crises and sudden stops. To garner the maximum benefits, domestic competencies, technologies and infrastructure have to be well developed so that the citizens can take full advantage of the spillovers that foreign-owned enterprises produce. And there is no better time than now for this to happen as there appears to be stability in the domestic political climate and together with the guarantee of adequate security, this is bound to create a conducive environment for foreign investors.

22

FDI Flows to Nepal: Benefits and Challenges*

Foreign direct investment (FDI) is an effective instrument for promoting sustainable development. Both the 2002 Monterrey Consensus on Financing for Development and its successor, the 2015 Addis Ababa Action Agenda on Financing for Development, acknowledged FDI as a mechanism that can facilitate sustainable development and the implementation of the Sustainable Development Goals (SDGs).

According to UNCTAD's *World Investment Report 2018*, global flows of FDI plummeted by 23 percent in 2017. FDI flows to developing economies remained stable at $671 billion, seeing no recovery following the 10 percent drop in 2016. Flows to developing Asia also remained stable at $476 billion. The region regained its position as the largest FDI recipient in the world.

FDI in structurally weak economies remained fragile as illustrated by the fact that flows to the least developed countries (LDCs) fell by 17 percent to $26 billion in 2017. This negative trend remains a matter of worry for policymakers in LDCs where international investment is indispensable for sustainable industrial development.

FDI can serve as a principal complement to domestic investment and capacity building for the growth and development of the LDCs. The unique aspect of FDI is that it brings in a package of resources—capital, technology, skills, management know-how, and marketing capabilities—together with production activities, to a host economy. While these resources and capabilities are

* *The Himalayan Times*, 17 July 2018.

utilized in the host-country affiliates and help optimize profits for the investing multinational corporations (MNCs), they also have an array of direct and indirect impacts that can, under suitable conditions, be very beneficial to the host economy. They can produce not only products for domestic consumption or for export, income and employment but also linkages and spillovers that bolster the capabilities of domestic firms and human resources, contributing to capacity-building and accelerated growth in the host economy. When the firm-specific assets that constitute the basis for international production through FDI are effectively leveraged and integrated with country-specific advantages of host economies, FDI has the potential to augment consumer welfare, create employment opportunities, increase labor and environmental standards, and contribute to improved living standards and poverty alleviation.

In Nepal's case, though FDI commitments surged to Rs 49.87 billion in the first ten months of 2017/18, the realization appears to be nominal. As per data of Nepal Rastra Bank, Nepal received FDI worth Rs 15.51 billion during the first ten months of 2017/18.

If the investment climate in Nepal is assessed against various parameters such as the condition of the infrastructure, policy stability, legal structure, capacity of the banking and financial sector, human resource profile, responsiveness of bureaucracy and internal security, Nepal would not pass this test as a number of reforms are required in many areas. The country can no longer depend only on low labor costs; it also needs to create high-quality, productive labor and sustain its comparative advantages. For potential investors, the ability to consistently fulfill product standards as well as production costs, skilled labor, ease of cross-border movement, and the availability of critical inputs (power, transportation, industrial land, among others) are some of the crucial factors in the decision-making process. Moreover, investor aftercare services have not been given due attention.

Despite the foregoing constraints, the country has been implementing a number of policy reforms to promote a competitive investment climate and create a range of investment opportunities—critical for the country in attaining its development goals of creating more and better jobs and the diversification of its export base. Some liberal acts pertaining to industrial enterprises and special economic zones have been brought into effect. However, foreign investors are still skeptical toward the quality of the domestic institutions and the enforceability of the law.

Nevertheless, with the right de-risking approaches, a commitment to directing FDI flows to productive sectors, and smart public-private partnerships, it is possible to attract more FDI inflows and generate positive linkages with the rest of the economy.

To conclude, while attracting FDI flows is essential for the country, it is only a small part of the story. Retaining investors is the key. The actual benefits emerge later on, as foreign firms bring in capital, employ local staff, share technology and know-how, and create spillovers that move a country up the value chain.

23

Boosting FDI Flows by Translating Pledge into Action*

Foreign direct investment (FDI) has a number of impacts on the economy of a host country by influencing the production, employment, income, prices, exports, imports, balance of payments, and general welfare. Flows of FDI are playing an instrumental role in building robust economic links not only between advanced and developing countries, but also among developing countries.

Acknowledging these positive aspects, developing countries nowadays aggressively seek to attract FDI, and to harness the dynamism of FDI projects for economic growth. This flow has several other positive effects including productivity gains, technology transfers, introduction of new processes to the local market, managerial skills and know-how, employee training and international production networks, among others. All of these benefits ultimately contribute to higher economic growth, which is the main instrument for alleviating poverty in those countries.

On deciding on whether to enter a new country, investors mull over a number of factors. One, a broad consensus in the host country in favor of FDI is crucial. In this context, a reasonably stable political environment, as well as conditions that support physical and personal security, is an important benchmark that is employed in judging the possibility of adverse changes in the investment climate for foreign-owned firms. Two, corruption and governance concerns have a major bearing on investment prospects. The investment regime and the environment for business—including the business licensing system, the tax regime,

* *The Himalayan Times*, 26 November 2018.

and the attitude and quality of the bureaucracy—are vital. Thirdly, a predictable legal system, which, among other things, respects the sanctity of contracts and facilitates a level playing field, is a must. Likewise, the countries that are best equipped to address infrastructure obstacles will procure larger amounts of FDI.

Based on the data of the Department of Industry, Nepal received FDI commitments equivalent to Rs. 55.64 billion in 2017/18 as against Rs 15.21 billion in 2016/17. However as per data provided by the Nepal Rastra Bank, only FDI equivalent to Rs. 17.51 billion flowed into the country in 2017/18 compared to Rs. 13.50 billion in the preceding year. This implies that with respect to FDI data, there are often significant time lags between approval and actual investment. As a matter of fact, the actual investment may not happen at all.

Analogous to other developing countries, FDI is crucial to Nepal in promoting economic growth by providing capital, technology, improvement of skills, efficiency and trade as well as by providing domestic small and medium-sized enterprises with linkages and markets for the supply of goods and services. Recognizing these benefits, the Government of Nepal undertook a number of policy reforms focused on making Nepal a favorable and predictable investor destination. In this respect, a number of rules and regulations were introduced including the *Foreign Investment and Technology Transfer Act of 1992* (with a new draft Foreign Investment bill, currently under review), the Foreign Investment and One Window Policy of 2015, the *Foreign Exchange Regulation Act 1962*, the Immigration Rules of 1994, *the Customs Act 1997*, *the Industrial Enterprise Act 2016*, and the *Special Economic Zone Act 2016*. However, despite these efforts, the country has not been able to tap its potential. Lack of roads, hydropower plants, and customs infrastructures for cross-border trading have been impediments to the high FDI inflow in Nepal. Moreover, the slow pace of decision making has always been a major concern for foreign investors. They complain that the authorities make them wait for inordinate lengths of time, sometimes for no apparent reason.

It should be recalled that an Investment Summit was organized in March 2017 to showcase Nepal's investment opportunities particularly to large scale investors. In that Summit, the government had signed letters of intent for investment tantamount to about $13.50 billion with foreign investors. However, it was not successful in capitalizing on the commitments. If the Government intends to organize another Summit in the near future, the aim should be to mobilize investors to expedite development in critical areas such as infrastructure, energy and agriculture. It is also crucial for the government to make sure that all FDI-related laws and policies are endorsed with necessary amendments prior to the Summit. Without these and other proper preparations, nothing concrete will be forthcoming and there will just be commitments with minimal or no actual inflows as in the past.

To conclude, while FDI is often superior in terms of capital and technology, spillovers to local economic development is not automatic. Appropriate policies to benefit from FDI include building up local human resource and technological capabilities to raise the absorptive capacity to capture productivity spillovers from multinational corporations. If FDI is tapped properly, it can play a much greater part than it presently does in Nepal's development process, contributing to job creation, upgrading of the enterprise sector and increasing living standards.

24

Marketing Nepal as a Potential Destination of FDI*

Foreign direct investment (FDI) has been playing an instrumental role in economic development of developing countries. However, abilities to attract and to benefit from FDI vary a great deal since socioeconomic, institutional, and cultural factors both enable and limit host countries in their efforts to attract and benefit from FDI.

Many countries strive to attract FDI hoping that knowledge brought by multinationals will spill over to domestic industries and increase their productivity. On the macro side, FDI could spawn new economic sectors, push an economy's technological frontier, and diversify exports. On the micro side, through knowledge spillovers and linkages between foreign and domestic firms, FDI could foster technology transfer, improve managerial and employee skills, and boost investment incentives and productivity in upstream and downstream sectors. Intensifying competition that results from foreign entry could incentivize local firms to upgrade their productivity, drive out unproductive domestic firms, and reallocate factors of production to more productive firms and uses.

An array of host country determinants influence FDI, such as economic, political and social stability, rules regarding entry and operations, market size, access to output markets, raw material, skilled labor, transport and communication costs, investment promotion, tax rates and investment incentives. Other important factors include the absence of crime and corruption, basic and specialized infrastructure and the effectiveness and functionality of the financial sector.

---

* *The Himalayan Times*, 21 March 2019.

There is also an important role played by institutional quality in determining FDI as low institutional quality denotes a higher cost of doing business and higher transaction costs. Similarly, macroeconomic stability is also a relevant driver of inward FDI. The absence of sharp fluctuations in inflation and exchange rates in a host country is a localization advantage that can attract FDI by lowering the risks associated with the expected value of assets and profits made abroad.

Policies also matter for reaping the full benefits of it. Foreign investors are influenced by certain factors: the return on their investment relative to their risks they are taking, especially political risks such as expropriation, convertibility and transfer restrictions and breach of contract by the sovereign; the ease with which subsidiaries' operations in a given country can be integrated in the investor's global strategies; and the overall quality of the host country's enabling environment.

In recent years, Nepal has stepped up its efforts to improve its investment climate. In many cases, amendments in FDI regulations have liberalized restrictions, provided for non-discrimination between foreign and domestic private investors, allowed profit repatriation, protected against expropriation, granted incentives and strengthened standards of treatment of foreign investors. Still, it is important to further simplify the processes and procedures for operating a business so that the cobwebs of traditional bureaucratic and administrative system do not aggravate the cost of doing business in the country.

The Foreign Investment Policy of 2015 is an indication of the government's growing confidence to liberalize the economy as well as the need to supplement the development efforts of the government with international private sector participation. However, it should be equally realized that FDI is not a panacea for all development challenges because if it is not aligned to the country's development priorities and if not managed properly, it can also create irreversible social, economic and environmental problems.

Nepal, so far, has not been able to draw on the potential technological and other contributions that FDI can make to the process of development. This underlines the need for effective policy interventions with a view to maximizing the benefits of FDI in an open environment. At the present juncture, many foreign investors still complain that corruption, bureaucracy, and a weak regulatory setting make investing in Nepal very difficult.

To market Nepal as a lucrative investment destination as well as to inform the investors about the political changes and the improvements in the investment climate, the government is organizing a second Investment Summit on 29 March 2019. To get the maximum benefit from it, however, it is vital that the investment-related laws and regulations are revised appropriately ahead of the Second Summit.

To conclude, it is imperative that the government and the private sector better understand the potential spillover benefits from FDI, particularly in how it helps increase the country's and firm's competitiveness. For this, the government will need to formulate an array of policies designed to enhance competitiveness, restructure the industrial base and support closer interface among the government, foreign investors, and the domestic business community. The local private sector, on its part, will have to devise strategies to harness the technical and managerial capabilities of foreign firms and ascertain greater forward linkages with them.

25

Improving Investment Climate for Quality FDI*

A number of global reports have painted a gloomy picture pertaining to Nepal's progress in improving the business climate for attracting more inflows of foreign direct investment (FDI). For instance, among 190 economies, Nepal slid five places in the ease of doing business index to land at 110th position in 2018 from 105th position in 2017 as per the World Bank's *Doing Business 2019*. It had attained an all-time high of 99 in 2016 and a record low of 123 in 2009 in the ranking.

Likewise, according to UNCTAD's *World Investment Report 2019*, Nepal obtained FDI equivalent to USD 161 million in 2018 compared to $129 million in 2017. The country was ranked 6th in the South Asia region with a share of just 0.32 percent.

Despite the meagre inflows of FDI into Nepal, it has been acknowledged that this financial inflow has the potential to bring in an array of benefits to Nepal. The advent of multinational corporations (MNCs) can promote efficiency through increased competition. It can also generate positive productivity spillovers as MNCs integrate domestic firms into their production processes through forward and backward linkages. Moreover, MNCs make new technology available and provide access to new markets, advancing the training and qualifications of the domestic labor force and raising wages and employment. The extent of these positive results, however, hinges largely on Nepal's absorptive capacity.

Currently, foreign investors encounter difficulties pertaining to restrictions on foreign exchange, including regulations linked to

---

* *The Himalayan Times*, 23 August 2019.

off-shore funds, borrowing and capital repatriation. Overlapping administrative procedures and a lack of transparency in regulatory and administrative systems have also frustrated investors seeking to undertake projects in the country. Dearth of skilled labor force and technological expertise, inadequate physical infrastructures, and exchange rate variability are the reservations of investors.

In order to encourage more quality FDI, the government of Nepal in recent times introduced some Acts including the *Public-Private Partnership and Investment Act, 2019*, the *Foreign Investment and Technology Transfer Act (FITTA), 2019* and *the Special Economic Zone Act (First Amendment)*. While the *Public Private Partnership and Investment Act* provides one stop service for any foreign investment of over Rs. 6.00 billion or a hydropower project over 200 MW capacity, the smooth and effective implementation of this Act to facilitate private investment can only happen if the government pushes for reforms to empower and improve the human resources of the bureaucracy and make them investment friendly.

Likewise, though the FITTA ensures national treatment for any foreign investment and an automatic route system has been incorporated to make the FDI-related processes simple and predictable, ambiguities relating to the provisions in FITTA still exist. One of the contentious clauses concerns contract manufacturing operations by MNCs. The FITTA specifies that MNCs can hire other firms only to produce accessories and supporting goods, but not to produce finished goods. Currently, many foreign investment firms are hiring contract manufacturers to produce finished goods for them. This has given the MNCs a comparative advantage due to various factors, including cheap labor, which lowers the production cost. But with the implementation of FITTA, multinationals may not be able to engage other firms to produce finished goods, and this could be a setback for prospective investors.

Another ambiguity concerns investment in the hydropower sector. While FITTA allows the Investment Board to issue production licence for hydropower projects with capacity above 200 MW, the Ministry of Energy, Water Resources and Irrigation would issue licence for hydropower projects regardless of their production capacities as per the Electricity Act

In the last Investment Summit held in Kathmandu on March 2019, investors had sought full implementation of the government's commitment to put procedural reforms and policies for investment security. Of the 77 projects that the government had showcased for investment, just 17 applications were filed for 10 projects. For the commitments to be converted into reality, however, the government needs to do regular follow-ups. Still, one lesson drawn from the Summit is that prior to holding a summit, it is vital to assess the needs of investors and the projects they seek as this would have a broader impact rather than just calling on investors to compromise with the available policies and projects.

Presently, the investors are keeping a close watch on what steps the government would take in providing investment security and removing administrative bottlenecks to that effect. They are also in 'wait and watch' state with regard to implementation of the various provisions in the different bills.

To conclude, the country needs to focus vigorously in creating a much more investment-friendly environment to attract quality FDI which will facilitate in achieving higher and more sustainable GDP growth over the long term.

26

Policy Intervention for Attracting FDI*

Foreign direct investment (FDI) is not only about capital, but also about technology and know-how. It no longer moves from 'North' to 'South', but also from 'South' to 'South' and from 'South' to 'North'. It has become part of the international production process through which investors establish a factory in one country to produce a good or a service that is part of a broader global value chain. It plays the instrumental role of satisfying the development, foreign exchange, investment, and tax revenue gaps in developing countries.

FDI's principal contribution to development is its unique productivity-enhancing effects, including a) improving export capacity and increasing imports of foreign-invested firms—both of which help domestic firms integrate into global production networks; b) inspiring technology transfer in production and management processes; c) enhancing training and skill development among workers; and d) bolstering competition and enterprise development.

However, it should be understood that while some factors that are vital in attracting FDI, including size of the market and availability of natural resources, cannot be induced by public policy, a number of other policy-related drivers—including human capital, the quality of infrastructure, and economic and political stability—can be influenced only in the medium to long run. In contrast, a number of components of a country's investment climate—such as the quality of its laws and regulations and the efficiency of its bureaucracy—can be affected in the short term.

---

* *The Himalayan Times*, 4 March 2020.

Nepal's policymakers acknowledge that the benefits of FDI can be enormous, such as technology spillovers, augmentation of competitive business environment, contribution to international trade and integration. In this respect, the country increased its efforts to improve its investment climate. As a result, according to World Bank's *Doing Business 2020*, Nepal climbed 16 spots and was ranked 94 out of 190 economies on the ease of doing business in 2019. Four vital reforms in a single year pertaining to construction permits, access to credit, trading across borders and contract enforcement helped the country reach this spot.

At the national level, a legislation is in place that has incorporated a variety of guarantees and opportunities for foreign investors. FDI regulations have largely liberalized restrictions, provided for non-discrimination between foreign and domestic private investors, permitted profit repatriation, granted incentives and boosted standards of treatment of foreign investors.

Though the government has been implementing a host of policy reforms to promote a competitive investment climate and generate a range of investment opportunities that is critical for the country in achieving its development goals, the reforms have not been successful.

A number of investors still maintain that investing in Nepal is difficult and risky due to corruption, bureaucracy, and a weak regulatory environment. While Nepal's legislation seems favorable, it still looks doubtful as to whether investment climate will be better once the legislation is implemented. Again, the country has not been able to pull on the potential technological and other contributions that FDI can make to the development process. This underscores the need and significance for effective policy interventions with the aim of optimizing the benefits of FDI for the country's prosperity.

The government had sought to entice foreign investors by holding the Nepal Investment Summit in 2017 and 2019. Still, FDI inflow has not improved. Despite political stability, the climate has not been accommodating for foreign investors.

The government and the private sector need to better understand how FDI supports in raising the country's and firm's competitiveness. For this, it is crucial that the government develop and implement a platform of policies aimed at enhancing competitiveness, restructure the industrial base, further strengthen the legal and regulatory frameworks that assist business, and support closer interface among the government, foreign investors, and the domestic business community. Moreover, the government will also need to look at selective interventions to inspire innovative programs with foreign investors such as linkages with domestic firms, academic organizations, and communities. For its role, the domestic private sector will have to formulate strategies to harness the technical and managerial capabilities of foreign firms, form more forward linkages with these firms, and detect techniques of increasing their competitive position.

Again, focus should be accorded in attracting quality FDI and ensure that each dollar invested contributes, in one way or another, to sustainable development and inclusive growth. If managed effectively and without any vested interest, FDI can become a vital avenue of capital for investment in infrastructure and other development projects.

To conclude, FDI inflows can play a pivotal role in economic growth of Nepal owing to their potential in accelerating growth and economic transformation through capital stock accumulation and technological spillover and the improvement of employment conditions and infrastructure. Attracting more of it through effective policy intervention leads to higher productivity which is the key to growth and development.

Section III: Remittances

27

Remittance Inflows to Nepal: Economic Impact and Policy Options*

Introduction

Development economics has traditionally taken into account foreign savings as the key to augmenting a nation's capital output ratio. Factors such as foreign direct investment (FDI), official development assistance (ODA), foreign trade, the transfer of technology and, more recently, remittances have been incorporated into these studies.

The macroeconomic effects of remittances enjoy a strong theoretical tradition dating back to Adam Smith, David Ricardo and the labor theory of value and comparative advantage. It advanced right up to the endogenous growth innovation in the 1980s assigning human capital a crucial role in modern production and exchange.

Generally, remittances refer to that portion of migrants' earnings sent from the migration destination to the place of origin. Even though they can also be sent in kind, the term "remittances" is normally limited to denote monetary and other cash transfers transmitted by migrant workers to their families and communities.

International migrant remittances have become an important source of external finance in developing countries. Remittances to these countries from overseas resident and nonresident workers are estimated to have risen by 8 percent in 2004, reaching US$ 125.8

* *Economic Review*, 18: 20-36, April 2006.

billion, making them the second largest source of development finance after FDI. That rise followed a 17 percent increase in 2003. Much of the 8 percent increase in 2004 happened in low-income countries, where remittances soared by 18 percent. Since 2001, remittances to developing countries have augmented by almost 50 percent. Low-income countries constitute almost half of the increase: the share of remittances flowing to low-income countries catapulted from 28 percent in 2001 to 35 percent in 2004.[1]

The major portion of the $41 billion increase in remittances to developing countries from 2001 to 2004 was concentrated in South Asia ($17 billion), Latin America and the Caribbean ($13 billion), and to a lesser degree, East Asia and the Pacific ($7 billion). The increases in remittance flows have been especially strong in China, India, Mexico, Pakistan and the Philippines.[2]

The upsurge in remittances flows over the past couple of years can be ascribed to a variety of causes. There have been noticeable reductions in remittance sending costs in some countries, for example, by 60 percent in the U.S.-Mexico corridor since 1999. Growing migration also play crucial roles. The sizable depreciation of the dollar against most other major currencies over the past three years has raised the dollar value of non-dollar remittances over time. Some portion of the rise in remittance flows can be attributed to improvements in data recording by central banks.

While the development community continues the search for additional resources to finance the Millennium Development Goals (MDGs), remittances—pro-poor and cyclically stable, compared to other capital flows—seem to be a promising source. In this context, a number of remittance initiatives are underway.[3]

Against the foregoing background, this paper first attempts to summarize some concepts and measurement pertaining to remittances followed by an investigation into the different theories for remitting. This is preceded by the general impact of remittances together with the use of remittance income. The impact of remittances on the Nepalese economy is then scrutinized followed by an analysis of the various initiatives undertaken by the concerned officials for encouraging remittance inflows through the official channel.[4] Before concluding, the paper attempts to provide some policy options for increasing remittances through the official channel as well as some measures to use remittance income productively.

Concepts and Measurement

Remittances fall under the group of items classified as transfers in the balance of payments (BoP). In the fifth edition of the *Balance of Payments Manual (BPM5)*, transfers are defined as offsetting entries for real sources or financial items provided, without a *quid pro quo*, by one economy to another. Putting it in another way, whenever an economy does not receive or provide recompense in the form of real resources of financial items for goods, services or financial items supplied to or received from another economy, it becomes a transfer for the purposes of BoP accounting.

Two kinds of transfer are identified in the *BPM5*: current transfers and capital transfers. While current transfers are recorded in the current account, capital transfers are recorded in the capital account.

Current transfers are categorized on the basis of the sector of the compiling economy into two main groups: general government and other sectors. General government transfers encompass current transfers, in cash or in kind, between governments and international organizations. Current transfers between other private sectors of the economy and non-residents consist of those occurring between individuals, between non-governmental institutions or organizations (or between the two groups) or between non-resident government institutions and individuals or non-governmental institutions. Moreover, the category of workers' remittances encompasses current transfers by migrants who are employed in other economies and considered residents there.

Standard measures on remittances are based on three items in the BoP reports (as incorporated in the IMF's *Balance of Payments*

Statistics Yearbook, 2005). These are in the form of a) workers' remittances (money sent by workers living abroad for greater than one year), b) compensation of employees (gross earnings of foreigners living abroad for less than one year, and c) migrant transfer (net worth of migrants moving from one country to another).

Motives for Remitting

According to the literature on remittances, a number of theories have emerged to explain the causes behind the migrants' decisions to send funds (cash and goods) to their relations back home.[5] An important research on the motivations to remit has been developed under the framework of the "new economics of labor migration" or NELM.[6] Families in migrant-sending areas, particularly rural communities, have indulged in migration by sending one or more members off as migrants (normally, sons and daughters of the household head), who subsequently share part of their earnings with the rural household, through remittances. The NELM theory states that imperfections in rural credit and risk markets (for instance, farmers' inability to obtain credit and insure against income loss) generate incentives to participate in migration by sending family members to work in the city or abroad. Migrants function as financial intermediaries, substituting for the missing rural bank or insurance institution. Once they are set up at their destinations, migrants provide the family members at the origin with required capital through remittances, and with income insurance, or simply the promise to remit if the origin household suffers an adverse income shock.

Generally, the motives behind remittances can be grouped under three headings: a) the altruistic motive; b) the self-interest motive; and c) implicit family contract: loan repayment and co-insurance.

Altruistic Motive

According to the altruism or livelihoods school of thought, remitting is an obligation to the household. A model of pure altruism would envisage that as migrant incomes rise, a portion of the incremental income is passed on to the origin household through remittances. Remittances are dispatched owing to affection and responsibility towards the family. The altruistic model states that sending remittances brings satisfaction to the migrant out of a concern for the welfare of his family. When motivated by altruism, remittances can vary based on the number of household members that migrate and the poverty status of the receiving household, though it has been shown that poorer households obtain a larger proportion of their total income from remittances than do non-poor ones.

Self-Interest Motive

A divergent motivation is to assume that the migrant is primarily stimulated by an economic and financial self-interest, when sending remittances to the home country. The argument supporting this line of theory is that at every point in time, the successful migrant in the foreign country saves. Subsequently, the migrant wants to know how (in which assets) and where (in which country) to accumulate his wealth. The home country is the obvious place to invest, at least part of his assets, by purchasing property, land and financial assets, among others. These assets could generate a higher rate of return than assets in the host country though their risk profile can also be greater.

Implicit Family Contract: Loan Repayment and Co-Insurance

Economic theory has devised explanations of the remittances process that take the family—rather than the individual—as the major unit of analysis.[7] According to this theory, families seem to develop an implicit contract among those who opt to reside abroad, the migrant, and those who stay at home. The implicit contract consists of an inter-temporal dimension, which could last for many years or even decades, as a time horizon.

The contract is a combination of the elements of investment and repayment. As per the loan repayment theory, the family invests in the education of the migrant and usually finances the costs of migrating (travel and subsistence costs in the host country). This is the loan (investment) element of the theory. The repayment part happens after the migrant settles in the foreign country and his income profile begins to rise over time and is in a position to begin repaying the loan (principal and interest) back to the family in the form of remittances. This implicitly connotes that the family invests in a higher yield "asset" (the migrant) who obtains a higher income level in the foreign country than other family members that live and work at home. The amount to be remitted will, however, be governed by various factors such as the income profile of the migrant.

A variant of the theory of remittances as an implicit family contract between the migrant and those at home is based on the notion of risk diversification. If it is assumed that economic risks between the sending and foreign country are not positively correlated, then it becomes an opportune strategy for the family as a whole to send some of its members abroad (often the most educated) to diversify economic risks. The migrant can then help to support his family in worsening times at home. Conversely, for the migrant, having a family in the home is insurance as bad periods can also take place in the foreign country. In this model, migration is a co-insurance strategy with remittances playing the part of an insurance claim. Analogous to any contract, there exists a potential problem of enforcement (for instance, ensuring that the terms of the contract are respected by the parties). Still, enforcement seems to be simpler, in principle, owing to the fact that these are implicit family contracts, helped by considerations of family trust and altruism.

Whatever the motivation to migrate and remit, the different uses to which the remitted funds are applied vary in their potential to reduce poverty and create economic security for the household and community. Remittances that form part of productive investment seem to have an effect on long-term poverty reduction, leading to less vulnerability at both the household and the community level. There could also be a reduction in inter-household inequality. Conversely, if remittances are utilized in domestic consumption, the impact could be only of short duration and may lead to a rise in inter-household inequality.[8]

Economic Impact of Remittances

Remittances can generate a positive effect on the economy through various channels such as savings, investment, growth, consumption, and poverty as well as income distribution. Workers' remittances flow in as a component of foreign savings and as such complements national savings by increasing the total pool of resources available for investment.

Remittances constitute an integral part of household livelihood strategies. They make a direct contribution to raising household income, while broadening the opportunities to increase income. They also permit households to increase their consumption of local goods and services.

At the community level, remittances create multiplier effects in the domestic economy, producing employment opportunities and spurring new economic and social infrastructure and services, especially where effective structures and institutions have been set up to pool and direct remittances. Where these have been set up and encouraged, and where the state is cooperative, remittances can bring about a change, especially in remote rural areas where state resources have not been effective.

The poverty reducing and income distribution effect of remittances is also significant.[9] This case is based on the fact that the recipients of remittances are often low-income families whose offspring left the country to work abroad. In this situation, migration is taken as a response to escape poverty at home and improve the income-earning capacity of the migrant by attempting to enter foreign labor markets in richer countries. Again, remittances assist in alleviating poverty of the family of migrants in the home country by supporting their income through transfers.

Remittances assist in augmenting national income by providing foreign exchange and raising national savings and investment as well as by providing hard currency to finance essential imports, hence curtailing any BoP crisis.[10] Since they bear no interest, do not have to be repaid, and their utilization is not tied to specific investment projects with high import content, they have a more positive effect on BoP than other monetary flows such as direct investments or loans.

Use of Remittances: Productive Versus Non-productive

It has been shown through a community- and family-level approach that remittances enable better health care, nutrition, housing and education.[11] However, spending patterns are governed by a host of factors such as the strength of the migrant's kinship ties and intent to return to the country of origin. Migrants who wish to return tend to remit than those who are permanently integrated into the host countries; hence, remittances may slow as ties weaken with time. Still, this argument supporting the "remittance decay hypothesis" remains anecdotal.[12] Although it is true that the propensity to remit, that is, the proportion of income remitted by a migrant, may go down over time, it rarely vanishes, since first-generation migrants (and often even second-generation migrants) continue to send money to their original communities. Even if the propensity to remit declines, the remittance volume rises with the sharp increase in income levels of migrants over time.

In many countries, a large portion of remittances are invested in real estate, demonstrating both a desire of migrants to provide housing to families left behind and a paucity of other investment instruments in the recipient. Whether remittances are utilized for consumption or purchasing houses, or other investments, they produce positive impact on the economy by stimulating demand for other goods and services. Moreover, the positive macroeconomic or development impact of remittances could become more effective if migrants form associations and their commitment to their home country becomes "institutionalized".[13]

While the contributions of remittances can be significant with positive growth impacts, the very act of the citizens migrating can also generate some negative growth impacts. This adverse growth effect will, however, depend largely on the type of migrant that left home, the state of the labor market and the productivity of the migrant. If the migrant was an unskilled worker of low productivity, or an unemployed person, demonstrating slack or excess supply in the labor market, it can safely be argued that the impact of migration on output in the home country will be meager. On the other hand, if the migrant is a highly skilled worker, such as a medical doctor or an information technology professional whose direct and indirect contribution to output was significant, for instance, then the negative growth impact will definitely be large. The permanency of remittance flows together with the macroeconomic importance would imply, however, that the negative effects of migration might only be a short-term phenomenon.

Still, some argue that remittances are utilized basically for non-productive purposes, and have concluded that they do little to stimulate development in the countries of origin. A few studies undertaken relating to the uses of remittances show that savings produced by remittances are frequently directed to purchases of non-productive assets.[14] Remittances were also seen to increase dependency. These inflows are quite volatile in the sense that countries that rely too much on them may encounter economic shocks when the flow is disrupted.[15]

The emergence of remittances as a central issue for development policy has generated some backlash and confusion among politicians and academicians pertaining to the nature of remittances. Some have cited remittances as promoting migration from poor countries, and hence leading to reduced labor pools, lower per capita incomes, increased income inequality, and negative "demonstration effects".

Others have associated remittances with the so-called 'Dutch Disease'.[16] This term has been loosely used to diagnose the exchange rate volatility, inflation, loss of competitiveness on international markets, and other effects, such as real estate appreciation, owing to an influx of foreign exchange (including remittances) into a country. Some are of the view that remittances enable governments to avoid reforms and to overspend on the bet of growing future inflows. Still, other researchers are of the view that geographic distance and asymmetric information between remittance senders and receivers lead to problems of moral hazard, whereby recipients may engage in activities contrary to the wishes of senders.[17]

Nevertheless, many of the research studies that question the benefits of remittances seem to understate several basic issues. In the first place, while remittances are no cause for celebration, they are not responsible for underdevelopment. The hard reality is that remittances exist since many countries cannot provide sufficient employment and income for their citizens. Thus, people move 'North' by the millions, and money flows towards 'South' by the billions. These flows have become a primary source of income for a large number of families. Indeed, it is impossible to envision social conditions in the absence of these resources.

Two, remittances do not typically produce optimal economic outcomes in recipient countries, but neither do other flows and economic activities in environments where poor economic incentives and weak institutions discourage households, businesses, and investors from saving, investing and undertaking risks.

Still, there are certain regulatory factors that can contribute to attracting or discouraging remittance flows and their investment.[18] The factors that hinder the sending of remittances, particularly through the formal channels include (a) monetary policies, such as foreign exchange restrictions or the channeling of all foreign exchange dealings through the central bank or a state bank, and (b) financial sector regulations that impact the availability or outreach of financial services.[19] The factors that obstruct the investment of remittances comprise (a) restrictions on foreign exchange holdings, such as foreign exchange-denominated bank accounts, (b) denial of repatriation of savings, c) indirect taxation of remittances through exchange rate controls or by withholding portions of remittances, and d) administrative hurdles to setting up a business.

Remittance Inflows and Impact on Nepal's Economy

In Nepal, much of early migrations were the result of push factors like excessive tax burden, exploitative agrarian relations and political instability. The more formal and temporary migration began after people started to work in the British army following the Sugauli Treaty that was signed on 2 December 1815. This Treaty permitted Britain to recruit Gurkhas for military service.[20]

While both the First and the Second World War created a huge demand for young army personnel from Nepal, in recent times the scope for out-migration for military services has declined and more and more people have migrated for other types of job. It was only after the 1990s that policy makers and academicians began to fully acknowledge the importance of remittances send by Nepalese employed abroad for enhancing the livelihoods of the households, including those in the rural regions.

There are basically three methods of measuring remittance inflows. The first technique is through the BoP estimates. The second mechanism is the household surveys of recipients of such flows, for instance, the Nepal Living Standards Survey (NLSS). The third technique is through banks or financial institutions in origin countries, that is, focusing on resource transfer institutions. The size of remittance flows examined in this paper refer to the workers' remittances under the current account of the BoP data compiled by the Nepal Rastra Bank (NRB).[21]

Conclusions relating to the impact of remittances can vary depending on the analytical approach adopted. Regardless of the approach employed, studies on the poverty impact of remittances have demonstrated that apart from possibly increasing inequality and dependency, remittances make a pivotal contribution to reducing poverty and vulnerability in most households and communities. In Nepal's case, according to the Central Bureau of

Statistics (2004), the impact of remittances on poverty has been positive since the poverty level, defined in terms of absolute head counts, declined from 42 percent in 1995/96 to 31 percent in 2003/04.[22] Other studies have also supported the government's findings on the significance of remittances.[23]

Currently, due to the widespread conflict in the country, many workers view foreign employment as their only viable option. Again, paucity of economic opportunities at home and growing employment prospects abroad have also tempted Nepalese to seek employment abroad.[24] According to the statistics of the Department of Labor and Employment Promotion, the number of workers going abroad for employment has increased by 14.7 percent in 2004/05 as compared to 2003/04.[25] With the increase in the number of workers, the inflow of remittances has also taken an upswing. Moreover, due to policy initiatives undertaken by the concerned authorities for enhancing the inflow of remittances through the official mechanism, the share of remittances incoming through the official channel has been going up.[26] For instance, in 2000/01, out of total remittance income of Rs. 47.2 billion, just about 20 percent flowed into the country through the official channel and 80 percent is estimated to have come through the unofficial channel. In 2004/05, on the other hand, out of total remittance income of Rs. 65.4 billion, 67 percent entered through the official channel and 33 percent is estimated to have flowed in through the unofficial channel.

The growing remittances have led to a surplus in the current account, thereby strengthening the overall BoP position. The share of remittances in total current account receipts, excluding grants, soared from 27.4 percent in 2000/01 to 38.2 percent in 2004/05. Remittances have relaxed foreign exchange constraints of the country. One of the prime causes for the 6.0 percent growth of convertible currency reserves of the banking system in 2004/05 compared to the previous year has been the rise in remittances. The strong external position has allowed the NRB to build official reserves to high levels, reducing its vulnerability to external shocks.

The impact of remittances on national economy can also be illustrated by the fact that it has surpassed exports as the top contributor in the foreign exchange earnings of the country after 2001/02. While the share of remittances in total foreign exchange receipts was 28.0 percent, 25.9 percent and 31.5 percent in 2002/03, 2003/04 and 2004/05, respectively, the corresponding share of exports was 26.2 percent, 24.4 percent and 28.8 percent. The share of travel receipts in total foreign exchange receipts, on the other hand, went down to 5.0 percent in 2004/05 from 5.7 percent in 2000/01. Likewise, the remittances to GDP ratio increased from 11.5 percent in 2000/01 to 12.3 percent in 2004/05.

Nepal's Efforts to Harness Remittances

Owing to the potential positive effect of remittances, the country has accorded priority in promoting overseas employment and mobilizing remittances so as to maximize the benefits from these transfers. In this respect, effective 29 March 2002, the NRB had begun granting licenses to private sector organizations interested in remittance-transfer business. As of 31 March 2006, 31 firms excluding the commercial banks were undertaking money transfer businesses as agents. Additionally, in order to make the money transfer business more competitive, the letter of intent was granted to 83 other firms to conduct this business directly as well as to act as agents.

Other policy initiatives have also been undertaken so that remittances could be directed through the banking channel. For instance, as per its Monetary Policy and Program for FY 2002/03, the NRB had arranged to provide 15 paisa per US dollar as commission to licensed private firms on top of the prevailing buying rate.[27] Moreover, permission was granted to manpower agencies, engaged in sending Nepalese nationals to work overseas, to open foreign currency account in the Nepalese commercial banks out of the foreign currency income that they realized under the prevailing rules.

As an increase in foreign employment generally leads to an increase in remittances, arrangement for employment is to be made by making the required provisions of training and loans to tackle the problem of unemployment by exploring foreign employment opportunities in FY 2005/06. Training programs that fall under the Council for Technical Education and Vocational Training, Ministry for Labor and Transport Management, Ministry of Industry, Commerce and Supplies and Ministry of Women, Children and Social Welfare would be undertaken to avoid duplication. These programs would be assessed to make them compatible to the requirements of foreign employment opportunities. Moreover, to further encourage foreign employment in FY 2005/06, provisions are to be made to provide loans from the commercial banks for those seeking overseas employment on the guarantee of Credit Guarantee Corporation.[28]

For FY 2005/06, continuity has been made to the arrangement of seed money for foreign employment loan programs targeted at providing loan for those seeking foreign employment. The program will bear up to 80 percent of the total expenditure incurred when seeking foreign employment.

Policy Options

Governments of labor-exporting countries have introduced a variety of schemes with these policy objectives in mind, namely (a) repatriable foreign exchange accounts to encourage the greater use of official channels, (b) foreign currency denominated bonds to encourage more use of financial assets in the home country[29], and (c) self-employment investment schemes to stimulate more direct investment in productive assets.

A favorable interest rate policy, a market-determined and realistic exchange rate and limited restrictions on withdrawals are also important. In building these products, policymakers should keep in mind that migrants and their families form a diverse group, ranging from white-collar workers to the illiterate and poor. Moreover, policies formulated to mobilize remittances should also be preceded by policies to promote other sources of foreign exchange to relieve the pressure on the foreign exchange pools and maintain stable exchange rates. Consistent interest rates should also be accompanied by policies to curb inflationary pressures.[30]

One of the biggest hurdles to private sector growth in Nepal is the paucity of credit for seed capital and working capital for enterprises, especially small and medium-size enterprises. Pooled remittances can provide such credit, thus supporting the growth of enterprises. Although residing abroad, many Nepalese migrants want to invest in enterprises in their home country, either to employ family members at home, earn additional income or to prepare for their retirement or eventual return. These types of investments on the part of remitters can lower poverty by expanding businesses in their home communities as well as generating jobs and income that would not otherwise exist.

To end this section, a few suggestions are made for improving the remittance market in terms of the roles to be played by each of the remittance market players: (a) remittance institutions, (b) public authorities; (c) civil society.[31]

Institutions conducting remitting business such as banks and money transfer companies should (a) disseminate all the information on total costs and transfer conditions, including all commissions and fees, foreign exchange rates applied, and execution time in a fully transparent way, (b) compete on the basis of fair and nondiscriminatory contractual arrangements and refrain from indulging in unfair pricing and applying high exchange rate margins, (c) use cost effective technology and deploy innovative platforms to slash costs, improve speed and security, and develop new products, (d) look for partnerships and alliances, including linkages between money transfer companies and financial institutions, in order to leverage capabilities and promote "cash to accounts" services, and other forms of financial intermediation, and e) deepen financial markets through inclusive and integrated services for remittance customers, such as current account services, savings, credit and mortgage products, among others.

The government and/or the NRB need to (a) facilitate remittance market and avoid attempts to tax, over-regulate or otherwise take actions that retard the remittances flow, (b) improve systems for collecting and reporting remittance market data and help to devise international standards for computing such data, (c) facilitate the mainstreaming of remittances into financial institutions by improving regulatory and financial sector frameworks, and (d) arouse awareness of the benefits of savings and other financial products.

The civil society and private sector organizations, on the other hand, should (a) systematically identify hurdles to leveraging the development impact of remittances, and engage and cooperate with all relevant stakeholders to address and eliminate such hurdles, and (b) support the social and financial inclusion of transnational families into their communities and build up innovative partnerships to promote training and domestic productive opportunities.

Conclusions

Remittances are potentially an important stimuli to economic growth. Despite the lack of accurate data on the real volume of funds transferred, there is ample evidence that remittance flows are substantial, stable relative to other forms of development finance, and well-targeted to vulnerable families, both as support during a crisis and as an income-smoothing mechanism.

In Nepal, during the last few years, remittances have been an important avenue of support for family members remaining at home. This has been partly the result of measures undertaken by the concerned officials to streamline financial systems, dismantling controls and creating incentives, with the aim of attracting remittances particularly through the official channel.

Economic growth, interest rate and exchange rate policies are crucial determinants of remittance inflows. In order to further encourage the inflow of remittances to the country through the official channel, it is imperative that the policies be conducive to these financial inflows.

Notes

1. These data taken from World Bank (2005) denote officially recorded remittances, which are sometimes estimated. Flows through informal channels, such as "hundi", are not captured in the official statistics but are assumed to be rather large.
2. The remittance flows to these countries are presented below:

(US$ billion)

Country	2001	2003
China	1.2	4.6
India	11.1	17.4
Mexico	9.9	14.6
Pakistan	1.5	4.0
Philippines	6.2	7.9

Source: World Bank (2005).

3. For instance, the Sea Island G-8 Summit in June 2004 called for better coherence and coordination of international organizations working to enhance remittance services and increase the development impact of remittance earnings. The World Bank, the IMF and the United Nations have constituted an interagency, intergovernmental technical group to improve remittance statistics. The Bank for International Settlements and the World Bank have set up a special task force on international retail payment systems to improve transparency in remittance transactions. Regional development banks, bilateral aid agencies and other international agencies have also begun ambitious programs to collect information and facilitate remittance flows.

4. It should be mentioned at the outset that internal remittances (defined as the money and/or goods sent to rural areas from urban areas by migrant workers) are equally important from a development perspective. For instance, Adams (1997) has demonstrated that in Pakistan while external remittances have a positive and significant impact on the accumulation of land, internal remittances have a significant and positive effect on the accumulation of agricultural capital. DeWind and Holdaway (2005) have also made a comprehensive analysis on the significance of internal remittances.
5. For an elaborated discussion, see Addison (2004) and Solimano (2003).
6. The NELM theory is examined in Stark and Bloom (1985).
7. For an extensive illustration on this issue, see Poirine (1997).
8. It should be noted that the theories pertaining to the motives for remittance transfers indicate that it is only in the altruistic case that there is a no "*quid pro quo*." Transfers take place solely out of concern for the family and fits into the standard definition of transfers in the BoP sense. The other motives behind transfers indicate that there may be a "*quid pro quo*" as in the case of implicit family contract, though this may not be immediate or binding.
9. For a comprehensive explanation, see Barham and Boucher (1998).
10. This aspect is delineated in Buch *et al.* (2002).
11. This has been illustrated by Chimhowu *et al.* (2005).
12. The "remittance decay" hypothesis indicates that the amount of remittances sent by migrants to their countries of origin declines through time. For details, see Greico (2004).
13. An example of such migrant associations is the Home Town Associations in the US, where organized migrants

from various Latin American countries such as El Salvador, Guatemala, Honduras, Mexico and the Dominican Republic come together and dispatch donations to finance investment for community projects in their home countries. For more on this, see Ellerman (2003).

14. Evidences from microeconomic surveys demonstrate that purchases of land, housing and other real assets, are the most common uses of remittances in the country of origin. In some instances, this led to ballooning prices of these real assets.
15. The Gulf war, for instance, put Jordan, Sudan and Yemen, among others, in difficulty owing to the massive return of emigrants. For details, see El-Sakka (1997).
16. This term is named for the economic effect on the Netherlands emanating from the discovery of natural gas in the North Sea. According to the Dutch Disease theory, the effects of capital inflows on resource allocation are traced through their effects on the real exchange rate. More precisely, it states that large inflows of capital can give rise to an appreciation of the real exchange rate and eventually a deterioration of the competitiveness of the sectors exposed to international competition, thus preventing the development of a dynamic export sector. For more on the Dutch Disease, refer to Bourdet and Falck (2004).
17. For details, see Chami *et al.* (2003).
18. The regulatory issues pertaining to remittances are discussed at length in Sander and Maimbo (2005).
19. Examples include regulations that require banks to operate full branches rather than allowing for less costly service points or restrictive licensing of money transfer operators that ties money transfer operator services exclusively to banks.
20. A historical perspective on foreign employment in Nepal is also provided by Singh (2006).

21. Since remittances are transmitted through different channels, it is an arduous task to capture the full amount in the BoP statistics. As a result, it is sometimes difficult to come up with strong and valid conclusions on the role of remittances in the economic development of the country.
22. Besides remittances, the other factors responsible for the decline in poverty included, among others, rise in agriculture wages, rise in non-agriculture wages and income, rise in urbanization and a drop in dependency ratio owing to a decline in fertility.
23. For instance, according to the Asian Development Bank (ADB), in FY 2003/04, the economic recovery was led by remittance-driven consumption expenditure. For details, see ADB (2005).
24. These causes have been discussed in detail by Seddon (2005).
25. The number of persons granted institutional permission for foreign employment was 121,769 in 2003/04. This figure was 139,696 for 2004/05. Country-wise data discloses that in 2004/05 Malaysia (47 percent) was the major destination for foreign employment followed by Qatar (30 percent) and Saudi Arabia (10 percent).
26. These policy measures are discussed in the next section.
27. See NRB (2002) for details on this incentive.
28. For details, see Ministry of Finance (2005).
29. For instance, foreign currency denominated bonds for development purposes were issued by the Egyptian Government to which Egyptians residing abroad were invited to subscribe on favorable terms and conditions. One of the most successful techniques to encourage formal remittances of hard currencies earned by emigrants was the introduction of a special import system called Own Exchange Import System (OEIS). As per this system, importers were provided an import permit if they were

able to demonstrate that they could provide the necessary foreign exchange on their own, that is, outside the official foreign exchange pool. The principal source of foreign exchange to the importers was the savings of emigrants. The OEIS was a very successful way of encouraging emigrants to utilize their savings to finance the country's needed imports from overseas. For more, see El-Sakka (1997).

30. In this context, domestic interest rates need to be quite competitive with those of the outside world. Lower interest rates in the country will provide incentives for the emigrants to put their savings abroad, or to direct their remittances towards non-productive uses with higher speculative intentions, such as investing in land and other real assets.
31. A list of suggestions is also delineated in Terry *et al.* (2005).

References

Adams, Richard H., Jr. (1997). "Remittances, Income Distribution and Rural Asset Accumulation." Available at: http://www.ifpri.org/fncd/dp/papers/dp17.

Addison, E.K.Y. (2004). "The Macroeconomic Impact of Remittances in Ghana." Available at: http://www.eldis.org/static/Doc/16957.htm

Asian Development Bank (ADB) (2005). *Asian Development Outlook 2005: Promoting Competition for Long-Term Development*. Manila: ADB.

Barham, B. and S. Boucher (1998). "Migration, Remittances and Inequality: Estimating the Net Effects of Migration on Income Distribution." *Journal of Development Economics*. 16:2.

Bourdet, Yves and Hans Falck (2004). "Emigrants' Remittances and Dutch Disease in Cape Verde." Available at: http://www.virtualcapeverde.net/news2/modules/ Downloads/ docs/emigration_dutch_disease.pdf

Buch, M. Claudia, Anja Kuckulenz and Marie-Helene Le Manchec (2002). "Worker Remittances and Capital Flows." *Kiel Working Paper*. No. 1130.

Central Bureau of Statistics (2004). *Nepal Living Standards Survey 2003/04*. Kathmandu: Central Bureau of Statistics.

Chami, R., Connel Fullenkamp and Samir Jahajah (2003). "Are Immigrant Remittance Flows a Source of Capital for Development?" *IMF Working Paper*. WP//03/189. Washington, D.C.: IMF.

Chimhowu, Admos O., Jenifer Piesse and Caroline Pinder (2005). "The Socioeconomic Impact of Remittances on Poverty Reduction." In Samuel Munzele Maimbo and Dilip Ratha, eds., *Remittances: Development Impact and Future Prospects*. Washington, D.C.: The World Bank.

DeWind, Josh and Jennifer Holdaway (2005). "Internal and International Migration in Economic Development." Available at: http://www.un.org/esa/population/ publications

Ellerman, D. (2003). "Policy Research on Migration and Development." *World Bank Policy Research Working Paper*. No. 3117. August.

El-Sakka, M.I.T. (1997). "Migration Remittances: Policy Options of Host Countries and Countries of Origin." Available at: http://www.cba.edu.kw/elsakka

Grieco, Elizabeth (2004). "Will Migrant Remittances Continue Through Time? A New Answer to an Old Question." *International Journal on Multicultural Societies* 6(2): 243-252. Available at: http://www.unesco.org/shs/ijms/vol6/issue2/art3

International Monetary Fund (IMF) (2005). *Balance of Payments Statistics Yearbook, 2005*. Washington, D.C.: IMF.

Ministry of Finance (2005). "Public Statement on Income and Expenditure of Fiscal Year 2005-06." Ministry of Finance: Kathmandu.

Nepal Rastra Bank (NRB) (2005). *Quarterly Economic Bulletin*. Kathmandu: NRB.

NRB (2004). *Monetary Policy and Program for FY 2004/05*. Kathmandu: NRB.

NRB (2002). *Monetary Policy and Program for FY 2002/03*. Kathmandu: NRB.

Poirine, Bernard (1997). "A Theory of Remittances as an Implicit Family Loan Arrangement." *World Development*. 25(4): 589-611.

Ratha, Dilip. (2005). "Workers' Remittances: An Important and Stable Source of External Source of External Development Finance." In Samuel Munzele Maimbo and Dilip Ratha, eds., *Remittances: Development Impact and Future Prospects*. Washington, D.C.: The World Bank.

Sander, Cerstin and Samuel Munzele Maimbo. 2005. "Migrant Remittances in Africa: A Regional Perspective." In Maimbo, Samuel Munzele Maimbo and Dilip Ratha, eds., *Remittances: Development Impact and Future Prospects*. Washington, D.C.: The World Bank.

Seddon, David, Jagannath Adhikari and Ganesh Gurung (2000). "Foreign Labor Migration and the Remittance Economy of Nepal." Final

Report Submitted to DFID. Overseas Development Group. Norwich: University of East Anglia. July.

Singh, Pranab (2006). "Remittance Economy." *Himal South Asian*. 18(5). March-April.

Solimano, A. (2003). "Workers Remittances to the Andean Region: Mechanisms, Costs and Development Impact." Mimeo.

Stark, Oded and David E. Bloom (1985). "The New Economics of Labor Migration." *American Economic Review*. 75(2): 173-178.

Taylor, J. Edward (2002). "Do Government Programs "Crowd In" Remittances? Inter-American Dialogue and the Tomas Riveria Research Institute. Available at http://www.iaidalog.org/publications/taylor.htm

Terry, Donald F., Steven Wilson and Pedro De Vasconcelos (2005). "Improving the Development Impact of Remittances." Available in: http://www.un.org/esa/population/ publications/ittmigdev2005/P10

World Bank (2005). *Global Development Finance: Managing Finance and Managing Vulnerability*. Washington, D.C.: The World Bank.

28

Recession and Remittances*

Introduction

The global recession appears to be getting worse rather than better. There are few signs of improvement. What is clear is that it is threatening countries all over the world. Around the world lay-offs and closures, bail outs and unemployment are the order of the day. The Nepalese economy would also be affected through reduced remittances from workers. At first there was hope that while the rate of growth of these remittances may decelerate, the remittances would be around what it has been in the last few years or slightly less. This expectation is diminishing as stories of layoffs of workers keep flowing in. Against this perspective, this article examines the recent trends in global remittances followed by the impact of the global recession on remittance inflows to Nepal. Some policy prescriptions are provided at the end.

Global Trends

International migration has an impact on the socio-economic conditions of both labor-sending and labor-receiving countries. There exists virtually no country that does not contribute to international labor migration either as a receiving country, sending country or country of transit. In recent years the issue of international migration has gained increased importance reflecting the impact of globalization and the explosive growth in the information and communications technology.

Correspondingly, international migrant remittances have become an important source of external finance in developing

---

* *Nepalese Economic Review*, 1(3): 98-105, June 2009.

countries. Evidence shows that for any given trade balance, positive remittances improve the current account and thus the external balance of a country. They can impact the domestic interest rate, foreign exchange rate as well as the credit-worthiness and external financing position of a country. Remittances are a source of income, consumption and investment for the recipient families, and can reduce poverty and raise spending on health and education.

According to recent World Bank estimates, in nominal dollar terms, recorded remittances sent home by migrants from developing countries reached $305 billion in 2008, a rise by about 15 percent from $265 billion in 2007. In real terms, however, remittance flows to developing countries fell from 2 percent of GDP in 2007 to 1.9 percent in 2008 and is projected to amount to 1.8 percent of GDP in 2009.

After robust growth for many years, remittance flows to developing countries, which doubled between 2002 and 2007, began to slow down in the third quarter of 2008. Because of the global economic recession, this slowdown is expected to deepen further in 2009 for the first time since the Asian financial crisis of 1997. Some migrants may lose their jobs and return to their countries of origin, but the more important impact of the recession on migration may be a slowdown in the deployment of new workers, especially to the higher-wage European and Gulf oil-exporting countries as well as to the East Asian countries such as Malaysia and Korea. Some sectors and corridors are expected to be more affected by the crisis, such as construction-related remittances moving from the Gulf States to South Asia.

Although there has been a slowdown in the level of remittances in 2008, the figures are not alarming for the short term. Several factors can be cited for the resilience of remittance flows during economic downturns. Remittances are sent by the cumulated flows of migrants over the years, not only by the new migrants of the last year or two. This makes it persistent over a longer period of time. If migration stops over a course of a decade or so, remittances then will stop growing. Again, remittances are a relatively small part of migrants' incomes, so they can continue to send even when hit by external shock. Remittances are economic responsibilities of migrants to their families and will not cease even under extreme economic duress. However, one cannot overlook the fact that migrant workers are one of the hardest hit by the economic downturn.

According to the World Bank, the environment for remittance flows to developing countries in 2009 and 2010 appears uncertain for four main reasons: (1) the economic slowdown in the high income OECD destination countries including the US and Western Europe (which constitute almost two-third of remittance flows to developing countries); (2) impact of the financial crisis on developing countries (which comprise half of migrants from developing countries); (3) impact of a fall in oil prices on the economies of the Gulf Cooperation Council (GCC) countries, a prime destination of migrants from developing countries in South Asia; and (4) volatility in exchange rates.

Remittance Trends of Nepal

In the Nepalese context, until the 1990s, most of the studies on Nepal emphasized the importance of agriculture in the national economy. It was only after the 1990s that policy makers began to realize the significance of paid employment outside the country for the livelihoods of the households. These changes also coincided with the present phase of globalization. Currently, one of Nepal's major exports is labor, and most rural households now rely on at least one member's earnings from foreign employment.

Again, due to the worsening political conflict and the shrinking job opportunities, the pace of foreign employment had, until recently, dramatically increased. In recent months, however, there seems to be a deceleration in the number of people going abroad for employment, largely attributed to the effect of the global recession. Although the number of workers going abroad for employment increased by almost 13 percent in 2007/08 as compared to 2006/07, on a monthly basis, in the ninth month of 2008/09, the number of Nepali foreign job-seekers dropped to 12,313 from 18,685 in the eighth month and 20,543 in the seventh month. The major destinations have been Malaysia, Qatar, Saudi Arabia and United Arab Emirates.

In the first eight months of 2008/09, workers' remittances aggregated Rs. 131.01 billion, a rise of 58.9 percent compared to the corresponding period of the previous year. This upsurge in remittances has led to a surplus of Rs. 28.94 billion in the current account, thereby strengthening the overall balance of payments (BoP) position. Consequently, the BoP is in significant surplus equivalent to Rs. 34.81 billion and the gross foreign exchange reserves are adequate for financing merchandize imports of 12.3 months and merchandize and service imports of 9.9 months as at mid-March 2009.

Similarly, the remittances to GDP ratio increased from 10.3 percent in 2001/02 to 17.4 percent in 2007/08. These figures clearly demonstrate that any significant decline in receipts from remittances could disturb the structure of the economy from the macro level. Thus, the notion that countries that have not fully opened up the capital account are less prone to adverse effect of the current financial crisis can be justified by the current development in the Nepalese economy.

Impact of Recession

So far, the data demonstrates that global recession has had a negligible impact on remittances. In Nepal's case, however, it should be noted that when unemployed Nepali migrants are forced to return home, this has led to a temporary boost to remittances as they repatriate their accumulated savings.

However, if the recession prolongs, foreign employment and remittances may be affected in the medium term. Of recently, taking a cue from the global economic meltdown, the Gulf countries, major markets for Nepali migrant workers, have started reducing workforce strength especially unskilled hands and those working in manufacturing and service sectors. A case in point is the government of United Arab Emirates which has decided to cut the number of foreign workers by 45 percent. Even the World Bank estimates that remittances from the Gulf region could decline by 9 percent in dollar terms in 2009, compared to a rise of 38 percent in the previous year. Again, the announcement by the Malaysian government to stop recruitment of foreign workers in the textile and services sector would also affect Nepal's labor market. Likewise, from February 2009, the Government of the Republic of Korea stopped issuing new visas to temporary migrant workers under the Employment Permit System. In Thailand, the government announced that it would not issue new work permits or renew the work permits of about half a million foreign workers in the hope that they leave the territory and that their jobs are taken up by Thai nationals.

Job losses continue to predominate, particularly in employment sectors sensitive to economic cycles such as construction and manufacturing, as well as financial services, retail and travel/tourism-related services, hence affecting migrants in these sectors. These job losses have been reported in many parts of the globe. In some countries (such as Malaysia and Singapore), deliberate policies have been formulated encouraging employers to retrench migrant workers first and/or to replace them with unemployed nationals.

All of these would have a detrimental impact on the Nepalese economy. With the rise in unemployment and the decline in remittances inflows to Nepal, there would be a reduction in household consumption and cutbacks in public spending. Spending on basic necessities such as food, electricity, medicine and schools fees would also decline. Moreover, the recession in the US, EU and other countries where the spillover effects of the current crisis have been observed will have an adverse impact on Nepal's external sector in the medium term.

Policy Measures Undertaken

The Nepal Rastra Bank (NRB) introduced measures for promoting foreign employment and encouraging the inflow of remittances through the official channel. Some of these measures, initiated prior to the onset of global economic recession, are summarized below.

A provision was made to include the commercial banks' loan of up to Rs. 100,000 per head for the individuals wishing to go abroad for foreign employment under the category of deprived sector credit. Likewise, an arrangement was made with the joint initiative of the NRB and Reserve Bank of India for remitting funds from India to Nepal through the National Electronic Fund Transfer (NEFT) system. Remittances could be sent through any of 40,000 NEFT enabled bank branches in India which would then be disbursed to beneficiary in Nepal through local commercial bank branches and money transfer agencies.

The NRB is monitoring the remittances data very scrupulously so that appropriate policies can be formulated in advance to withstand any adverse impact on the country's external stability. In this light, a circular was issued by the NRB to the commercial banks and money transfer companies to provide country-wise data on remittances on a monthly basis.

On the Government's part, to tackle the adverse impact on foreign employment and remittances, it formulated a consultation mechanism between the Foreign Ministry and Ministry of Labor and Transport Management at the Secretary Level; it also gave instructions to the diplomatic missions abroad to monitor and assess the situation regularly.

Focus Areas

Although the global recession, if protracted, would have a negative impact on foreign employment and remittances, it is exigent to continue to accord priority on formulating and implementing concrete measures for promoting foreign employment and remittances. Nepal should push ahead with effective economic diplomacy and relationship management through its foreign missions so as to minimize the adverse effects of job losses. The government's policy to provide a labor attaché to a country with more than 5,000 Nepali workers needs to be broadened to include more countries.

The role of Nepalese missions in labor receiving-countries needs to be redefined, with priority being given to the protection of the rights of migrant workers. Labor attachés and concerned officers at the missions who deal with Nepalese workers should undergo orientation training before they take up their assignments abroad. There is also a need of a sound inter-ministry coordination especially between the Ministry of Labor and Transport Management and the Ministry of Foreign Affairs and its missions in different countries.

Human capital should be developed in accordance with the demands of the international labor market and this should constitute an integral part of the overseas employment process in Nepal. Again, the country needs to devise mechanisms for encouraging retention and absorption of return migration of its workers. Returning migrants, particularly qualified workers, bring back knowledge and experience, thus converting "brain drain" into "brain circulation."

A national policy of remittances could build up the framework under which the endeavors of the NRB, Department of Labor and Employment Promotion, poverty alleviation agencies and the Ministry of Foreign Affairs, could be aggregated and coordinated towards the attainment of common goals. This policy could support in placing the topic of remittances on the national development agenda, particularly in a country like Nepal where remittances to GDP ratio is quite high.

Conclusion

A decline in remittances would make a serious dent on the BoP. It is the reality that when people go to different countries for work, their per capita earnings would increase, and, as a result, it would multiply the inflow of remittances. For Nepal, to reap the benefits from this great potential remains a challenge, especially in the present context of global economic recession.

References

Pant, Bhubanesh (2009). "If the Money Should Stop." *The Kathmandu Post.* 17 March.

Pant, Bhubanesh (2008). "Mobilizing Remittances for Productive Use: A Policy-oriented Approach." *NRB Working Paper*. NRB/WP/4. December.

Ratha, Dilip and Sanket Mohapatra (2009). "Revised Outlook for Remittance Flows 2009-2011." *Migration and Development Brief 9.* 23 March.

Seddon, David. (2005). "Nepal's Dependence in Exporting Labor." Available at: http://www.migrationinformation.org/Profiles/display

World Bank (2008). "Global Financial Crisis: Implications for South Asia." Washington, D.C.: World Bank. 21 October.

World Bank (2006). *Global Economic Prospects: Economic Implications of Remittances and Migration*. Washington, D.C: World Bank.

29

Harnessing Remittances for Productive Use in Nepal*

Background

Since the end of the 1990s, there has been a renewed interest in the financial resources that migrants send back to their countries of origin. The main reason for the renewed attention is the growing volume of official remittances to low income countries and their potential contribution to the economic development of the receiving regions.

According to IMF (2009: 272), remittances denote "household income from foreign economies arising mainly from the temporary or permanent movement of people to those economies. Remittances include cash and noncash items that flow through formal channels, such as *via* electronic wire, or through informal channels, such as money or goods carried across borders. They largely consist of funds and non-cash times sent or given by individuals who have migrated to a new economy and become residents there, and the net compensation of border, seasonal, or other short-term workers who are employed in an economy in which they are not residents."[1]

Until the global financial crisis of 2007-09, remittances had proven to be a dependable source of income for households in developing economies, with robust growth regardless of the state of the business cycle. However, as the real-sector spillovers from the financial crisis were quite severe, and had a deleterious effect on developed and energy-exporting countries, total remittances dropped in 2009 for the first time in decades. The World Bank

---

* *Economic Review*, 22: 1-20, April 2011.

estimated that remittance flows to developing countries reached US$ 307 billion in 2009, a decline by 5.5 percent in contrast to the growth of 16.7 percent in 2008. Because of improved prospects for the global economy, however, remittance flows to developing countries are expected to rise by 6.0 percent in 2010 and 6.2 percent in 2011 (Mohapatra *et al.*, 2010).

Remittance, as a source of development funding, are directly linked to migration. In many instances, particularly in the vulnerable countries, this migration has been forced either by civil conflict, political persecution or economic hardships. For people from the least developed countries (LDCs), migration is often a case of running away from a very difficult situation, rather than a matter of preference. The irony of it is that having escaped their countries, migrants then assist in sustaining the economies of those very countries through remittances.

Remittances can contribute significantly to local, regional and national economic development in migrant-sending countries and also play an instrumental role in reducing poverty as they flow mainly to poor and marginalized families. In many instances, remittances form a significant percentage of total household income, acting as a substitute for earned income lost to unemployment, illness, retirement, emigration, falling wages and crop failure, among others, and ultimately protect poor families against the erosion of what are already basic household assets.

Remittances can also contribute to stability by lowering the probability of current account reversals. Since they are a cheap and stable source of foreign currencies, remittances are likely to stem investor panic when international reserves are taking a downward trend or external debt is rising.[2]

A significant portion of relevant literature on remittances argues that they are primarily spent on consumption, housing and land, and are not utilized for productive investment that would contribute to long-run development. In this context, the distinction between "productive and non-productive" uses of remittances needs to be reexamined. The recognition that only a small proportion of remittances are utilized to establish small businesses, improve agricultural practices, or on other forms of "productive" investment created disillusionment over the development impact of remittances among researchers and policy makers in the 1970s and 1980s. In recent years, the distinction between consumption and investment has been criticized by researchers that expenditure on 'consumption' items such as health and education should be understood as investment in human capital. As an example, in both the short and long run, investment in education denotes an improvement of the educational infrastructure of the labor exporting economy. Migrants, in combination with high productive physical capital, yield returns that are normally much higher than they would have been if the migrants were employed in their home country. The migrants' family members that stay behind in their home country, enjoy a higher standard of living through the migrants' savings. Hence, expenditure on consumption and housing produces indirect multiplier effects, which encourage investment and output in related industries. Thus, making a distinction between the productive and unproductive remittances seems quite blur, and both contribute to livelihoods and development, with productive uses contributing more.

Based on the above analysis, the major thrust of this study is to recommend measures for the productive use of remittances. The rest of this paper is planned as follows. The next section examines some general policy measures for utilizing remittances productively followed by the experiences of South Asian countries. Nepal's experiences are then examined along with the impact of the growing remittances on the economy as well as some measures initiated for attracting more remittances through the official channel. Before concluding, some policy alternatives for mobilizing remittances for productive use are spelled out.

General Policy Measures

There are a few policy instruments the government can employ to improve development impact of remittances and enhance the flow through the formal channel. Which policy instruments the government opts depends on the desired goal it intends to achieve. First, if the government's objective is to capture a portion of remittances for development purposes, then the policy instrument could be to impose taxes or levies on remittance transfers, or to explore voluntary check-off for charitable purposes. However, taxing remittances may be counterproductive as this could redirect remittances from the formal channels to informal channels, thus, worsening the balance of payments (BoP). Second, if the government's objective is to stimulate transfers through formal channels and to stimulate capital availability, then the policy instruments could focus on the sale of remittance bonds, opening of foreign currency accounts, premium interest rate accounts, promoting transfers through microfinance institutions, promoting financial literacy, and banking the unbanked. Foreign currency accounts and bonds have proven to be a feasible technique of raising funds. This should be targeted at the Diasporas' middle-to-upper income members.[3] Moreover, if the goal is to stimulate investment of remittances, then the government could reach out to remittance receivers through microfinance infrastructures. The government could also reach out to its migrants abroad through migrants' service bureaus and tax breaks on imported capital goods by migrants.

Since a long time, governments of migrants' home countries have employed a large variety of policy measures that target different elements in the system. Multilateral agencies such as the World Bank and the IMF and bilateral development agencies such as the Department for International Development of the UK have also analyzed different policy options and recommendations. Based on this array of experiences, a list of policy measures, including the ones mentioned earlier, is illustrated in Table 1.

Table 1: Policy Measures to Enhance the Development Impact of Remittances

Objective	Measure
Capturing a share of remittances for development purposes	Taxation of emigrants Duties or levies on remittance transfers Voluntary check-off for charitable purposes (or transfer forms)
Stimulating transfers through formal channels and/or stimulating capital availability	Remittance bonds Foreign currency accounts Premium interest rate accounts Promoting/enabling transfers through microfinance institutions (MFIs) Promoting financial literacy/banking the unbanked
Stimulating investment of remittances	Outreach through MFI infrastructure Outreach through migrants' service bureaus Tax breaks on imported capital goods SME schemes (financial, infrastructural, or innovative) Training programs
Outreach to migrant collectives/ Hometown Associations (HTAs)	Matched funding Public-private ventures Competitive bidding for development projects
Influencing consumption patterns	Promoting consumption of local goods & services Enabling migrants to spend on their relatives' behalf

Source: Carling (2004).

A few examples as how to tap the skills of the Diasporas are discussed in Box 1 below.

Box 1

Tapping the Diaspora

Efforts have been undertaken to tap the skills, networks, funds and savings of the Diaspora population. The Chinese Diaspora and Indian information-technology specialists have either reinvested in their countries of origin or have gone home to set up their own businesses; some have even established a commercial presence in other countries. Other government initiatives targeted at assisting the reintegration of returning migrant workers and stimulating investment include the provision of facilities for importing capital goods and raw materials, business counselling and training, access to loans, and encouraging entrepreneurship for development.

Sending governments could consider the following mechanisms to mitigate the adverse effects of brain drain: requiring migrants to perform public service for critical occupations such as those relating to health care and education; bearing a partial cost of their education if they do not complete the mandatory domestic employment requirement; and encouraging return migration by acknowledging their training abroad and giving them visiting scholar positions or other honorary positions and encouraging them to serve as trainers.

Other examples include arrangements requiring some compensation from host countries for every foreign worker taken in; exploring the possibility of inviting some of their own experts, practitioners and specialists to conduct training on the advances in the field on a regular, short-term basis as a form of compensating for the loss of skilled workers; and establishing a special visa scheme to ensure the temporariness of the workers' employment and stay in the host country, thus ensuring return migration.

Source: Puri (2007)

To pinpoint possible policy options for augmenting the benefits of remittances, it is important to take into account the links between remittance usage now, and development and consumption in the future (Figure 1). In this model, "development" denotes remittance-independent development, that is, future livelihoods that are not dependent on future remittances.

Figure 1: A Model of Remittance Use and Development Impact

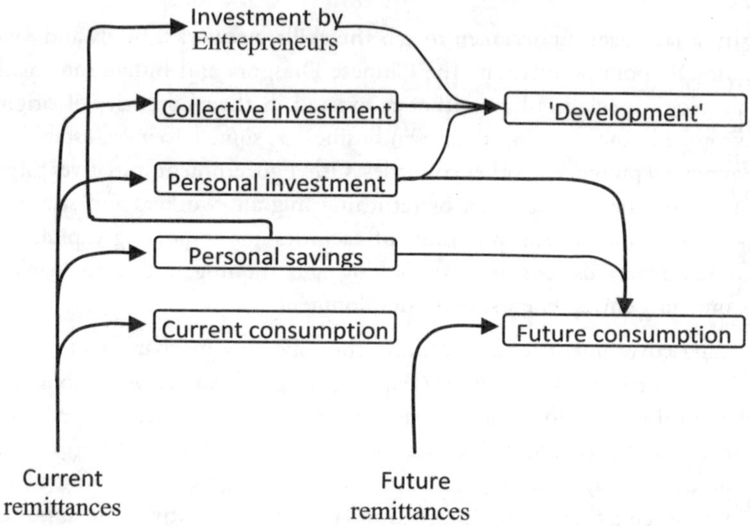

Source: Carling (2005).

If remittances today are just spent on consumption, future consumption needs to be financed by future remittances (or other sources of income). However, if remittances are saved or used for investment, this could assist in financing future consumption. Collective investment in development projects will not result in direct future returns to the individual investors; however, this would directly benefit the community. When remittances are saved in financial institutions, this augments credit availability and can enable entrepreneurs to realize investments that have a positive impact on development. This could be a more realistic way of stimulating investment of remittances than promotion of entrepreneurship by migrants or remittance receivers themselves.[4]

Policies in South Asia

It is growingly acknowledged in South Asia that foreign labor migration helps promote national economic growth, eases the pressure of unemployment, brings in much-needed foreign exchange through remittances and increases consumption, savings and investment at both the household and macro levels.

The Governments of Bangladesh, India, Pakistan and Sri Lanka have devised a legal framework encouraging their citizens to send foreign remittances into their countries of origin. Generally, the non-resident citizens of these countries are granted the following facilities, among others: a) maintenance of bank accounts in both foreign and local currencies without tax implications; b) investments in securities/shares, and deposits with local firms/companies; and c) investments in immovable properties in the respective countries. Again, most of the South Asian Governments have established special institutions such as migrant workers' welfare funds and have appointed community welfare officers/attaché in embassies in the receiving countries to promote and protect the interest of migrant workers.

India witnessed an upsurge in returns and investments of its Diaspora population especially after 2006 when it introduced registration certificates called Overseas Citizens of India for persons of Indian origin. They are analogous to green cards, and allow non-resident Indians (NRIs) most of the benefits of citizenship while maintaining their foreign passports. They cannot, however, obtain an Indian passport, vote in Indian elections, own agricultural and plantation properties in India or work for the Indian government. Incentives for returnees include attractive job opportunities, particularly in the areas of software and other information-technology-related jobs, finance, telecommunications, pharmaceuticals and research and development. Many programs have also been launched to attract NRI intellectuals and professors to Indian universities.

India has a wide-ranging package of activities and incentives that accords top priority to building stronger links with its Diaspora communities. These are all orchestrated by the Ministry of Overseas Indian Affairs that was set up in 2004. This Ministry seeks to persuade its Diaspora to invest in long-term ventures, rather than just sending wire transfers and short-term remittances. For meeting this goal, the Government in 2008 launched an Overseas Indian Facilitation Centre, a one-stop shop to help overseas Indians invest in India. Some other initiatives being undertaken by this Ministry include the following:

- Setting up an ICT-driven Diaspora Knowledge Network to draw on India's Diaspora knowledge resources as well as to provide impetus to projects in the Public–Private Partnership mode.
- Establishing a single window for overseas Indian investments to function as a single point of contact.
- Operationalizing the electronic remittance facility for overseas Indians that combines the qualities of economy, speed and convenience.
- Launching the scholarship program for children of overseas Indians to study in India.
- Expanding the Know India program so that the Diaspora youth would gain knowledge about India.
- Fully operationalizing a new Overseas Citizenship of India scheme (UNCTAD, 2009).

Because of these and other facilities provided to its non-resident citizens, India has been able to attract enormous remittances from their respective non-resident citizens and has been the world's top remittance earner for more than a decade. It was the largest recipient in 2009 with US$ 55.0 billion, followed by China at US$ 48 billion and Mexico with US$ 26 billion (Mohapatra *et al.*, 2010). This figure of US$ 55.0 billion was up 7 percent from US$ 51.6 billion in 2008, and just two billion dollars a year in the late 1980s.

The rise in remittances in 2009 came despite the global economic slowdown which had been expected to affect migrant labor. The Reserve Bank of India attributed the higher remittances to India to a rise in interest rates on non-resident deposits and new investment products.

Other factors have also been responsible for the surge in remittances to India. The Government of India eased regulations and controls, eliminated the black-market premium on the rupee, and created convenient remittances services. The Indian and international banks systematically shifted some remittances from the informal "hundi" channels to formal channels. Indians abroad also responded to several attractive deposit schemes and bonds offered at home. Again, the Indian Investment Centre devised mechanisms that assist Indian companies to collaborate with NRIs (see Box 2).

Box 2

Indian Diaspora's Investment Potential

To facilitate the development of enterprises in India, the Indian Investment Centre developed mechanisms that enable Indian companies to collaborate with NRIs to identify sources of capital and technology. The agency maintains an industrial information service that provides the status of industries and profiles for potential industrial projects. Furthermore, the agency's website provides nonresident Indians with answers to an expansive list of investment questions on bank accounts, repatriation of profits, and investments in securities, shares, company deposits, and property. The site also offers special facilities to NRI investors repatriating funds.

Source: Azad (2005).

With regard to Bangladesh, the Bangladeshis working abroad sent home a record US$ 10.7 billion in 2009, as remittances continued to scale new heights despite the global meltdown. This figure was 19.4 percent higher than what the country's more than six million workers had remitted in 2008.

To ensure productive use of remittances, the government, Bangladesh Bank and Schedule Banks designed a number of savings and investment schemes for wage earners abroad. These included the following:

- A migrant can open a non-resident foreign currency deposit account in any branch of Bangladeshi and foreign banks that possess an authorized dealership license. The account can be opened for different periods, are renewable and can be maintained for an indefinite period even after the return of the wage earner.

- The remittances of Bangladeshi migrants abroad can be invested in Bangladeshi currency in five-year wage-earner's development bond which is also renewable. The profits are investable in Bangladesh and principal is freely transferable abroad in foreign currency.
- US Dollar Premium Bond and US Dollar Investment Bond are also available at attractive interest rates.
- The non-resident Bangladeshis are granted permission to invest in "Industrial Development Bond" scheme of the Agrani Bank, one of the nationalized banks of Bangladesh.
- A non-resident Bangladeshi can purchase shares in both primary and secondary markets including the debentures of Bangladeshi companies. A 10 percent reserve quota has been fixed for a non-resident Bangladeshi in initial public offering (IPO) of the local companies.
- Foreign investors including the non-resident Bangladeshi do not require any approval to set up a new industrial unit, but only have to be registered with the Board of Investment (BOI). They receive priority in obtaining industrial facilities like procurement of land, electricity, gas and sewerage connections, import of capital machinery and raw material and tax rebate, among others.

Another aspect that calls for discussion in the case of Bangladesh is the Migrant Welfare Fund (MWF) that was set up from the subscription charges levied on migrants before they leave the country. Passport renewal fees and attestation fees also accumulate in the MWF. Some of the aims of the Fund include the following: a) provision of hostel-cum-briefing centre for the prospective migrants; b) provision of orientation briefing; c) welfare desk at Dhaka Airport; d) burial of dead bodies and providing help to the family of the deceased; e) providing assistance and treatment to the handicapped laborers; and f) establishment of clubs in destination countries.[5]

In Bangladesh, the institutional mechanisms for dealing with remittances are quite exhaustive and have performed their tasks efficiently (Box 3). In order to disseminate the information pertaining to the available remittance services, savings and investment options to the migrants in host countries effectively and timely, the following communication channels have been employed: a) pre-departure briefings for migrant workers by the government's Bureau of Manpower Employment and Training (BMET); b) migrant worker briefings in social events and meetings in host countries, supported by the labor wings of embassies of Bangladesh; c) press releases/advertisements in print and electronic media channels popular with the migrant workers in host countries and also in Bangladesh for information of families/beneficiaries of migrant workers; d) information booklets/brochures/pamphlets in hard copy made available through banks in Bangladesh and their clearing arrangement counterparts abroad; and e) websites of the government, central banks, commercial banks and embassies abroad.

As Bangladesh is one of the pioneers in issues involving micro-finance and micro-credit schemes on the one hand, and the successful implementation of linking microfinance institution (MFIs) to remittances in other countries on the other, MFIs involvement in remittances in Bangladesh has been one of the most promising approaches for maximizing the development impact of remittances. MFIs in Bangladesh have operated as distribution agents in remote areas, and administered schemes which support the utilization of remittances for savings and investments for development.[6] This experience of Bangladesh could be emulated by LDCs such as Nepal.

Box 3

Managing Overseas Employment in Bangladesh

There are five government ministries dealing with international labor migration in Bangladesh, the Ministry of Expatriates' Welfare and Overseas Employment being the principal one. The others include the Ministries of Home Affairs, Foreign Affairs, Finance and Civil Aviation, and Tourism. The Bureau of Manpower, Employment and Training (BMET) is the executing agency of the Ministry of Expatriates' Welfare and Overseas Employment in charge of processing labor migration. In particular, the BMET is responsible for a wide range of functions, including control and regulation of recruiting agents, collection and analysis of labor market information, registration of job seekers for local and foreign employment, development and implementation of training programs in response to specific labor needs for national and international labor markets, and resolving legal disputes among key stakeholders.

The government enacted an Overseas Employment Policy in 2006 with the main objectives to: (i) ensure opportunities at reasonable cost for both short-term and long-term migration; (ii) enhance migration opportunities for the skilled and professionals; (iii) manage the recruitment process efficiently; (iv) encourage remittances through formal channels; (v) encourage long-term and short-term migrants to invest in Bangladesh; (vi) assist returning migrants in social and economic reintegration within the country; and (vii) arrange coordination work among related institutions.

Source: Raihan *et al.* (2009)

Meanwhile, Pakistan registered a high level of remittance inflows equivalent to US$ 7.8 billion in 2009, a rise by 21.1 percent compared to the inflows of US$ 6.5 billion a year earlier. A number of factors were responsible for this state of affairs including the return of some of the expatriates, diversion of remittances partially from informal to formal channels, and increased outreach of the banking sector.

In Pakistan, a number of incentives were announced in 2001 reflecting the significance that the government placed on remittances as an instrument for economic development. Linked to a minimum remitted amount (US$ 2,500 to US$ 10,000), overseas Pakistanis were provided privileged access to higher education, public housing and share offerings as well as free renewal of passports and import duty exemption for US$ 700 per year.

Pakistan introduced a "non-repatriable investment scheme" under which overseas Pakistanis were permitted to import machinery and equipment at concessionary rates of duty to establish manufacturing enterprises. The rate of duty rebate varied, that is, projects in relatively underdeveloped areas were granted a higher rate of rebate. The Investment Advisory Service of Pakistan conducted pre-feasibility studies to facilitate the choice of investment projects. Pakistani migrant workers were also permitted to invest in export processing zones (EPZs) which enjoyed complete duty exemptions on machinery and raw material imports.

In order to provide an ownership structure in Pakistan for remittance facilitation, State Bank of Pakistan, Ministry of Overseas Pakistanis and Ministry of Finance jointly launched the Pakistan Remittance Initiative (PRI) on 22 August 2009. The objective of PRI is facilitating and supporting faster, cheaper, convenient and efficient flow of remittances. The PRI focused on providing information about the remittance channels and other facilities to overseas Pakistanis.

Remittances to Sri Lanka, on the other hand, increased by 14 percent to US$ 3.3 billion in 2009 compared to 2008. This increase in remittances was ascribed to the information and financial education provided by the Sri Lanka Bureau of Foreign Employment.

Sri Lanka was the first labor-exporting country in Asia to introduce an entrepreneurship development program for return migrants. The main objective of the program, launched in 1982 by the Sri Lankan Ministry of Labor in collaboration with the Merchant Bank of Sri Lanka, was guiding returning migrants in business creation. Many lessons were learnt from this initiative. First of all, return migrants belonging to higher occupational categories were suitable for an orientation program of this type. Secondly, it was realized that the possibilities for guiding candidates into business were limited unless accompanied by steps to facilitate the access to capital. Three, the ability to identify and develop a project, together with managerial skills needed to run a business, could not be imparted just through a program of class instruction.[7]

The government also made it mandatory for those going abroad for employment to open non-residential foreign currency accounts. Again, Sri Lankan domestic aides working in West Asian countries were sent for employment only after signing a legal employment agreement. Moreover, the efforts of the government authorities to hold talks with the labor authorities abroad had made it possible to get salary increments for domestic aides in the respective countries.

In Sri Lanka, the Government attempted to encourage investment and long-term financial planning by return migrant workers by offering different types of credit schemes. The credit schemes did not focus solely on investment, but also catered to other identified needs of migrant workers, making them more realistic in application.

Nepal's Experiences

Nepalese workers have sought foreign employment as both the agricultural and non-agricultural sectors struggle to generate new employment opportunities. With limited arable land, landlessness is pervasive and the number of landless households has steadily increased in the agricultural sector. In the nonagricultural sector, the slowdown in growth, especially since 2000/01, due to the Maoist insurgency and exogenous shocks has further retarded the pace of employment creation. The conflict had also, until recently, created difficult living and security conditions, especially in the rural areas.[8] It had also prompted people to look for overseas employment.

India has been a traditional destination for Nepalese migrants. The primary reasons for this are geographical proximity, historical and cultural links, and a large and open porous border. The 1950 Treaty of Peace and Friendship between India and Nepal formalized free border movement of the people. The bulk of these migrants are employed in the private, informal sector. These migrants hold semi-skilled and unskilled jobs in restaurants and factories or are employed as domestic workers, security guards, and maids. However, a significant proportion of the remittances from India are not recorded in the BoP as they are brought in by the migrants themselves or sent through relatives and friends.

An increasingly larger share of remittances now comes from countries other than India, reflecting changing migration patterns and higher earnings in these locations. Moreover, the composition of skills of the labor flows is different among destinations. While migrants to the Middle East are employed mostly as security personnel, chauffeurs, and construction workers, the demand from South East Asian countries is more for employment in industrial enterprises.

A number of other policy measures were also initiated for encouraging the transfer of remittances through the official channel. A recent measure was the issuance of a five-year Foreign Employment Bond in July 210 with an interest rate of 9.5 percent per annum. The main objective of issuing this bond was to utilize remittances of Nepalis working abroad and bring in the money through the banking channel. This issuance of the bond was expected to facilitate the overseas workers to invest their money in the bond that would be utilized for the government's development programs.

Remittances rose from Rs. 65.5 billion in 2004/05 to Rs. 209.70 billion in 2008/09. Moreover, the share of remittances incoming through the official channel has been going up. For instance, while in 2004/05, out of total remittance income, just about 27 percent flowed into the country through the official channel as against 73 percent through the unofficial channel, in

2009/10, on the other hand, almost 90 percent entered through the official channel and the rest through the unofficial channel.

The upsurge in remittances had led to a surplus in the current account, leading to a strengthening of the overall BoP position. For instance, the share of remittances in total current account receipts rose from 38.2 percent in 2004/05 to 56.7 percent in 2008/09 (Table 1). This in turn had enabled Nepal to maintain a comfortable level of foreign exchange reserves.

Similarly, the remittances to GDP ratio increased from 11.1 percent in 2004/05 to 21.2 percent in 2008/09. These figures clearly indicate that any significant decline in receipts from remittances could disturb the structure of the economy from the macro level. And this is exact what happened in 2009/10, thanks to the delayed impact of the global recession that started to bite the Nepalese economy.

Table 1: Remittances Data

Heading	2004-05	2005-06	2006-07	2007-08	2008-09	2009-10p
Total remittances (in Rs. billion)	65.5	97.7	100.1	142.7	209.7	231.7
Share of remittances in current a/c receipts excluding grants (in %)	38.2	46.7	45.3	51.1	56.7	59.3
Ratio of remittances to GDP (in %)	11.1	14.9	13.8	17.5	21.2	19.6

p: provisional
Source: NRB.

As a result, in 2009/10, remittances aggregated Rs. 231.7 billion, a rise by just 10.5 percent compared to its significant growth of 47 percent in the previous year. While both in 2007/08 and 2008/09 the upsurge in remittances was responsible for the surplus in the current account and BoP, in 2009/10, the deceleration in the growth of remittances led to a current account deficit of Rs. 32.4

billion, thereby weakening the overall BoP which also registered a deficit of Rs. 2.6 billion. Analogously, the gross foreign exchange reserves were adequate for financing merchandize imports of only 8.6 months and merchandize and service imports of 10.3 months as at mid-July 2010 compared to 12.3 months and 10.0 months respectively in mid-July 2009. The remittances to GDP ratio fell by 1.6 percentage points to 19.6 percent in 2009/10.

On the basis of data provided by the Department of Foreign Employment, the number of workers going abroad for employment increased by 35.4 percent to 294,094 people in 2009/10 compared to 217,164 people in 2008/09.[9] With the increase in the number of workers, the inflow of remittances should have taken an upswing. However, this did happen.[10]

While remittances shielded the economy during difficult situations in the past, the global economic crisis has brought a new challenge to the role of remittances. Weak global demand for goods and services and slower economic growth, along with consequent rise in unemployment in host countries, has put the demand for Nepali workers and their remittance transfers at risk.

In terms of uses, however, it has been revealed that remittances in Nepal have been used very little for productive purposes. A small study undertaken by the NRB (2002), that took into account 10 districts and 160 sample households, revealed that the remittance earnings were primarily invested for household purposes, purchase of real estate and house, paying off the loan, purchase of jewellery and as bank deposits.

A few explanations are provided in Box 4 as to why remittances have been used less for productive purposes.

Box 4

Possible Causes for Less Productive Use of Remittances

The following are some of the reasons as to why migrant workers do not invest in productive uses:

a. Paucity of promotion support in terms of information, advisory, training and other services pertaining to investment in new and potentially successful sectors.

b. Less risk involved in the purchase of land and construction of houses.

c. Hardly any knowledge on investment opportunities.

d. Top priority accorded to household expenditure.

e. Lack of expertise in the remittance receiving household for undertaking a business.

f. Lack of investment-friendly climate.

Policy Alternatives

Policies need to be devised to encourage the use of remittances for promoting longer-term growth and income security. Nepal has to formulate policies that (i) encourage workers to send more remittances through official rather than unofficial channel; (ii) raise the levels of remittances by encouraging migrants to hold their savings in financial assets in the country rather than holding them abroad (or spending their savings on consumer goods); or (iii) encourage migrants to become investor in productive assets in the country.

Encouraging self-employment and small business formation amongst returning migrants and their relations back home should be acknowledged as opportunities by the government, and schemes must be aimed to support investment in business activities. In this light, microfinance could address the demand for remittance-linked financial services, particularly among poor and/or geographically isolated populations. Microfinance institutions (MFIs) have revealed a competitive advantage based on a host of techniques that reduce the high transaction costs of outreach to poorer clients. By broadening the remittance-linked services to the "unbanked", MFIs have the potential to promote broad-based development, as well as expand the volume of remittance flows mediated through the financial system. In this respect, MFIs in Nepal could also expand their micro and small business portfolio, while the government and NGOs could provide services such as training, business advice and marketing assistance for micro and small entrepreneurs.

Pooling remittances in MFIs in terms of deposits enables them to finance a wide range of activities, and generate a potentially greater economic and social impact than what could be viable with special targeted business development programs. Moreover, MFIs themselves can utilize remittances to leverage more funds in the commercial markets to finance their growing lending operations. This will enable the MFIs both to diversify their funding sources and also increase the breadth and depth of their outreach. Over time, with more experience, innovative MFIs will find different ways of turning workers' remittances into a productive business that would contribute to their social mission and profitability. Those who receive remittances may also find that MFIs' involvement will provide better ways to manage their inflows. These improvements in both the supply and demand sides can make a significant contribution to increase the welfare of the poor and low-income households.

Banks could make MFIs their working partners in the rural sector for operating microfinance activities. The MFIs would act as loan service agents, and collaborate with social entrepreneurs to set up greenfield MFIs. Under this arrangement, each bank or group of banks could develop microfinance loan portfolio by accumulating the remittances they receive from migrant workers and establish a network that could eventually distribute a range of financial services throughout the rural areas. As a result, commercial banks would also benefit from the potential of the microfinance sector.

An increasingly recognized policy route is to provide matching funds to the collective remittances sent by migrant organizations abroad, commonly referred to as Hometown Associations or HTAs. Most frequent examples are from Mexico and El Salvador. The local or federal governments in these two countries allocate US$ 2 or more for every dollar migrant organizations remit back in their communities. The pooled funds are normally used to finance infrastructure and social projects, such as remodeling schools.[11] This mechanism could also be considered in Nepal's case.

Pre-departure orientation program, coupled with awareness-raising initiatives for both migrants and their families, and information dissemination in the destination countries could address the problem of limited awareness about the costs and benefits of seeking employment opportunities abroad and could also act as a powerful tool in raising awareness about remittance methods and utilization. In the destination country, regular meetings should be organized by the Nepalese mission and information should be disseminated through different media by the Government of Nepal. Moreover, returnee migrants also have an important role to play as they can share their experiences with future migrants and their families. Overall, the involvement of a variety of actors (migrant associations, NGOs and governmental bodies) is instrumental in the success of these initiatives.

Financial education can provide remittance receivers with the knowledge and skills to evaluate their options and choose the most suitable financial products, to understand how product features differ, to calculate and compare costs and to determine what they can afford and what products are best suited to their requirements. It empowers the remittance receiver with the knowledge and skills to indulge in a dialogue with the sender about various options for sending remittances through formal channels and how remittances can be used to meet the financial goals of both the sender and the receiver.

It is crucial to encourage migrant knowledge transfer and organization of migrant groups for business development. Diaspora communities are not only a source of funding for projects, but also an important source of human capital, which could well be used in Nepal. Due to their attachment, many migrants could thus be mobilized to assist in projects in Nepal, not just through financial contributions, but also by offering time and knowledge.[12]

At the point of origin, as the majority of remittances are utilized to repay loans borrowed from money lenders at high interest rates, it is important to explore the possibilities of indulging self-help groups to set up a social fund, which would provide loans with lower interest rates and develop access to institutional credit. This would lower the debt burden of households. Other options such as vocational training, increasing and disseminating information flows pertaining to rural investment opportunities, the provision of loans from financial institutions, and developing market linkages for at least some selected non-farm products and services should be delved into by government and non-governmental agencies. The development of entrepreneurial competence would definitely enhance investment in productive activities.

The governments of Brazil, Mexico and the Philippines had employed an array of inducements to attract remittance funds to specific saving and investment vehicles, including migrant pension plans, preferential loans or grants for business ventures, preferential access to capital goods and raw material imports for recent returnees, and investment and advisory services for business start-ups.[13] Nepal can learn a great deal from the experiences of these countries.

Likewise, the experiences of South Asian countries in terms of using remittances productively could be very beneficial to Nepal. These include, among others, the incentives provided to its expatriates by the Government of India and the mechanisms devised by the India Investment Centre to help Indian companies collaborate with NRIs, the different savings and investment schemes for wage earners abroad designed by the Bangladesh Bank as well as the role of MFIs for the productive use of remittances, the PRI and the non-repatriable investment scheme launched by the Government of Pakistan and the Sri Lankan Government's entrepreneurship development program for return migrants.

Nepal needs to develop a website to make available information to migrants on remittances transfer mechanisms, prices, and speed and reliability that could improve transparency and further competition in the remittance industry. The website could also provide information on investment opportunities back home, immigration policies in destination countries and links to websites of the Nepal government and non-government institutions that work with the Diaspora, return migrants, and micro-credit institutions.

The setting up of a special category of deposit accounts at commercial banks where migrant workers can deposit their money earned abroad is one of the common incentives utilized in many countries to attract money transfers from abroad. These special deposit accounts grant migrants preferential interest rates and the choice to have accounts denominated in foreign currency. Other incentives schemes include special training schemes for migrants to open small businesses back home, and granting premium interest rates on remittance funds.

With regard to the global recession, it is exigent to conduct continued assessment of the impact of the worldwide financial meltdown on the economic situation in those destination countries where there are a large number of Nepali migrant workers. This would assist in forming the basis for estimating job losses for Nepali migrants and the number of returnees.

Conclusions

Remittance flows are a crucial policy concern since they are very large in size, are relatively stable and provide a cushion for economic shocks, and are unique in providing direct benefits for households. However, remittances do not automatically contribute to national development. To carry out effective and efficient public policies to channel remittances into productive projects, the government has to look at what motivate Nepalis to send money home particularly beyond individual family remittances, and craft its policies to take advantage of it. While the policies and initiatives undertaken so far to augment the impact of remittances are primarily aimed at encouraging the sending of remittances through official channels, the utilization aspect of remittances has been largely ignored by the government authorities.

Hence, directing remittances to productive investments is a challenge for the government. Families of migrant workers should be encouraged and trained so that they are able to undertake small businesses. This will generate jobs and help improve the domestic economy. In the long run, migrant workers can come back and be reintegrated in the country, bringing in better skills and technology.

Notes

1. IMF (2009) also discusses the standard components in the BoP framework pertaining to remittances, including compensation of employees, personal transfers as well as supplementary items related to remittances.
2. These beneficial impacts are particularly strong for countries where remittances are above 3 percent of GDP as illustrated by Bugamelli and Paterno (2006).
3. For example, India and Pakistan maintain interest rates on foreign currency accounts that are higher than domestic or Euro-currency deposits.
4. Moreover, there is always a possibility that investors will direct funds into uses with high yields, which could be different from uses with high development impacts. When migrants do invest, their emotional attachment to their regions of origin can help compensate for the disadvantages of these regions in the eyes of purely profit-seeking investors. For details, see Carling (2005).
5. For other details on the MWF, see Murshid *et al.* (2002).

6. A comprehensive examination of the role of MFIs in the utilization of remittances in Bangladesh is provided in Bruyn and Kuddus (2005).
7. Details of this program are given in Puri and Ritzema (1999).
8. This is elaborated in IMF (2006).
9. Out of the total number of people that were given approval for foreign employment, Malaysia was the top destination with a share of 38.5 percent followed by Saudi Arabia, Qatar and the United Arab Emirates.
10. Major factors included the lagged impact of sending remittances as well the lack of awareness for sending money through the official channel. Moreover, a large number of manpower agencies held workers' money for overseas agents that assisted them in securing job orders. For details, see *Republica*, 11 September 2010.
11. Hence, these HTAs could act as a conduit for development projects. At the same time, once set up, the pooling of resources could also be used to finance local entrepreneurial activities, with the advantage that it could offer returns to investors. For further elaboration, see Agunias (2006).
12. An example is the case of Algeria where its government realized the potential benefit from human capital, and formed an Algerian transnational network of researchers and engineers; thus, students that remain in the host countries (Europe and the US) transform the brain drain into brain gain. The underlying idea is that contributions by these groups of migrants can stimulate small and medium starts-up in high-tech sectors such as biotechnologies for agriculture which is strongly needed to improve productivity. For details, see European Investment Bank (2005).
13. These mechanisms of different countries are cited in Sander (2003).

References

Agunias, Dovelyn Rannveig (2006). "Remittances and Development: Trends, Impacts and Policy Options." Available at: http://www.migrationpolicy.org/pubs/ mig_dev_lit_review_091406.pdf

Azad, Abul Kalam (2005). "Migrant Workers' Remittances: A Source of Finance for Micro-Enterprise Development in Bangladesh?" In Samuel Munzele Maimbo and Dilip Ratha, eds., *Remittances: Development Impact and Future Prospects*. Washington, D.C.: World Bank.

Bruyn, Tom de and Umbareen Kuddus (2005). "Dynamics of Remittance Utilization in Bangladesh." *IOM Migration Research Series*.

Bugamelli, Matteo, and Francesco Paterno (2006). "Workers' Remittances and Current Account Reversals." *Bank of Italy Economic Research Paper*. No. 573. Rome: Bank of Italy.

Carling, Jorgen (2005). "Migrant Remittances and Development Cooperation." *PRIO Report*. Oslo: International Peace Research Institute.

Carling, Jorgen (2004). "Policy Options for Increasing the Benefits of Remittances." Paper presented at the Ninth International Metropolis Conference. Geneva. 27 September-1 October.

European Investment Bank (2005). "Study on Improving the Efficiency of Workers' Remittances in Mediterranean Countries" FTF/REG/0/2005. Available at: http://www.eib.europa.eu/attachments/countryfemip_workers_remittances_en. pdf

International Monetary Fund (IMF). 2009. *Balance of Payments and International Investment Position Manual (BPM6)*. Washington, D.C: IMF.

IMF (2006). "Nepal: Selected Issues and Statistical Appendix." IMF Country Report No. 06/45. February.

Mohapatra, Sanket, Dilip Ratha and Anil Silwal (2010). "Outlook for Remittance Flows 2011-12." *Migration and Development Brief 13*. 8 November.

Murshid, K.A.S., Kazi Iqbal and Meherun Ahmed (2002). "A Study on Remittance Inflows and Utilization." Dhaka: International Organization for Migration.

Nepal Rastra Bank (2002). *Foreign Employment and the Remittance Economy of Nepal* (in Nepali). Kathmandu: Nepal Rastra Bank.

Pant, Bhubanesh (2008). "Mobilizing Remittances for Productive Use: A Policy-oriented Approach." *NRB Working Paper*. NRB/WP/4. December.

Puri, Lakshmi (2007). "Assuring Development Gains and Poverty Reduction from Trade: The Labor Mobility and Skills Trade Dimension." Geneva: UNCTAD

Puri, Shivani and Tineke Ritzema (1999). "Migrant Worker Remittances, Micro-finance and the Informal Economy: Prospects and Issues." *Working Paper*. No 21. Available at http://www.gdrc.org /icm/ remittance/shivani.html

Raihan, Selim, Bazlul H. Khondker, Guntur Sugiyarto, and Shikha Jha (2009). "Remittances and Household Welfare: A Case Study of Bangladesh." *ADB Economics Working Paper Series*. No. 189. December.

Sander, C. (2003). *Capturing a Market Share? Migrant Remittance Transfers and Commercialization of Microfinance in Africa*. Bannock Consulting. July.

UNCTAD. (2009). "Contribution of Migrants to Development: Trade, Investment and Development Linkages." Note by the Secretariat for the Ad-hoc Expert Group Meeting. Geneva. 29 July. Available at: http://www.unctad.org/en/docs/ ditctncd20092

Republica, 11 September 2010.

30

Role of Remittances in Recovery and Reconstruction*

During the past decade, developing countries have been increasingly exposed to natural disasters with severe consequences with respect to output, trade, and fiscal balances. Especially, low income countries are highly vulnerable to natural disasters including earthquakes because of their limited ability to absorb large external shocks affecting the economy. These disasters hamper sustainable development initiatives and exacerbate other financial, health and environmental shocks. As a result, the policy debate is refocusing on these countries' vulnerability. Given the precarious public budgetary stance, asset destruction caused by natural disasters could largely hamper capital accumulation and growth potential. In this respect, external resources for post disaster reconstruction can be sourced from multilateral development banks, regional development banks, bilateral development partners, international NGOs, private philanthropies and charities, and remittances. Among these different resources, the role of remittances in reconstruction and recovery of earthquake-affected economies is briefly examined in this article as the dynamics of earthquake-induced remittance flows and the possibilities of leveraging remittances for post-earthquake development have been meagerly researched so far.

Country experiences demonstrate that remittances can play a distinctive role in reconstruction and recovery programs of earthquake stricken countries. Literature reveals that migrant remittance flows increase in the aftermath of large earthquakes, and act as a safety net for households that have migrants abroad.

* *The Himalayan Times*, 24 August 2015.

Migrants transfer more funds during difficult times to assist their families and friends. In this light, the "Sendai Framework for Disaster Risk Reduction 2015-2030" that was adopted at the Third United Nations World Conference, held from 14 to 18 March 2015 in Sendai, Japan has recognized migrants as germane community-level stakeholders in disaster risk reduction and has also acknowledged the value of migrants' knowledge and skills in building community resilience.

Generally, after an earthquake strikes, almost all households experience loss of income arising from the destruction of productive assets, the loss of local jobs, the return of wage earners from overseas countries or the disruption of remittance flows. However, households whose livelihoods include remittances appear less vulnerable to the earthquake's effects, and possess considerably more livelihood resilience. According to the World Bank, the rise in remittances makes up for 13 percent of income losses in the year of the natural disaster and 28 percent within four years; in contrast, increases in development assistance make up for approximately 26 percent and 21 percent, respectively, during a four-year period.

As an immediate upshot of the great earthquake of 25 April 2015, there appeared to have been a large increase in remittance inflow to Nepal during the tenth month (mid-April to mid-May) and the eleventh month (mid-May to mid-June) of FY 2014/15. Remittances aggregating about Rs. 63 billion flowed into the country during each of those months compared to an average inflow of Rs. 47 billion in the earlier months. This surge has been attributed to migrant workers transferring money to rebuild their damaged houses after the quake. Another factor for this rise is the decline of remittances through the "hundi" as several banks and remittance companies provided an exemption in service charge while sending remittance following the earthquake.

Remittances can be an invaluable resource for post-earthquake reconstruction. They act as a type of insurance that improves a family's ability to respond to a crisis. The fact that, especially in the recovery and rebuilding process, remittances are generally spent on local goods and services, means that their impact is multiplied, providing a further incentive to restore them. Their application, however, is governed by a favorable policy environment and effective coordination among different sectors and development actors. To maximize the contributions of post-earthquake remittances for poverty alleviation and national development, collaboration among a wide range of stakeholders is crucial.

Policymakers in Nepal should better incorporate remittances as a formal means to hasten post-earthquake reconstruction and recovery. The continuation or restoration of remittance flows while other income and means of livelihood go down or only slowly recover are obviously critical to the recovery of households receiving these remittances. But, it is important that remittances do not become a substitute for structural development. There are other downsides to remittance-dependence, too. Small economies such as Nepal with massive inflows of remittances and little absorptive capacity may witness exchange rate appreciation, inflation, and an erosion of external competitiveness. Still, the inflow of remittances can support reconstruction in earthquake-affected Nepal, but it cannot sustainably be a replacement for investment and reconstruction. Likewise, although remittances are an important mechanism to help families prepare and recover, the long-term financial sustainability of such a system needs to be further examined.

31

Remittances and Microfinance: Risks, Hurdles and Opportunities*

There have been ample discussions on the proposition that linking remittances and microfinance has a positive development impact on recipient communities. This is because many similarities exist between the goals of microfinance and remittances; both are targeted at poverty reduction, both can increase a safety net for households and families, and both have the potential for employment generation and economic development through investment in small and micro-enterprises. The involvement of microfinance institutions (MFIs) in the remittance transfer process is, thus, a promising means for expanding financial services access to the poor, particularly in rural areas that do not have access to commercial banks.

While remittances have the potential to spur development, relying too much on them can create problems. Coordinating with the microfinance sector could help in counterbalancing many of these risks. One risk is that people might become so dependent on the remittances to the extent that they stop to undertake economic activities at home and instead concentrate on dispatching young adults abroad to make money and send remittances home. This would restrain economic development in the home country and stimulate the "brain drain" wave. Hence, it is crucial to leverage the potential for remittances to raise job creation in recipient communities.

Likewise, though remittances ameliorate the lives of those who procure them and have a positive multiplier effect on the domestic

* *The Himalayan Times*, 16 March 2016.

economy, there exist hurdles to effectively investing remittances into micro and small enterprises. Recipients who might otherwise be encouraged to begin a small business are constrained by the absence of a safe place to save their remittances, the inability to leverage the remittances through a loan, and the paucity of an infrastructure for participating in a market. In this respect, combining microfinance opportunities with remittances could mitigate these gaps and thus improve the prospect of developing lasting and sustainable business ventures.

Hence, microfinance is quite appropriate for remittance-associated financial services. Since they are poor, many remittance recipients lie outside the typical bank client profiles, but are well within the market segment targeted by MFIs. Likewise, MFIs can render a money transfer service in underserved areas and at a lower cost than mainstream providers owing to their social mission of serving the poor and unbanked people. By employing lending techniques that take into consideration the lack of collateral and low individual sums, MFIs are often better prepared than commercial banks to overcome the information asymmetries that thwart the poor from having access to credit. Studies have also revealed the potential for microfinance loans that can help recipients establish new businesses.

Despite their potential, however, MFIs face several obstacles in linking remittances with financial services. For instance, though MFIs match the socio-economic profile of remittance receivers better than traditional banks, they often do not have the institutional capacities for complex cross-border transfers in terms of liquidity management and information-management systems, among others. Moreover, there could be regulatory controls with respect to activities in foreign currencies or restrictions in offering certain financial services. Likewise, for the productive use of remittances, technology-leveraged banking, such as card-based transactions or mobile banking, demand infrastructure that may be beyond the resources of most MFIs.

In the case of Nepal, the tie between microfinance and remittances has taken an upward trend in recent years with a focus on linking the inflows of remittance money to MFIs who are often better positioned than banks to offer money transfer services to remittance recipients in remote rural areas with low-cost transfer products due to their close proximity to client groups and communities that receive remittances. MFIs can support clients' family members in developing micro enterprises through entrepreneurship development by extending access to finance and enabling them to meet the capital needs of their enterprises. Likewise, the remittance business can be a crucial avenue of income and funds for MFIs because most of them rely predominantly on interest income and are vulnerable to potential volatilities in the income from this source. MFIs, on their part, could also offer special deposits, investment loans and other type of loans to the families who receive remittances.

Over time, with increasing experience, innovative MFIs will find concrete ways of transforming workers' remittances into a productive business that would contribute to their social mission and profitability. However, for all of this to translate into reality, the regulatory and legal aspects need to be properly addressed and appropriate policies need to be designed and implemented. An example of the policy kit could be the formulation of apposite regulatory measures for permitting remittance recipients to open accounts in MFIs.

All in all, MFIs can act as a conduit through which remittances can be saved and reinvested in rural communities. With an upsurge in the number of Nepalese migrant workers and subsequent inflow of remittances, it is the extensive network of MFIs that has the potential to leverage remittances as one of the sources of development finance for setting up sustainable rural enterprises.

32

Remittances: Responding to Emerging Challenges*

The significance of remittances to national economies is well known and there is little debate over the value of these flows that have the proven capacity to protect people from income shocks and lifecycle risks. Remittances augment household incomes and are thus an effective anti-poverty force in developing countries, paying for basic needs and education, enhancing their ability to withstand risks pertaining to unemployment or illness, and building their resilience to external events including climate change or natural disaster. When there is a dearth of well-functioning credit markets, these flows can also provide migrants and their families with the financial resources to invest in enterprises.

To the extent that migrants are inspired by altruism as well as solidarity motives and dispatch more money home during periods of economic distress, remittances may actually seem countercyclical.

Still, the potential of these flows for development is greater than their existing impact. Currently, remittance transfers are just partially integrated with financial services since a number of remittance senders and recipients do not have bank accounts. Connecting remittance families to banks and other financial institutions gives them the potential to access loans, build credit histories, securely save for the future, and insure themselves. In many low income countries, a paucity of products and services designed to particularly respond to migrant demands, encourage savings and incentivize entrepreneurial activities is impeding the potential that remittances have for asset building and investment.

---

* *The Kathmandu Post*, 2 March 2018.

Similarly, from the migrants' perspective, poor infrastructure, corruption, distrust in government institutions, the lack of appropriate public policies (schooling, health care, and land reform, among others) and market failures dissuade them from undertaking the risk of investing their money in their countries of origin and lower their incentive to return. Hence, migration impacts appear to be quite context-sensitive and based on the specific development context, migration and remittances may enable people to move away from, just as much as to invest in domestic economic activities.

Moreover, studies have also divulged about a negative link between development and remittances including the fact that large volume of remittance inflows would result in currency appreciation as well as exacerbate inequalities by distorting local income levels. The effect of remittances on inflation and local prices, particularly for land, property and construction are also worrisome. Further, it has been illustrated that these financial flows may encourage dependency and undermine motivations to work in the home country as well as curtail the local workforce.

In Nepal's case, remittances have been providing a vital lifeline for many of the country's most vulnerable and poor households, both by contributing to basic needs including food, health care, education and housing, and by helping to cope with external shocks and fluctuations in income. These inflows have operated as a form of household insurance against loss of income and other financial adversities and also helped in reducing the overall incidence of poverty as well as maintaining a healthy BoP.

One of the principal developmental challenges for Nepal's policy makers is to inspire senders and recipients of remittances to undertake their money transfer operations *via* formal financial institutions so that remittances could become formal savings and deposits in financial institutions and, in turn, have a multiplier impact. Currently, however, the informal channels seem to be more efficient and normally tend to fulfill the special requirements of the migrant and his or her family. Discouraging the informal channels while encouraging migrants to send remittances through official channels can bolster the country's foreign currency reserves, strengthen the financial system, and make more credit available to nurture the local economy even more.

While remittances appear to have largely benefited the macro-economy, it has also allowed the government to evade the crucial task of labor policy reform for generating employment opportunities, which would have improved the performance of the domestic economy. The impact of migration has been clearly witnessed in the rural sector that has suffered largely on account of employment losses.

Again in Nepal's case, the full promise of technology is yet to be realized, largely due to the lack of infrastructure in a number of receiving areas. Mobile phone networks, internet-based tools and digital money in various forms present a potentially transformative force for sending and receiving remittances, reducing costs and saving time, and can also become a gateway to financial inclusion.

Though the Government introduced some policies to increase remittance flows and to channel them to productive uses, such measures have not been very fruitful. For the developmental potential of remittances to be fully realized, a collaborative effort involving the government, migrant groups, the local community, and non-governmental organizations is a must for exploring ways of encouraging the flow and creating an atmosphere for more sustainable investment of remittances.

Despite the growth in significance of remittances as a source of development finance in Nepal, its instability and risks, such as vulnerability to sudden external shocks and distortions in economic priorities, connote that remittances should not be seen as a substitute for a sustained, domestically engineered development effort. Even the World Bank's *Nepal Development Update 2016* had earlier warned that Nepal's overdependence on remittance to maintain its foreign exchange earnings is quite a risky strategy as the country is susceptible to external shocks. Hence, a key challenge for our policymakers is to find alternatives and develop ways to reduce this dependency, so that the country can cope with the situation if such inflows start to decline, adversely impacting the BoP position and ultimately the overall economy. And this is already beginning to take shape as BoP data for the first half of 2017/18 divulge that workers' remittances fell by 0.5 percent to Rs. 34.5 billion in contrast to an upsurge by 5.7 percent in the corresponding period of 2016/17. As a result, the current account registered a deficit of Rs. 75.7 billion with the overall BoP also remaining at a deficit of Rs. 6.6 billion in the first half of 2017/18. Hence, to alleviate the economic and social risks flowing from these developments, the government must begin to acknowledge the gravity of this issue and respond proactively.

33

Fostering Remittances for Meeting Development Objectives*

Migrants' remittances, one of the largest and reliable source of external funds for developing countries, have been soaring in recent years. Although they are second only to FDI inflows with respect to scale, they are more than three times official development aid and eight times private capital. This upsurge as well as the potential for remittances to lower poverty and economic vulnerability, improve family welfare, and accelerate economic development has renewed academic and public policy interest on this issue.

According to World Bank's latest *Migration and Development Brief* released on April 2018, remittance flows to low- and middle-income countries (LMICs) rose by 8.5 percent to $466 billion in 2017. The increase is expected to continue in 2018 to reach $485 billion. Likewise, remittances to South Asia increased by 5.8 percent in 2017 following a decline by 6.1 percent in 2016. This trend is also likely to prevail into 2018 owing to stronger economic conditions in developed economies (especially the United States) along with a modest increase in oil prices that should have a positive impact on the GCC countries. An important challenge for governments of South Asia is to employ remittances to nurture their financial sectors and invest in targeted development projects, especially in infrastructure.

Macroeconomic studies demonstrate that though remittances are affected by the economic cycles of source and host countries, they provide a crucial avenue of foreign currency, boost national income, finance imports and contribute to the balance of

---

* *The Kathmandu Post*, 7 May 2018.

payments (BoP). While other capital flows appear to rise during favorable economic cycles and fall in periods of economic downturn, remittances seem to react less violently and exhibit incredible stability over time. Likewise, remittances seem to be better targeted at the requirements of the poor than foreign aid or FDI, as recipients generally rely on remittances to cover daily living expenses or to undertake small investments in business. Likewise, migrants have been sending more money to their families back home in periods of economic downturns, financial crises, or natural disasters.

Theoretically, remittances are guided by different motives, which can also justify their behavior during business cycle fluctuations. For instance, if the motive is generally altruistic, remittances are likely to be countercyclical, that is, they rise when a recipient economy is in a slump. Another view looks at remittances as an investment by migrants in their home country, encouraging them to send more money to garner higher future returns. In these instances, remittances can be procyclical. In the case of low income countries, however, unlike other types of capital flows, remittances respond basically to the needs of households and not the profit-seeking aims of investors.

Global evidence indicates that recipient households generally have higher levels of consumer spending and lower incidences of extreme poverty than those who do not obtain remittances, implying that remittances have been playing an instrumental role as a 'powerful anti-poverty force'.

According to the International Fund for Agricultural Development, about forty percent of total remittance flows are directed to the rural areas, thereby facilitating the growth of the agricultural economy, improving food security and creating employment opportunities, especially for the youths.

With respect to Nepal, remittance transfers often consist of relatively small amounts in themselves but connote a lifeline for the recipients, contributing a sizable share of GDP (about 29 percent in 2017). This income has been increasing the standard of living, particularly of those of the rural areas and also covering basic needs such as food, education, health and housing. It has also created opportunities to save, invest, and build assets. Moreover, it has also acted as a form of insurance for the country against exogenous shocks such as the great earthquake of April 2015 where it played a pivotal part in the rehabilitation efforts in the country.

While there have been apprehensions about brain drain, remittance-dependence, and the adverse impact of remittances on Nepal's export competitiveness due to the pressure on currency appreciation, remittances so far seem to have made positive contributions to the economy. However, different case studies of Nepal have divulged that remittances have been primarily utilized to finance consumption rather than being channeled to increase productive capacity. Still, spending remittances on consumption often leads to improved health, education and human capital, augmenting both private and public welfare. Similarly, a large portion of the remittance-related investment have also increased the stock of wealth of the migrant household in the form of land and housing, all of which have indirect macro-economic impacts on development.

Remittances, as private flows, can be leveraged *via* incentives that safeguard migrants' rights while allowing them to make use of their earnings in pro-development ways. In this respect, projects need to be based on the requirements and priorities of the local population. Likewise, financial services need to be customized through novel means. While financial services can, on the one hand, incentivize savings and investment behavior, they also need to consider the diverse needs of remittance recipients, on the other. However, this is not happening in Nepal.

Overall, the positive impacts on poverty and development become greater when remittances can be saved and invested in infrastructures and productive capacity. Moreover, the development impact of remittances can only be fully achieved in partnership with sound and realistic public policies and priorities, along with private-sector initiatives.

34

Encouraging Remittance Inflows Without Creating Dependency Syndrome*

The inflow of remittances is an old topic in the study of migration, but one that has stimulated renewed policy focus in recent years. As global remittances are taking an upward trend to a degree that is on par with global development assistance and foreign direct investment (FDI) in the developing world, it is not surprising that this subject is of interest to policymakers.

Many reasons have been cited as to why migrants send money home. These include explanations of remittance behavior such as "altruism" which indicates that remittances go up when the economic requirements of families back home rise, the notion of "exchange" which suggests that migrants are effectively repaying family and relatives for investments in the education or travel of the migrant, and the notion of "co-insurance" where both migrants and family provide monetary and in-kind transfers to safeguard the other against short-lived shocks. It is generally agreed that remittances are likely to be higher in conditions where the migrant leaves the country due to economic rather than social or political factors, where they have temporary rather than permanent resident status, and where they are young, but married with family left behind.

The 2019 United Nations Report on the world's progress toward Sustainable Development Goals (SDGs) divulges that personal inflows of remittances from migrant workers are the largest source of external financing for low and middle-income

* *The Himalayan Times*, 9 December 2019.

countries (LMICs). According to World Bank's latest *Migration and Development Brief,* remittance flows to LMICs grew by 9.6 percent in 2018 (up from the 8.8 percent rise in 2017), to reach a record $529 billion. They represent more than three times the size of official development assistance. Moreover, as FDI has been taking a downward trend in recent years, remittances stood close to the level of FDI flows in 2018. Further, in 2018, remittances represented more than 30 percent of GDP in countries such as Tonga (35.2 percent), Kyrgyz Republic (33.6 percent), Tajikistan (31.0 percent), and Haiti (30.7 percent), For Nepal, the figure was 28.0 percent.

Remittance flows to Nepal have a direct impact on recipient households by lowering poverty and inequality and increasing consumption and social well-being. They also have a positive impact on the financial sector developments such as increasing the access and use of financial intermediaries, particularly in the rural areas. They support in improving credit ratings of countries and help raise external financing.

Nepal's Budget for FY 2019/2020 and the Monetary Policy for 2018/19 have accorded priority in directing remittances through banking system as well as mobilizing remittances towards productive use (such as micro and small industries, agricultural enterprise and employment-oriented services). These issues have always been given attention in previous budgets and monetary policies also. Unless the Government and the Nepal Rastra Bank take concrete steps in implementing these policies, no tangible results will emerge.

Moreover, though there is a host of advantages of remittances, the remittance market, to a large extent, has not been exploited for prospective financial services. Furthermore, remittances are often not directed into productive investments owing to a variety of factors including a) dearth of investment knowledge of the remittance clients, b) inconsistency in remittance transactions, and c) inappropriate investment-friendly climate.

An important disadvantage is that remittances also encourage more migration of labor as family members obtaining remittances realize that they would be better off moving to other destinations and earn more money rather than staying back in their home county. Another drawback is that the country's dependence on remittances increases. And, this could be alarming as an abrupt stop in these financial inflows could lead to a financial debacle.

There are also detrimental outcomes of being over-dependent on remittances. For example, too much dependence opens up Nepal to exposure to external shocks linked to remittance-sending countries. Likewise, remittance inflows have had a knock-on effect in terms of imports. With exports dwindling, trade deficit has been expanding at an alarming rate.

Still, the overall impact of remittances in comparison to other types of international financial transfers has been encouraging and should be fortified more with appropriate policies by the government without creating a dependency syndrome.

To conclude, remittances to Nepal have been generally observed as an important tool to reduce poverty and inequality, to impart social benefits, to act as buffers against economic shocks, and to produce other positive impacts. Still, their full developmental potential has not been realized so far. The successful mobilization of remittances for productive purposes basically hinges on the capacity of the government to build a "development-centered" macroeconomic environment along with supporting the establishment of a viable and inclusive financial sector. Likewise, joint and intensive efforts must be aimed at establishing and improving the mechanisms through which the principal actors, especially the individual remittance senders and recipients, can leverage these flows for developmental purposes.

Index

D

E

F

G

N

O

P

Q

R